State, Securit

STATE, SECURITY, AND SUBJECT FORMATION

Edited By

Anna Yeatman
and
Magdalena Zolkos

continuum

NEW YORK • LONDON

2010

The Continuum International Publishing Group Inc
80 Maiden Lane, New York, NY 10038

The Continuum International Publishing Group Ltd
The Tower Building, 11 York Road, London SE1 7NX

www.continuumbooks.com

Library of Congress Cataloging-in-Publication Data
A catalog record for this book is available from the Library of Congress.

ISBN 978-0-8264-9226-5 (Hardcover)
        978-0-8264-4284-0 (Paperback)

Typeset by Newgen Imaging Systems Pvt Ltd, Chennai, India
Printed in the United States of America

Contents

Contributors

Charles Barbour is lecturer in philosophy at the University of Western Sydney. Along with a number of book chapters, he has published articles on social and political theory in journals such as *Theory, Culture, and Society, Philosophy and Social Criticism, Telos, Seattle Law School: Law Review,* and *The Journal of Classical Sociology.* With George Pavlich, he has co-edited the volume *After Sovereignty: Essays on the Question of Political Beginnings* (forthcoming, Routledge-Cavendish).

Barbara Evers is about to complete a PhD at Murdoch University, Western Australia. Her research interests include studies of personae/histories of person formation, sociology of culture, and historical sociology.

Paul Hoggett, BA Social Psychology, University of Sussex, professor of politics and director of the Centre for Psycho-Social Studies, University of the West of England, Bristol. Recent books include *Emotion, Politics and Society* (Palgrave, 2006; with Simon Clarke and Simon Thompson), *The Dilemmas of Development Work* (Policy Press, 2008; with Marj Mayo and Chris Miller) and *Politics, Identity and Emotion* (Paradigm Publishers, 2009).

Ian Hunter is an Australian Professorial Fellow in the Centre for the History of European Discourses at the University of Queensland. His research has two main focuses. For the last decade, he has been working on the history of early modern political, philosophical and religious thought. During this time his publications have included *Rival Enlightenments: Civil and Metaphysical Philosophy in Early Modern Germany,* Cambridge, 2001; *Natural Law and Civil Sovereignty: Moral Right and State Authority in Early Modern Political Thought,* Basingstoke, 2002 (co-edited with David Saunders); *Heresy in Transition: Transforming Ideas of Heresy in Medieval and Early Modern Europe,* London, 2005 (co-edited with John Christian Laursen and Cary J. Nederman); *The Philosopher in Early Modern Europe: The Nature of a Contested Identity,* Cambridge, 2006 (co-edited with Conal Condren and Stephen Gaukroger); and, most recently, *The Secularisation of the Confessional State: The Political Thought of Christian Thomasius,* Cambridge, 2007. Since 2004 he has also been working on the "history of theory" project, which is an intellectual history of the 1960s "theory boom." Several papers from the latter project have appeared, including "The History of Theory" (*Critical Inquiry,* 2006), "The Time of Theory" (*Postcolonial Studies,* 2007), and "Talking About My Generation" (*Critical Inquiry,* 2008).

Robert van Krieken is associate professor of sociology and director of the Socio-Legal Studies Program at the University of Sydney. He holds a BA (Honours 1) and a PhD in Sociology from the University of New South Wales, and a LLB (Honours 1) from the University of Sydney. His publications include *Norbert Elias* (Routledge 1998), "Cultural Genocide," in *The Historiography of Genocide* (edited by Dan Stone; Palgrave Macmillan,

2008) and "The barbarism of civilization: cultural genocide and the 'stolen generations'," *British Journal of Sociology* 50(2) 1999: 295–313.

Jeffrey Minson works across the fields of political, legal, and cultural theory. He has written on the political and ethical aspects of Michel Foucault's work, on ethics of state, citizen, and on questions of citizenship from the ethical demands of democracy to sexual harassment and cultural policy. He is currently working on a comparative study of the styles of political civility associated with rival political and cultural theories.

David Saunders is professor emeritus at the Socio-Legal Research Centre, Griffith University (Australia) and Visiting Research Professor at the Centre for Research in Socio-cultural Change, Open University (UK). His books include *Authorship and Copyright* (1992) and *Anti-lawyers: Religion and the Critics of Law and State* (1997). He is co-editor (with Ian Hunter) of *Natural Law and Civil Sovereignty: Moral Right and State Authority in Early Modern Political Thought* (2002) and of *Samuel Pufendorf: The Whole Duty of Man According to the Law of Nature* (2003). His research concerns the consequences of European religious settlements for modern political-legal order.

Gary Wickham is professor in sociology at Murdoch University, Western Australia, where he has worked for 24 years. His books include *Foucault and Law* (Pluto, 1994, with Alan Hunt; translated into Japanese 2007), *Using Foucault's Methods* (Sage, 1999, with Gavin Kendall; translated into Japanese 2007), and *Cultural Studies: Culture, Order, Ordering* (Sage, 2001, with Gavin Kendall). His recent journal articles have appeared in: *Journal of Sociology; Journal of Classical Sociology; Forum Qualitative Sozialforschung; Journal of Law and Society; Griffith Law Review; Cultural Studies Review; Social and Legal Studies;* and *Chicago-Kent Law Review.*

Nigel Williams is a senior lecturer in the Centre for Psycho-Social Studies at the University of the West of England. He is a psychotherapist and supervisor. He works with organizations that deliver clinical services, and helps psychotherapists develop research into psycho-social issues.

Anna Yeatman took up an appointment as professor and Foundation Director of the Centre for Citizenship and Public Policy at the University of Western Sydney in mid-2008. Before this, she was a Canada Research Chair in Political Science at the University of Alberta for five years, prior to which she was the chair of sociology at Macquarie University for ten years. An interdisciplinary political theorist, Anna engages in both political theory and its applications to especially but not only matters of citizenship and public policy. Her book *Individualization and the Delivery of Welfare Services* was published by Palgrave in 2009. Her current research falls into two areas: (1) the idea of the state in relation to contemporary debates concerning citizenship, human rights, nationalism and cosmopolitanism; (2) an ecology of the human subject. She is also a trained practitioner of the Feldenkrais method of somatic education.

Benjamin Zachariah read history at Presidency College, Calcutta, and at Trinity College, Cambridge. He is Reader in South Asian History at the University of Sheffield, currently on secondment to the Zentrum Moderner Orient, Berlin, as Research Fellow. He has written on the social and intellectual history of colonial and postcolonial South Asia, on the developmental imagination and the Indian state, on anticolonial nationalisms, and on political culture, political rhetoric and standards of political legitimacy in colonial and postcolonial India.

Magdalena Zolkos is research fellow in political theory at the Center for Citizenship and Public Policy, University of Western Sydney. She has published academic articles on reconciliation, transitional justice, collective trauma, and testimony in *European Legacy, Studies in Social and Political Thought*, and *International Journal of Transitional Justice*. She is the author of a forthcoming book *Transitional Justice and Subjective Life. Trauma Testimony as Political Theorizing in the Work of Jean Améry* (Continuum).

Preface

This volume is a product of a research collaboration initiated in the planning and the event of an international workshop on "Security, State and Subject Formation," held at the Department of Political Science, University of Alberta in October 26–27, 2007. Interdisciplinary in nature, this event brought together academic researchers from the areas of sociology, law, history, history of political ideas, political theory, psychoanalysis, and international relations. The papers had been distributed in advance among the participants and were the basis for roundtable conversations on the conceptual history as well as the current politics and predicaments that underscore the intersection of state, security, and the subject. However, the contributions included in this volume are more than mere revisions of the papers presented at the workshop. They are also, and possibly more importantly, an outcome of the participants' in-depth and comprehensive engagements with the topic at hand and each other's works. As a result, the contributions to this volume relate to each other not only through their situation within the common conceptual and thematic framework of the state, security, and the subject, but also at a more intimate and nuanced level of cross-referencing, as well as argumentative and polemical mediations. Thus in order to emphasize the multileveled connectedness among the contributions the editors have decided not to introduce any sectional divisions into structure of the volume.

In workshop discussions we came to use the shorthand, "the civic project." By this we meant a project in which the goal of peaceful coexistence on equal terms for all participant subjects assumes paramount status, and supplies the raison d'être of the political organization of society. Such political organization has three integrally connected aspects: the sovereign state that has both power and authority to impose pacification on those who come under its jurisdiction; those who comprise the political society so bounded and given a territorial specificity by the state; and an ethics of civil conduct that enters into how the individual subject is educated and formed (for the latter, see especially Wickham and Evers, this volume). Historically, the civic project was first enunciated in early modern political thought of the kind that offers a de-confessionalized conception of the state (see Hunter, this volume), namely, a state that does not institute a particular profession of faith or values as the terms of belonging to the political community. This conception of the state has informed the modern liberal-republican tradition of democratic constitutionalism that has found expression in the constitutions of Australia, India, Canada, to name but a few examples. However, if such a tradition counts as an achievement, it is not to be taken for granted. Its fragility is exposed in the present when there is a reassertion of different kinds of attack on the de-confessionalized or "secular" idea of the state (for such attacks in context of contemporary Indian political debate. see Sen 1998), and of the parallel proposition that the conditions of possibility of any state reside in its being the expression of some underlying community of faith or shared values.

The chapters focus on the following question: within different historical *cum* place-situated constellations of the state, security, and the subject, what are the historical, theoretical and normative trajectories of their "civic" formation, as opposed to past and/or contemporary manifestations of public confessionalism (religious, nationalist, ethnic, or moralist, etc.). This query is informed by the preoccupation with the possibilities of achieving (and the conditions of preserving) an institutionalized ethos of public togetherness that ensures civility and peacefulness and that is, importantly, "this-worldly" and "supra-confessional" in character. First, the "this-worldly" quality of the civic nexus of the state, security, and the subject relates to the broadly defined notion of secularism, which is a conceptual and etymological derivative of the Latin word *sæcul-um,* meaning "pertaining to this era; this world; this generation." It is thus explicitly antagonistic to any form of theological incursion into the idea of political community that points to a transcendent direction of, inter alia, religious order, organic national unity, or value homogeneity, as formative of that community and its political life. Second, the reference to the "supra-confessional" character of the political society that comes into being with the establishment of the sovereign state under law indicates a conception of political togetherness that is "above," "beyond," or more simply "outside" the various forms of confessional difference. This does not mean, however, that it is synonymous with discrimination against, repression, or suppression of such manifestations. In other words, this volume assumes that civic order works with an idea of political society and a politics of world-making (a world that its members and participants have in common). Participation in political society and this project of world-making does not demand of subjects that they somehow step outside their faith- or value-based convictions but that, instead, when they bring them into the public domain of political society that they neither profess nor assert them in a way that undermines the fundamental and defining feature of civic order: that each enjoys the status of the person as the subject of right, someone who is entitled to live life as his or her own, a status that is constituted and specified in accordance with the principle of nondiscrimination by the state, and that is enacted in practices and protocols of civility by individual citizen-subjects of the state/political society.

An important aspect of the nexus of the state, security, and the subject explored in this volume is thus the idea of civility. If civility is to inform relationships between subjects and how they interact with the state as the public authority, then they have to have both a subjective disposition to civility and the capacity to practice it. The subject of the civic state has to be educated in the norms, practices, and protocols of civility (an ethos that demands today an education in value pluralism and standpoint plurality). The subject has to be able to practice not just civility in relation to his or her others, but to have an inner life that makes such practice both psychically meaningful and possible. The question of how a subjective capacity for civility is to be understood is one that is touched on by a number of the chapters in this volume (see chapters by Minson, Hoggett and Williams, and Wickham and Evers).

The state is the authoritative and coercive enforcer of civil order while political society denotes the distinctive kind of sphere of sociality that comes into being when the subjects of the state interact with each other as persons. "The State" and "political society" are two sides of the same coin, for political society is not possible without the coercive framing, containing, and constituting of its conditions of possibility that the state supplies; and the state cannot function as the public authority unless it finds support in such functioning in the living of an ethos of civility by those who comprise the body of those who come under the state's jurisdiction. Accordingly, we can say that civil order has both involuntary and voluntary aspects. The involuntary aspect concerns the power of the state as it imposes subjection on those who come under its jurisdiction. The voluntary aspect concerns how subjects themselves engage with the authority and power of the state. It also concerns how they comport themselves in everyday life both within civil society and family/domestic life, for the ethos and ethic of civility has to be the orientation for relationships between subjects in all spheres. The state has a role to play in providing an authoritative set of expectations of civility from all spheres of society, just as those spheres need to have sufficient independence of the state in order to expect that the state live up to the conditions of its legitimacy—namely, that it actually function as the public authority that is dedicated to securing the status of the person for all those who come under its jurisdiction.

Just how civil order relates to democracy depends on what idea of democracy is in view. If it is a constitutional conception of democracy, then it is one that is already imbued with the ethic of civility. Ideas of radical and plebiscitarian democracy are more equivocal in this regard. At the point at which they privilege "the voice of the people" as the paramount value, they drift away from the ethic and ethos of civility for the identity of the people is presupposed as something that is independent of its formation as the specific political society that attends on a specific state. When "the people" or some radical democratic conception of political community is posited as a foundational normative reference point for evaluating the state, the state cannot be permitted the autonomy the civic project requires it to have. At the same time if the constitutional conception of democracy is to enable civility to be a lived practice, there must be an inclusive conception of participation in political society that is constantly reiterated in relation to new demands for inclusion, to "more differentiated identities and potentialities" (Saward 2008:417).

Some of the contributors to this volume interrogate the conceptualization of the relationship between faith and state in the seventeenth century political thought (in particular writings of Thomas Hobbes)—a time when religious wars were endemic and profoundly destructive. The volume also includes texts that work with contemporary twentieth and twenty-first century approaches to the question of security, for instance in context of Agamben's critique of "the state of exception" (see chapters by Saunders and Barber). Still other chapters focus on the issue of subjective capacity for peaceful coexistence. These include (i) an investigation of Norbert Elias's ideas on the establishment of a personality structure of "individual pacification" through the civilizing force of social norms (see the chapter by Van Krieken); (ii) texts concerned with the psychodynamics of the self (see the chapter by Hoggett and Williams); and (iii) explorations of collective narratives that construct and organize meaning in the process of reconciliation after historical violence (see the chapter by Zolkos). Such narratives are central to the anthropology of subjectivity, shaped by the experience of complexity, loss, trauma, and knowledge of the dark side of oneself ("the depressive position").

It follows from the different disciplinary allegiances of the contributors that this volume does not work with a unitary methodological perspective. Some of the contributions employ historical and conceptual methods, while others take more sociological, political, normative-theoretical, and/or critical approaches. However, the civic nexus of state, security, and the subject formation, discussed in greater detail in the introductory chapter to this volume written by Anna Yeatman, provides the individual contributions with a conceptual platform, which is not to say that they take the same position as she does. The tripod of state, security, and subject formation incites a perspectival flexibility of response from the contributors. While individual contributions take under consideration all three elements of the state, security, and subject formation, many tend to give interpretative priority either to one of these elements or to one of their connections, which subsequently serves as the "lens" for contextual and thematic investigation of the whole nexus. The result is a creation of numerous (and numinous) interpretative and analytical possibilities, which tend to be more limited in research frameworks deriving from conceptual architecture resting on binary oppositions.

All that said, the contributions to this volume do not represent a unified and unqualified endorsement of the civic model of the state, security, and the subject. For instance, some of the contributions imply that the possibility of realization of the civic ethos beyond the narrow geopolitical and historical space of the modern Western state is doubtful, thus suggesting that the civic project itself, its universalistic aspirations notwithstanding, needs to be considered as a specific cultural and/or ideological creation. Other contributions question the extent to which the civic project ever acquired a real purchase over historical processes of state–society–subject formation. However, what brings these contributions together is a shared commitment to serious academic exploration, both affirmative and critical, of the civic idea of state, security, and subject formation. This is also what links the historically specific contributions and those of more contemporary provenance. The historical analysis of the emergence of early modern confessional understandings of state institutions share the contemporaneous normative orientation to the history of political thought that characterizes Quentin Skinner's work for example (see Skinner 1998). Such inquiry into the early modern civic project is something more than the development of an historical episteme. Rather, such research is designed to provoke self-reflexivity in the contemporary reader about the (deficiencies of) existing state conceptualizations and practices. It gives insight into once valued political ideas, which had subsequently been downplayed or all together forgotten, but which, it is suggested, we nevertheless should try to regain and recover for our world.

Some of the contributions intimate that there are historical, cultural, ideational, and thematic contexts to which the civic idea might be "foreign," or at least "more distant." Directly or indirectly, they raise the question of what are the benefits, difficulties, and dynamics of its recontextualization into the diversity and complexity of the contemporary world. What is at stake in these problematizations of the civic idea are difficult, yet potentially productive, negotiations between its universality and a range of context-bound (thematic, cultural and theoretical) "particularities." Perhaps a useful way to think of the recontextualizations and, inevitable, renegotiations, of the civic idea is what Judith Butler (2000:14) calls "cultural translation." Processes of such translation indicate an interpretative and political practice with "counter-colonialist possibilities" that exposes "the limits of what the dominant language can handle," and where the (universal) master signifier "loses some of [its] claim to priority and originality precisely by being taken up by a mimetic double" (Butler 2000:36–7).

This volume argues that the civic project can exist only if it commands both understanding and, at least in its fundamentals, assent. As such the civic project (i) provides important themes for academic research, (ii) calls into question the current reassertion of confessional influence of different kinds in relation to the public sphere, and (iii) inspires a secular and metaconfessional project of world-making. The contention is that the current condition of the civic ethos is rather fragile, not to say endangered. One of its main adversaries is the institution of a state that not only privileges, but also is grounded in, a community of faith or national values. The examples we had in mind included not so much contemporary Islamic theocratic conceptions of the state as the various Western state discourses of "national values" as enunciated by George W. Bush for the United States of America, John Howard for Australia, Tony Blair for the United Kingdom, and Stephen Harper for Canada. In this state model, the protection of a particular confessional tapestry becomes highly securitized as a matter of its own preservation and the assertion of its international presence, in an often forceful, violent, and imperial manner. The idea and practice of the state that is founded upon a community of faith or a community of values institutes a particularly reductive view of the human subject, whose primary modality of identification becomes that of (degrees of) non-/belonging to that confessional community. By offering this rich collection of texts, this volume hopes to contribute to the critique of public forms of confessionalism, to testify to its destructive and violent possibilities, and to articulate some politically viable and academically fruitful alternative paradigms of thinking about the state, security, and subject formation.

As a way of acknowledgement, the editors would like to thank the Department of Political Science at the University of Alberta for hosting the workshop and also the Canadian Canada Research Chairs program for affording Anna Yeatman the research funding for the event. Thanks are also due to Joanne Faulkner and George Pavlich, for serving as paper commentators during the workshop; to Alexa DeGagne and Deniz Ferhatoglu, for their technical assistance during the workshop; to Azadeh Etminan, for her careful and high quality work of copy-editing the volume; and to Marie-Claire Antoine, Political Science Editor at Continuum. Finally thanks are due to several workshop contributors who for different reasons did not pursue their papers into book chapters but whose conversational contributions to the development of this project were rich and generous: Jeremy Webber, Emilian Kavalski, Riaz Hassan, Jan Ruzicka, and Kamila Stullerova. We remain particularly indebted to Kamila Stullerova for her valuable contribution to this project, her insightful critique of its ambitions and her comments on individual papers.

Anna Yeatman
Magdalena Zolkos

CHAPTER ONE

State, Security, and Subject Formation— an Introduction

Anna Yeatman

The Question of Security

"Security" is a prominent preoccupation in our era. Just what security means, whose security is in view, and how security is to be attended to, are pressing questions. Here I offer an introduction to the preoccupations that shaped the enterprise that became this book; I do so not with the intention of binding the contributors, for not all would agree with what I have to say, but with that of indicating the nature of the terrain that was the center of our discussion.

There is a fundamental normative question concerning the idea of security. It turns on whether security is conceived as a public or private good. A public conception of security is one that is inclusive, universal, and cooperative. Essentially it is structured by the premise that my or "our" (understood particularistically) security cannot be bought at the expense of yours. Elaborated, this argument repeats the now familiar logic of Hobbes's *Leviathan*, namely, that private strategies of security seeking end up compounding the conditions of insecurity precisely because they license private agents to engage in preemptive attacks on those who may threaten their security. The only effective way of overcoming private strategies of security seeking is the establishment of a state that, as public authority, imposes the terms of pacification on all, inclusively, and, without fear or favor. Thus, the public conception of security combines a normative ethics of inclusion with a pragmatics of enforced universal cooperation, the state being the agency that both mandates cooperation and ensures that the mandate is carried out.

In referring to the state as the public agency of universal pacification, I am reiterating a state-centric conception of political order and of the polity that such order makes possible. The res publica or domain of things public cannot exist except as it is actualized both in and by means of the sovereign state. If the idea of the state is an abstract universal specified in terms of a normative conception of things public, it is also as this abstract universal jurisdictionally specific. Without such specificity, the state cannot exist. It has to be a bounded entity dedicated to the question of how best to secure those who come within these boundaries in such a way that they may flourish. In its actualization, the state becomes a particular state contextualized or situated in relation to the determinations of place (on the idea of place, see Malpas 2006) so that the idea of the res publica, jurisdictionally specified as it is, takes on the complexities and dynamics of these determinations of place. As such the state is unique, an individual of the class of similar individuals (other states).

The individuality of any one state is like all instances of individuality both possible and meaningful only in relation to the presence of other individuals, in this case, the existence of other states. Thus the challenge of the domestic project of pacification for any one particular state is and must be imbricated with the challenge of this project for other states. What presents as an issue of domestic civil order for one state, will see other states being caught up with the same issue as it is given contextual particularity for other states. The issue of reconciling slavery with a modern conception of citizenship, for example, was never an issue just for one state but for all states sharing in the historical era of this particular civic challenge. Instances of domestic terrorism, fuelled as they are by a politics of ressentiment associated with a deep sense of historical injustice and injury, are always internationally networked for those who bear the sense of injury ally with others who have a similar basis of ressentiment. Whether a state's interest in the imposition of civil order is expressed in the peaceful evolution of an already established national-civil project, or as an emergency-driven use of state-sanctioned violence against the threat of terrorism, what one state does on these fronts is necessarily linked to what other states do. This is not to suggest that all states do the same thing or that they have an equal commitment to the terms of civility as they are historically specified. Clearly this is not the case. A state that consistently abrogates the terms of civility—Zimbabwe under Mugabe for example—is a state that positions itself in a "rogue" relationship to other states and the international order of civility they uphold. Whatever may be the conduct of a particular state, its individuality is defined only in relation to the conduct of other states, an individuality that is articulated in the discursive institutions of the interstate order.

Put differently, the state cannot be considered independently of the order of relationships between states. It is useful to make the distinction between the empirical state and the idea of the state as the public authority. We cannot assume that an empirical state will actualize the idea of the state or that, if it does, it does so consistently and coherently. What is of consequence is how far an empirical state understands and commits to the idea of the state. Such understanding and commitment at the level of the individual state is profoundly influenced by the empirical discourses and practices of statehood that prevail at a particular time.

"Mission Drift"—the Corruption of Things Public by Their Subjection to Private Ends

Historically, the empirical state has at different times been more adequate to its civic mission than at others. Marxists have argued that the idea of the state is merely a legitimating cover for the real conduct of the state that is given to the use of the power of the state to advance the private economic interest of capital (or the interest of the bourgeoisie as the class that owns capital). There can be no doubt that at times the political configuration of the empirical state does operate in something like this fashion. Yet should the state abandon its civic mission—its duty to secure on a nondiscriminatory basis those who come under its jurisdiction and to respect the sovereignty of other states—it forfeits legitimacy. At other times, the empirical state is sometimes politically configured so that its civic mission prevails over and contains class power. State formation after the Second World War in the era of a new human rights discourse, postcolonial independent statehood, and the international legal conceptualization of crimes against humanity, invited a civic conception of nation-building that deserves to be more closely studied with a view to understanding the global discursive conception of the state at this time. This was a time, for example, when the social-democratic idea of the welfare state in established state societies was matched by a Nehruvian idea of civic development in the new state of India (for the latter, see Benjamin, Chapter 10, this volume; and Khilnani 1999 especially chapter 1) that belonged to a wider postcolonial conception of civic development offered by the economist Amartya Sen and others.

At the same time in both foreign policy and imperialist ventures, the established states of the modern West have rarely given up an opportunity to advance their private interest as states even if at the same time they use their power to impose a new civic order in a context where it has broken down or never been established. The "domestic" civic project has never been matched in the international arena by a clearly conceived obligation of the state to do what it can on an impartial basis to contribute to the civic order elsewhere.

The postwar era of state formation in a civic mold did not last. The era of independent statehood for erstwhile colonies of Western imperialist powers decisively ended discussion and debate concerning the colonizer's obligation to regulate and restrain the "private empire of money" and market forces (Von Tunzelman 2007:15) in the colonies in order to ensure that some kind of public purpose and civic order were established. Now private market forces could operate globally without restraint. The new international legal regimes of free trade and human rights developed in parallel with there being no require-ment of global trading interests to comply with human rights. In this context, the power of private capital both in eluding the public jurisdictional effectiveness of states and in developing new global reach has been extraordinary. With such power, the model of the unregulated market economy (the ideology of "laissez-faire"') has been reasserted in public policy both within states and their international agencies.

The reassertion of laissez-faire as the orientation for public policy has caused a process of "mission drift" for the state. Public ends and processes have been displaced by private ends and processes associated with the dynamics of the market economy. The substance of civic professionalism on behalf of things public has been displaced by the economic value of productivity with its emphasis on efficiency (maximizing output, doing more with less, etc.). Measuring performance understood in terms of output has displaced political judgment concerning public policy and its delivery (see Radin 2006). It would not be correct to view this process of mission drift in terms of the reassertion of the class power of the bourgeoisie over the state. It is more complex than that. Arguably the champions of the "performance movement" have been the bureaucratic leaders of large complex organizations both public and private. We need an account of how the late twentieth century and early twenty-first century political society has permitted a form of dedifferentiation, specifically, the displacement of the distinctive claims of the civic project as an inherently public project by the distinctive claims of the economic. Domestically, this has opened up the civic project of the state to a form of corruption that follows on the contracting out of public services to private for-profit agencies. The cor-ruption resides in the state's reliance on private commercial motivation to undertake the work of the state. Internationally, a parallel sort of corruption prevails: instead of the possibility that privileged states, ones that enjoy stability and resources, might lend their strength to assist other states in stabilizing their own civic project, there is a tendency for states in the former category to conceive such assistance so that it furthers the interest of their own national private economic firms.

Corruption does not designate only dishonest, unlawful, and deceitful uses of public power and funds. Substantively, it designates any use of the public authority of the state to serve private ends, which being so, are necessarily exclusive and irreconcilable with the ethical universality of the state. So regarded, the mission drift to which I have been referring is an invitation to the corruption of the state qua public authority by private interests of one kind or another. This occurs even when the trappings of transparency, accountability, and public audit are maintained. When private agencies, both for-profit and nonprofit, are permitted by the state to take over its work, the private ends of civil society readily displace the public ends of the sovereign state if these are not rethought and enunciated to fit the situation.

Human Rights and the Idea of "Humanitarian Intervention"

The adoption of human rights "as the master discourse of international law" (Yeatman 2001:108) after 1945 ended the right of the sovereign state to do as it pleased with those who came under its sovereignty with the exception of foreign nationals who belonged to the jurisdiction of another sovereign state (see Yeatman 2001:109). Now the state was obliged to respect the rights of those subject to it, and to be held to account in this respect. Paul Sieghart (cited in Yeatman 2001:110) proposes that this meant that the "strict doctrine of national sovereignty has been cut down in two crucial respects":

> First, how a State treats its own subjects is now the legitimate concern of international law. Secondly, there is now a superior international standard, established by common consent, which may be used for judging domestic laws and the actual conduct of sovereign States within their own territories and in the exercise of their internal jurisdictions, and may therefore be regarded as ranking in the hierarchy of laws even above national constitutions.

It is this last claim of Sieghart that is the most contentious one. If the international law of human rights enjoys supremacy over national constitutions, it would seem that the state no longer enjoys sovereignty. This is a contradiction in terms for reasons I explain below: if the state is not sovereign, it is not an effective state.

This is a large and complex topic that I will not attempt to canvass here. It is relevant, however, to refer to the idea of humanitarian intervention with a sovereign state in order to protect the human rights of those subject to this state, an idea that has assumed currency in both practical international politics and contemporary political thought (see Cohen 2008).

The international discourse of humanitarian intervention licenses an international coalition of states in violating the sovereignty of an individual state in the name of rescuing its subjects from what are said to be gross violations of human rights. It is however impossible to disentangle the particular, or private interest of the states participating in the coalition from their shared public interest in securing an international set of conditions for civic order. On the terms of political thought of the kind that Locke and Hobbes offer, it is not clear that anyone other than those subject to the authority and power of the state have a right to determine when that state has forfeited its legitimacy from which it follows, I think, that those who do not belong to this particular political community of interest have no right to impose the terms of civil pacification on those who do belong to it. However, it is reasonable to propose that the political community of states has an interest in conserving civic order both internationally and within states, for as I have proposed, these two aspects of civic order are integrally linked. From this line of argument, one would expect to see the elaboration of a case for harnessing the international capacity of states to assisting in building the effectiveness of individual states that, for some reason, are faltering in their civic mission.

In short, it is more important to sustain the effectiveness of a sovereign state than it is to destroy it in the name of allegedly human values as "human rights" have come to be conceived at least in the contemporary West (see Cohen 2006; Cohen 2008). When the discourse of human rights is invoked by a particular party in the interstate order to claim legitimate force in relation to another state, the burden of proof surely is to demonstrate that this is not the imposition of a private conception of security, namely one that in some way advantages some state or group of states in relation to another.

A Private as Distinct from Public Conception of Security

A private conception of security, then, is one that compromises, displaces, or cancels a public conception of security by conceiving the nature of security such that it makes some safer as persons and in the conduct of their affairs than others. A private conception of security is inherently discriminatory while a public conception of security is not. A private conception of security is just that, privative, depriving at least in relative terms others of their right to security in order to protect the security of a particular interest, be this that of a state or community of states, of private firms, or individuals. As Hobbes put it so clearly in the *Leviathan*: a private orientation to security leads the subject in question to do all that it can do to enhance its power in relation to others, a rationality that makes it sensible to preemptively and unilaterally "by force or wiles, . . . master the persons of all men he can . . . till he see no other power great enough to endanger him" (Hobbes 1996:88). Security seeking in such a setting assumes the shape of the private accumulation of power: there is only power, there is no right—"there be no Propriety, no Dominion, no Mine and Thine distinct; but onely that to be every mans, that he can get; and for so long, as he can keep it" (Hobbes 1996:90).

The question of security, then, is entirely different depending on whether it is considered to be private or public in nature. Framed in terms of Carl Schmitt's conception of the political as based in the distinction between friend and enemy (see Barbour, Chapter 4, this volume), the question of security necessarily assumes a private cast. For it is the security of the homogeneous community of identity (those that constitute us and our friends) that is legitimately to be protected in relation to those we understand as our enemies. Within this framework, we cannot make our way to a public conception of security, one that suggests that it makes neither ethical nor pragmatic sense to privilege the security of one group in relation to another. Notwithstanding Schmitt's appropriation of Hobbes (see Schmitt 1996 [1938]), Hobbes did not operate on the terrain of an exclusivist identity politics of the kind that Schmitt presumes. Hobbes is able to offer a public conception of security precisely because he confers an equality of standing on all the subjects who find themselves, in context of private security seeking, in a war of all against all. He rejects all forms of identity-based distinction that legitimize the assertion of one subject's power over another. Vickie Sullivan (2004:90) rightly emphasizes the radical nature of Hobbes's conception of equality among human beings, which he supported by claiming "the faculties of the mind are equally distributed among humankind" (Sullivan 2004:90). Significantly, Hobbes argues that "those who seek superiority resist a common authority, whereas those who do not seek pre-eminence welcome such an authority." A competitive orientation to the private accumulation of power, one that leads the subject to feel justified in doing what is necessary to "kill, subdue, supplant, or repel the other" (Hobbes 1996:70) is fuelled by the dynamics of vainglory, the assertion of the primacy of one's own identity, and the needs based in it over those of others. Hobbes's argument discloses the hidden dimension of Schmitt's antagonistic conception of the political (the friend/enemy distinction): it is based on a rejection of human equality and on an embrace of a competitive struggle for preeminence that must necessarily be structured as a series of competitive identity claims reductive in the end to the simple structure of such a claim—I am better than you, or, you think yourself better than me, and, you are wrong. In this context, consider at more length Vicki Sullivan's discussion of Hobbes's commitment to the premise of equality:

> Hobbes finds a fundamental divide between those who seek to elevate themselves over others and those who do not. The Englishman explains that "considering the great difference there is in men, from the diversity of their passions, how some are vainly glorious, and hope for precedency and superiority above their fellows, not only when they are equal in power, but also when they are inferior; we must needs acknowledge that it must necessarily follow, that those men who are moderate, and look for no more but equality of nature, shall be obnoxious to the force of others, that will attempt to subdue them.'" As he says here, there is a great diversity in men, a diversity that arises from the diversity of the passions, but he points to only one fundamental division, that between those who seek superiority and those who do not. Those who are dissatisfied with equality will victimize those who are content with it (Sullivan 2004:95).

A public conception of security implies that we concern ourselves with the challenge of peaceful coexistence as this challenge is given shape and specificity by the historical context in which it appears. Considered as a political end, peaceful coexistence is oriented by an ethics of human equality and subjective right. It turns on a contextually responsive and publicly oriented consideration of the standing of each human being as someone entitled to live their life in as secure a manner as possible. Such consideration leads in the direction of asking what it is that the state as the public authority must do in order to secure the standing of each human being as a subject of right, a person. The state as the public authority is the state under law, and, thus global consideration of the terms of peaceful coexistence demand a conception of law that can work with a genuinely universal, in the sense of nondiscriminatory, conception of human rights that can be implemented within the state as the only possible guarantor of the right to have rights. A nondiscriminatory conception of human rights has always to be contextually specified, and such specification in order to remain nondiscriminatory has to be subject to public accountability and critique both within any particular state and the international community of states. In a public conception of security, there can be no legitimate privileging of the security of one group, nation, culture, or civilization over that of another. If, in fact, the security of the state as the body politic—that is, a publicly constituted jurisdiction that includes those who are subject to this jurisdiction—is under threat from either internal or external forces, it must defend its integrity, but it will do it in the name of its integrity as a state, not its integrity as a community of identity.

This may seem a puzzling claim in the face of a development with which Hobbes did not have to reckon: the specification of the idea of the state in terms of a nationalist conception of "the people." In fact, the schema of the state offered by civil philosophers such as Hobbes and Locke precludes an idea of the state as expressive of the identity of a particular people, understood as a prepolitical given. In both accounts, the political community, comprising those individual subjects whose right is now guaranteed by the state as sovereign public authority, comes into being only with and by means of the agency of the state so understood. Without the state understood as the guarantor of the security of each on a nondiscriminatory basis, there can be no political community, for this community exists only as a shared subjection to a state that imposes the terms of peaceful coexistence on these individuals. Individualism is inherent within the ethical commitment to equality: it is as individuals that each human being is a subject of right, someone whose security matters, and therefore demands the protection of the state. Political community so understood can be expressed in a civic nationalism that holds itself accountable to human rights both domestically (within the nation-state), and, so far as this does not interfere with the integrity of other states, internationally. But political community in this civil sense cannot be reconciled with an identity-based nationalism; one that being so makes the claims of the identity-based group prior to those of the individual and advances the claims of this group as precedent to those of other identity-based groups.

This book was conceived as a response to the privately oriented discourse of security that has prevailed since 9/11 within the West. This is a discourse that realizes Carl Schmitt's conception of the political as a zero-sum game of antagonism between friend and enemy. Whether it is the vantage point of Jihad, or that of Western civilization, the assumption is that one's own (group-based) identity is that of a superior morality or civilization, and that this being so, it makes sense to do what is necessary to defend this morality or civilization in the face of the antagonism of the other. Each antagonist calls its enemy into being and lends it its rhetoric, the difference being only the valuing of the one in relation to the other. The idea of civilized conduct as practices of civility that enable the terms of peaceful coexistence to be sustained is rejected; a universalistic civility is discounted and, instead, a defensive and competitive assertion of values in the face of an assumed enemy is made. A particular identity is represented as the home of a true or genuine civility that the enemy is said to lack.

Here civility is trumped by culture (this is a point that Anne Phillips, 2007, can be taken to be arguing in her important book *Multiculturalism without Culture*). Perhaps the most egregious expression of this contemporary development is the view that civil philosophy is merely an identity game—the expression of Western civilization understood in culturalist terms. The value of equality is made to seem simply the expression of a particular, in this case "Western" culture, a strange complicity with a Western sense of civilizational superiority that maintains an invested ignorance of the attachment to equality that can be found in Buddhism or, in the Indian context, in a long-standing tradition of critique of caste hierarchy in the name of equality.[1] An ethical orientation to the standing of the individual as a person who deserves consideration and security of being in his or her own right, and thus to some form of pragmatics of peaceful coexistence, is not the prerogative of any one culture or civilization. It is an achievement of human society; where it exists, authority is conceived and instituted so that it functions on behalf of this orientation. In the modern type of large scale organization, this authority assumes the form of the state, supported as it must be by the agencies of civil society (including the professions) and by the civic comportment of individuals.

The displacement of civility by cultural identity is a political outcome that represents a defeat for all those who would be advocates of a contemporary civil philosophy. It is an outcome that is worked for by those who are interested in a competitive struggle for power associated with some conception that, by right, their identity should take precedence over that of others. As I have said, a political ethic of civility is tied to an equalitarian conception of the individual as a subject of right, a person. Such an ethic is earthbound, as Hannah Arendt (1998 [1958]:3) might have put it. The integrity of the individual as a living being—as a self who has a right to be preserved (see Yeatman, Chapter 8, this volume)—assumes importance only if, in Hobbes's (1996:46) phrase, the "felicity of this life," the joys and challenges of engaging in the business of being alive, is valued as the central point of reference for what it is that we as a political community need to consider. Why is it that war should be the option of last resort? Surely it is because we share a frame of reference that brings to light the nature of the destruction that war involves—the destruction of human lives not just in the present but carried over into the future as those who have suffered war trauma continue to suffer it and pass their suffering onto new generations; the destruction of other creatures and their habitat; the legacy of intercommunal hatred; and, not least, the conversion of scarce resources that might be used for peaceful ends into weapons of war. What all such facets of war-induced destruction have in common is the negation of the desire to get on with everyday living on the part not just of humans but also of other species and living organisms. Such claims are made to seem far less important than those associated with the prosecution of war that is driven by identity politics.

Mary Kaldor (1999:6) suggests that what makes contemporary wars "new" is that they are driven by identity politics: "By identity politics, I mean the claim to power on the basis of a particular identity—be it national, clan, religious or linguistic." In concert with my argument in this chapter she (1999:10) proposes:

> The key to any long-term solution is the restoration of legitimacy, the reconstitution of the control of organized violence by public authorities, whether local, national or global. This is both a political process—the rebuilding of trust in and support for public authorities—and a legal process—the re-establishment of a rule of law within which public authorities operate. This cannot be done on the basis of particularistic politics.

Kaldor's conception of new wars seems to fit the contemporary mode of warfare whether reference is to the Palestinian–Israeli conflict, to the Pakistani–Indian war over Kashmir, or to the Western interstate coalition's War on Terror.

The historical achievements of a res publica associated with the development ("nation-building") of a particular state are readily undone by war that is driven by identity politics. By a res publica, I mean not only the institutional order associated with public schooling, a publicly funded health system and other social services, but an ethical comportment on the part of state services that is civil in nature—that is, services are designed and delivered so that they contribute their part in securing the integrity of each individual considered as a person or subject of right. It is not just that war takes over resources that might otherwise have been spent on schools and public health; it is not just that war devastates the environment of those who live in it, and that prolonged war leads to perpetual environmental devastation; the more fundamental problem is that those who prosecute war in the name of identity politics have a studied contempt for the quotidian and prosaic claims of ordinary lives and ordinary living.

Genuinely defensive war on behalf of the terms of peaceful coexistence does not share this contempt for ordinary lives and ordinary living, but is dedicated to the restoration of the terms on which getting on with such ordinariness is possible. Great public institutional achievements are possible in the context of such war so that they continue to be built upon after the war has ceased, in peacetime. I have in mind the Second World War and its aftermath in places such as Australia and the United Kingdom, a war where the allies saw themselves in a coalition of defense of sovereign constitutional statehood against the threat posed by the Nazi and Japanese states.

The stakes are high indeed when we confront the fundamental question of security: is it to be a public or a private conception of security? As I have indicated, this question is not new. In context of the religious wars of the sixteenth and seventeenth centuries, the early modern civil philosophers clearly recognized these stakes. Thus it was they so clearly enunciated the terms of a public conception of security, and of the state as the only possible agency by which this conception can be imposed.

The State as the Guarantor of Subjective Right

The essential and defining nature of the state as the public authority is that its purpose is grounded in doing what the state can do to assist in and to secure the self-preservation of each individual who comes under the jurisdiction of the state. The authority of the state so understood resides in its protection of the subjective right of the individual where the core of subjective right concerns the self-preservation of this individual. The early modern theorists such as Locke and Hobbes gave prominence to the subjective right of self-preservation. With rare exceptions, the significance of so doing has gone unremarked: either the idea of subjective right as the right of the individual to self-preservation is evacuated into an empty humanism that assumes precisely that which should be argued, or, it is displaced by a cynical proposition that, in suggesting this right is more often contravened than observed, tacitly relies on the normative force of this idea of right without bothering to take responsibility for its advocacy.

The right to self-preservation is a right, and this is why it requires the combination of authority and power in the state to both positively specify and practically secure this right. It is a right to live as the uniquely individual subject that one is (for elaboration, see Yeatman, Chapter 8, this volume). It is a right that precedes all other rights, and thus constitutes the most fundamental right, what Blandine Kriegel, following early modern natural law theorists, terms *status libertatis*: "*Status libertatis* has to do with liberty and personal security, the right of each person to his own body, the right to life" (1995:35).

The legitimacy of the state resides in its orientation and practice on behalf of the security of subjective right qua *status libertatis*. When a state acts in such a way as to neglect, abandon, compromise, or violate the subjective right of those or some of those who come under its jurisdiction, it loses legitimacy in relation to these acts. Should such action become the dominant patterning of how a particular state operates, it loses legitimacy in general. In civil philosophy, the presumption is that it is only those who are subject to the action of such a state who have the right to call it to account for its dereliction and commission of wrong; it is only they who can judge at what point the state has lost any legitimacy it might claim and what it is they need to do to overthrow it.

The right to self-preservation constitutes the individual as someone who deserves the status of a person. To be a person is to count as someone whose being is valued and who therefore others cannot treat in such a way that abrogates or violates his or her distinctive being. As persons, individuals are equal, but this does not mean that, in other respects, they are equal, for they clearly are not. Some kinds of inequality demand that the status of the person be adapted so as to take them into account differences in developmental maturity, for example.

The personhood of the baby is to count, but it requires a different kind and modality of recognition than that of the experienced and skilled older adult. Gender difference also can be socially recognized in ways that are congruent with a shared equality of status between men and women as persons. When we understand that the right of each individual to self-preservation is the core of the status of the person, it is much easier to see how subjective right so understood can be reconciled with acknowledgment of the many differences between people.

Properly understood, a politics that is normatively oriented in terms of the right to self-preservation is as normatively radical now as it ever was. The right to self-preservation or "right to personal security" (Kriegel 1995:40) has, Kriegel argues, "pride of place among all individual rights." Kriegel elaborates further on the primordial nature of the right of self-preservation:

> It is the only one that is nonnegotiable. More importantly, it is the only *civil* right. . . . *Homo homini lupus*: the anarchical and collective law of force poses a constant threat to each person's physical safety. In the civil state, by contrast, the sovereign's confiscation of all acts of war, his monopoly on the sword of justice, brings about individual security by means of the rule of law. (1995:40)

The real force of Hobbes's argument for the sovereign state is this: under the conditions of large-scale social organization, there can be no consensual political authority based on a community of faith or values for it is the nature of such organization to be involved in differences in matters of fundamental belief. The only kind of authority that can command obedience because it is able to function publicly on behalf of the self-preservation of all individuals that come under its jurisdiction, without fear or favor, is the state. The state binds and brings into being the political community of those who come within its jurisdiction. It obliges them to interact on the terms of peaceful coexistence. Within the containment that a shared political order supplies, conflict between values, identities, and professions of faith has to be peacefully articulated and negotiated. This is more easily achieved if the state both respects and cultivates regional polities that permit an anchoring of public policy in locally transacted relationships and challenges. People have to learn how to comport themselves so that they are capable of peaceful coexistence even under conditions where there are fundamental and deep disagreements dividing them.

The terms of peaceful coexistence have to be determined and negotiated in relation to the specific historical context that informs the body politic. They are never settled once and for all but have continually to be addressed anew so that the state as the public authority is ready to learn about new fault lines and bases of conflict, and to determine how they are best addressed if they are to be effectively contained within civil order. Thus the state as the agency of an effective and practical political community of peaceful coexistence has to welcome, facilitate, and resource the opening of public spaces within which conflict, dissension, and discussion about the terms of peaceful coexistence can occur. These public spaces have to be permitted an independence in relation to the state so that the stability as well as sovereignty of the state as a set of institutional practices is not compromised by the discursive openness of public spaces, the quality of conditionality that characterizes the positions taken in public debate, and the unpredictable fluidity of the twists and turns in public debate.[2] It is through participation in public space—including the public spaces that the everyday environments of schools, families, neighborhoods, and workspaces—that people learn how to practice a civility that fits the specific historical demands of how they interact and converse with their fellows as well as learn from them.

It is the state that is the sovereign power with regard to the conditions of possibility of the body politic. To be sovereign is to have the right and the power to impose the terms of civil order as these terms fit the demands of the day. Sovereignty and the idea of the state are mutually defining terms. To cite Kriegel again with reference to the early modern doctrine of power as sovereignty: "Supreme power, as Bodin defined it, is also as Loyseau emphasized, the *very essence of the state*: 'Sovereignty is the form which gives being to the state; it is inseparable from the state; without it, the state vanishes'" (Kriegel 1995:15). Sovereignty denotes the absolute power of the state to impose, institute, and maintain political order. It is absolute because no one, and no truth claim, can be exempt from submission to the political order so far as the question of civil order is the question that is to hand. Thus, sovereignty trumps all theological claims that privilege the claims of a sacral authority over civil life. It also (a point insisted upon by Saunders, Chapter 5, this volume) trumps the secular liberal version of such claims, that outside and prior to the positive law instituted by the state, there is some ideal law of reason that is to be privileged over the laws that the state brings into being.

For sovereignty to be sovereignty, it must be absolute in nature. However, this does not mean that sovereignty is not self-limiting. The very basis of sovereignty, residing as it does in the right of the individuals who come under its power and authority for self-preservation, indicates that it must be both absolute and self-limiting (this is a point that both Hunter [Chapter 2] and Saunders [Chapter 5] stress in this volume). Its exercise cannot be such as to arbitrarily and unlawfully violate the right of the individual to self-preservation. Nor can the exercise of sovereignty extend beyond the sphere of what is involved in the constitution and protection of a civil community of coexistent persons, each accorded the right of self-preservation. Kriegel (1995:31) points out that, if absolute sovereign power were unlimited, "sovereignty would be no different from feudal domination," where the subject has no right, but is simply subjected to domination and force. Thus, the military and police arms of the state are required to be self-limiting to develop a professional ethics that demands that they practice a disciplined art of force, oriented to securing the right to self-preservation of those they are charged to protect, and limited in its exercise by respect for the rights of ordinary criminals and enemy aliens. Furthermore, beyond the concern of the sovereign state with securing the right to self-preservation, and a body politic in which the terms of peaceful coexistence are enforced, it has no authority over how its subjects live, what they consider truth to be, or how they conduct their business.

Subject Formation

Only subjects who know what it means to value civility and why it matters will commit to the practice of civility. Only subjects, who have learnt how to act as someone who takes responsibility for their own action, and to regard others as persons in their own right, are capable of practicing civility. Political authority has a role to play in the cultivation of the valuing and practice of civility. It does this best when it models the valuing and practice of civility as distinct from engaging in a didactic pedagogy of civility. People learn far more about what civility involves and why it matters if they enjoy membership of a political community where in everyday life it is clear that the authority of the state upholds a nondiscriminatory value of respect for each individual as a person and expects that people will treat and interact with each other on the basis of such respect. People will also learn the art of civility if political authority deploys it; thus, for instance, the art of listening carefully to those who hold different opinions from one self is best demonstrated in the modus operandi of political authority in all contexts of its operation.

The civil professions have a key role to play here. These are the professions that include not just those who are charged with conducting the business of the state but also the professions that attend to the claims of the person considered as a self (see Yeatman et al. 2008b, Part I, especially chapter 2). Such professions include nursing, social work, teaching, medicine, and management. The civil professions are those that realize in different ways the ethical orientation of the state to security for individuals as distinct selves. To offer some examples of what I have in mind here: an ethic of public service that includes all stakeholders and brings them into conversation with officials in the design, implementation, and evaluation of policy in a particular area; classroom practice that cultivates in each child the ability to listen to others and to use such listening to inform his/her conduct; a general practitioner who enters into a clinical alliance with the patient to treat his/her suffering in a way that maintains respect for the patient and his or her lifeworld and builds the patient's capacity for intelligent and reflective self-care; public health nurses who provide both support for new mothers in coping with the demands of parenting and an early intervention service for babies; and a social worker who facilitates his/her client in learning how to stay out of jail, acquire new life skills, and engage in ongoing, legitimate employment.

In his book *The Politics of Uncertainty*, Peter Marris (1996) argues that the individual's history of attachment influences what pattern of managing uncertainty seems to make most sense to him or her, whether it be a competitive or cooperative approach to the management of uncertainty. Marris (1996:43) comments:

> Three aspects of attachment are especially relevant to how we experience uncertainty and try to deal with it. First, because our security in childhood is so fundamentally

associated with the attachment figures who take care of us, our sense of security continues to be intimately connected to attachment relationships throughout our lives. Second, the particular nature of that childhood experience of attachment will profoundly affect the confidence or anxiety, trust or ambivalence, with which approach attachments later in life. Third, in learning how to manage our need for attachment, we are learning at the same time about the nature of power and control, the sources of consistency, predictability, order and chaos, and we apply what we have learned to many other kinds of relationships.

The attachment history of an individual shapes his or her capacities for trust in the availability of cooperative, openhearted, and optimistic possibilities of working with others. If the individual acts on the premise that such possibilities are real, then he or she will contribute to shaping a pattern of relationship with others where these possibilities become real. In order to trust, however, an individual has to have been fortunate enough to be able to trust in the care and protection those charged with his or her parenting offered him or her. If this bond of trust is broken through serious neglect, abandonment, or abuse at the hands of others, then it is less likely that the individual can approach possibilities of connection with others in a trustful, optimistic, and cooperative way. The cooperative option as distinct from the competitive one makes sense only to those who have experienced it. Where individuals have been forced to rely on their own resources in a competitive relationship to others, this pattern of self-reliance is likely to be their default option.

The attachment histories of individuals are not independent of their social experience. While public policy cannot make up directly for parenting that has not been "good enough" in D. W. Winnicott's phrase (see Abram 1996:193–4), it can do a great deal to assist people in being good enough parents, thereby helping to create not just for the child a positive attachment experience but enabling a wider societal environment of support for such experience. There is much that can be done in this area including, not least, the reduction of poverty.

There is a close relationship between individuals' subjective experience and their capacity to practice civility. Contemporary political society seems more willing than in the past to know something of subjective experience. There are a number of protocols for civility—for example, those of restorative justice—that are designed to facilitate individual self-awareness and to support individuals so that they do not have to revert to "splitting." Splitting is a psychic defense whereby the individual shores up his or her sense of self by splitting off what is good from what is bad, casting the bad outside him(her)self, and seeking to hold together what is left inside by identifying it with the good. While this is a genuinely defensive structure designed to protect the individual's sense of self, it is a profoundly self-defeating one. It brings about a severe depletion of self with the casting out of all that the individual thinks of as bad about him or herself; it then creates an external persecutory force of the bad in relation to an individual whose boundaries are already brittle and weak, and who consequently becomes paranoid in relation to others; in turn, it justifies the individual in refusing to trust those who he/she sees as persecutory; and, finally, split violently off from the bad, the good is idealized in such a way that it cannot possibly be exemplified by actors who are in Nietzsche's phrase human, all too human, thus leading to chronic disappointment of the individual in both others and him/herself. Of course, an individual whose psyche is structured in this way (it is the paranoid–schizoid position first conceived by Melanie Klein and discussed by Hoggett and Williams in Chapter 6, this volume) will act as though external reality is the same as his or her internal reality. An individual's tendency to idealize others (to ask them to be emblematic of the good) is not a way of living alongside and cooperating with all too human fellow beings; and his or her tendency to compete with others who he or she fears as potential persecutors is not a way of inviting others to engage in shared civility with them.

It is not appropriate in my view to map the inner dynamics of the individual psyche onto the dynamics of social life, but Marris is right surely: there is a connection between them. A society that invites people to think in terms of simple either/or moral distinctions between virtue and evil and to project these distinctions onto a cast of characters, those like us who are committed to virtue, and the Other who is committed to evil, is a society that is also inviting people to engage in the psychic mechanism of splitting. This is the argument that Hoggett and Williams make in their chapter (Chapter 6). A society that is interested in cultivating civility will be one that embraces knowledge of the internal complexities of subjective life, of how the good folds into the bad, and back again. It will seek to know more about how the state can provide both policy and funded support for the development in individuals of a subjective capacity for civility.

Conclusion

The security I have argued concerns the right of each individual to self-preservation. Of course, just what self-preservation involves is something that needs discussion since it refers to something quite other than mere survival (see Yeatman, Chapter 8, this volume; and Yeatman 2008a). Essentially, it is the right of the individual to live a life that is his or her own, free from the domination of an arbitrary will, and secure access to the goods that constitute human welfare. Right is inherently relational because it refers to the standing of the subject within his or her relationships to other subjects. In this case, the subject of right is the individual, thus implying all individuals, in how they are positioned vis-à-vis each other. The question then becomes one of how to secure the right to self-preservation on a universal and nondiscriminatory basis.

I have argued that Hobbes's insight was profound: security cannot be achieved through private effort because it is the nature of private effort to be self-preferential, inclusive of the interest of others only when it serves or, at least, does not contradict the private interest of the one (whatever the nature of the subject who constitutes the one). In other words, a private orientation to security ensures that the security of one or some is bought at the expense of the security of others. For those who have more power than others, a private orientation to security is always the tempting path to follow. It was Hobbes's genius to decisively demonstrate that such a path creates worse conditions of security for all, an endless vicious cycle that brings about a chronic situation of war, fear, and a competitive approach to the management of uncertainty (Marris 1996).

More simply we can say: subjective right is an inherently public matter. More emphatically, I would argue that "things public" (the res publica) understood in a modern sense takes on meaning only with reference to the idea of subjective right and the institutional order that is designed to secure it. I have argued that this institutional order is that of the modern (democratic constitutional) state as it supplies the framework, containment, and processes of civic order. Civic order refers to an ordering of human relationships that ensures that those who are involved in these relationships are secure—that they enjoy terms of peaceful coexistence, and that they have recourse to the protection of the public authority if they are subject to the discriminatory, abusive, or domineering will of another. Some would call this a rather straitened view of public life for it eschews the championship of an idea of the good life beyond that, which is involved in the establishment of a civic order for all to enjoy their respective and individual right to self-preservation. Yet it is the only one that guarantees that the individual is not subjected to the imposition of someone else's conception of the good life. It is not quite right to call this position "liberal" for liberalism is a coat of many colors, and it can accommodate a view of politics as the adjudication of group claims. Group claims by the standards of subjective right are inherently privat(iv)e in nature: not only do they presume their own priority in relation to the claims of other groups, but, of nature, a group claim subordinates subjective right to the integrity of the group. Group claims cannot be reconciled with what I have called subjective right.

It is not liberalism but civil philosophy that is oriented to what is involved in conceiving subjective right (the right to self-preservation) as the primordial political right, and to a conception of the state as the agency of the res publica, understood as a shared individual interest in security for subjective right. Ian Hunter and others have shown that seventeenth century civil philosophy was remarkable for the clarity by which it offered these conceptions, a development in thought that was provoked by a long period of chronic religious warfare. We seem again to be in an historical position where we are provoked to rethink the nature of civil philosophy in terms that fit the demands of the present.

Notes

1. Anne Phillips' (2007:35) example is grist to my mill: "Indian notions of caste differences are sometimes cited as evidence that the idea of a fundamental human equality remains alien to many cultures. Amartya Sen notes, however, that dissident voices have spoken against caste differences at least as far back as the *Mahabharata*, as in Bharadvaja's comment that 'we all seem to be affected by desire, anger, fear, sorrow, worry, hunger, and labour: how do we have caste differences then?'"
2. This conception of the decoupling of the state and a discursive public sphere is offered by Dryzek (2005) but I have formulated it more in terms of an earlier argument concerning the relationship of state to civil society offered by Alberto Melucci (1988).

CHAPTER TWO

The Man and the Citizen: the Pluralization of Civil Personae in Early Modern German Natural Law

Ian Hunter

Introduction

In the preface to his *De officio hominis et civis* of 1672, the Saxon natural law political philosopher Samuel Pufendorf (1632–1694) introduced a set of distinctions that he hoped would reshape the relations between law, religion, and politics in natural law thought.[1] Pufendorf argued that it is necessary to separate civil law, natural law, and moral theology by accepting that the first concerns laws derived from the commands of a sovereign, while the second pertains to norms for civil conduct derived from natural reason, and the third to norms for man's spiritual welfare derived from divine revelation. Moreover, natural law and civil law pertain only to man's external conduct, while moral theology concerns his inner moral condition. He then continued:

> But by far the greatest difference is that the scope of the discipline of natural law is confined to the orbit of this life, and so it forms man on the assumption that he is to lead this life in society with others. Moral theology, however, forms a Christian man, who, beyond his duty to pass this life in goodness, has an expectation of reward for piety in the life to come and who therefore has his citizenship [*politeuma*] in the heavens while here he lives merely as a pilgrim or stranger. (Pufendorf 1991:8–9)

In Pufendorf's separation of the Christian man whose salvation is the concern of the theologian from the political subject or citizen whose civil conduct is the sole concern of the positive and natural jurist, we encounter a central and characteristic instance of the pluralization of moral personae in early modern German natural law thought. In Pufendorf's natural law, this pluralization formed part of a deep and wide-ranging program to separate political authority from spiritual discipline—citizenship from religious community—and to reconfigure the relations between them. At the centre of this program stands the figure of the civil sovereign no longer concerned with spiritual felicity of his subjects as Christians, but focused solely on the governance of their civil conduct as citizens (Hunter 2001; Seidler 2002).

THE MAN AND THE CITIZEN 17

This pluralizing and secularizing program was neither uncontested nor destined to sweep the field as the harbinger of a rational and enlightened modernity. It was vehemently attacked by contemporary Christian natural jurists and philosophical theologians, and by their secular surrogate, the savant metaphysician Gottfried Wilhelm Leibniz (Schneider 1967; Schneider 2001). In a critique that would be relayed into the twentieth century via Kant, Leibniz argued that the civil conduct of citizens is inseparable from their transcendent aspirations and expectations, which means that there is no sharp division between the personae of citizen and man, and that theologians and metaphysicians should continue to play a key role in determining the norms of civil conduct (Leibniz 1972; Pufendorf 2003). Leibniz's views too formed part of a larger project, according to which the prince or state cannot restrict civil law to the secular purpose of maintaining social peace, as the law itself is beholden to a transcendent justice grounded in divine ideas and acceded to by philosophical theologians rather than political jurists (Hunter 2003). In this regard, though, Leibniz was updating at the end of the seventeenth century doctrines of Christian natural law and *politica Christiana* from the century's beginning, which were in fact the doctrines against which Pufendorf's program had first been elaborated (Schneider 2001). Legal, political, and religious authority were so mutually enmeshed within the cultural and political institutions of the early modern Holy Roman–German Empire—and so profoundly overdetermined by the religious and political conflicts of the sixteenth and seventeenth centuries—that all attempts to reconfigure them could only be regarded as programmatic and interested, hence as intrinsically contested by other programs and interests.

This suggests a necessary corrective to modern attempts to understand such programs from the standpoint of a monovalent normative moral or political philosophy (Denzer 1972; Schneewind 1996). Whatever their merits as normative philosophy, these accounts are anachronistic in relation to the actual intellectual character and cultural-political uses of early modern natural law. Natural law was not a surrogate for systematic philosophy and, prior to the end of the eighteenth century, it had no interest in seeking a formal foundation for moral and political norms. Rather, it was a shifting matrix for an array of positive disciplines—theology, positive law, moral philosophy, and political science—loosely framed by the idea of a law that is "natural" in two senses: in being grounded in man's moral nature, and in being acceded to via natural as opposed to revealed knowledge. The arguments that took place within this framework—over the character of man's moral nature and the relations between revealed truth and natural reason—were irredeemably interested and programmatic (Friedeburg 2003; Hunter 2004a).

It was this disciplinary-matrix character of natural law that permitted exchanges to take place between several domains of personhood—legal personality, metaphysical and theological anthropologies, moral psychologies, and political theories of duty and office—forming the shifting and contested field in which the conceptualization of moral personae took place. Rather than being formal philosophies of law or politics, the different forms of natural law, with their rival constructions of man and citizen, were in fact competing "theory programs." The role of these theory programs was to provide the intellectual architecture for different orderings of the relations between law, religion, and politics, suited to different kinds of political authority. We should not presume, then, that philosophy can supply a normative adjudication of these programs based on insight into the principles of human reason and morality. This is not least because philosophies promising such insight were themselves among the competing programs, which deployed rival conceptions of human reason and moral personality. As one of the disciplines contained within early modern natural law, philosophy was in no position to transcend the programmatic and contentious character of its rival forms.

What made natural law into the predominant cultural-political discourse of the German territories during the seventeenth century was its capacity to act as a clearing-house for academic disciplines that played a key role in the cultural and political order of the empire and its constituent polities (Dreitzel 2001). This applied above all to the discipline of law whose preeminence arose from the fact that the political order of the empire—the relation between the empire and the church, and between the empire and the imperial states and estates—was shaped by imperial public law and by the juridical institutions (*Reichskammergericht, Reichshofrat*) enforcing its jurisdiction. For this reason, German polities relied on university-trained jurists as their imperial representatives and domestic political advisers, giving rise to the powerful stratum of academic jurisconsults to which both Pufendorf and Leibniz belonged (Hammerstein 1986). If natural law conceived of politics juridically, and if it was natural law rather than philosophy that organized political discourse, this is because it allowed religious, political, and ethical questions to be formulated in an overarching juridical language, in terms of the shifting relations between divine, natural, and civil law.

Scarcely less important than jurisprudence among the natural law disciplines, however, was theology. This was in part because the churches were themselves an integral part of early modern judicial systems, maintaining their own courts and participating in positive law via the dual jurisprudence of Romano-canon law (Padoa-Schioppa 1997). It was also because in the wake of the great scholastic systems, philosophical theology (metaphysics) staked a powerful claim to be the "natural knowledge" for deriving natural law norms, hence for establishing transcendent norms for positive civil law (Dreitzel 2001). From the early sixteenth to the mid-seventeenth century, Protestant natural law was dominated by theologians and philosophical theology, initially by Melanchthon's natural law but then in the increasingly metaphysical forms elaborated by such figures as Balthasar Meisner and Joachim Stephani. The Christian natural law of Protestant scholasticism established the terms for a religious reception of positive law and formed the target for Pufendorf's anti-scholastic campaign to expel philosophical theology from natural law in favor of a Hobbesian civil philosophy.

What sent natural law discourses into overdrive, though, and impelled the elaboration of competing programmatic forms, were the unplanned outcomes arising from the interaction of two extraordinarily consequential historical developments. These were the fracturing of Western Christendom into rival confessionalizing religions during the sixteenth century, and the roughly synchronous emergence of dynastic territorial state-building in a form that would prove difficult to contain within the legal order of the Holy Roman–German Empire. From these twin developments arose context-specific alliances between (rival) confessionalizing churches bent on imposing a new level of spiritual discipline on populations, and state-building princes' intent on enclosing populations within consolidated territorial borders and subjecting them to centralized forms of law and government. Such alliances witnessed the birth of a new political reality, the early modern confessional state. This was the princely territorial state in which a centralizing and unifying government of the population was executed through the juridical and pedagogical enforcement of a particular theological confession and form of church. It was the attempt to build confessionalized princely territorial states within the framework of the empire—together with the resistance to such efforts mounted by diversely confessional- ized nobilities and cities (the "estates")—that drove natural law to ceaselessly reconfigure the relations between law, religion, and politics. This gave rise to forms of natural law designed to support the relations characteristic of the confessional state and also to those forms, like Pufendorf's, that were intended to dissolve and recast these relations, in part through the pluralization of civil personae. Before discussing these developments, then, we need to offer a brief account of the interaction of confessionaliza- tion and state-building in the emergence of the confessional state.

Confessionalization and State-Building

The splitting of the "universal" imperial church at the beginning of the sixteenth century, together with the three waves of confessionalization—Lutheran, Catholic, and Calvinist— that swept across central and northern Europe during the second half of that century, represents a set of historical developments central to any understanding of the relation between religious and political community, especially with regards to the "formation of the subject.'" Formulated by historians as a means of absorbing and relativizing the idea of the Reformation, the concept of confessionalization is designed to capture a crucial historical phenomenon: namely, a series of campaigns by rival churches to carry religious discipline into the daily lives of whole populations in an unprecedented manner. The concept takes its name from the confession, or definitive theological formulation of the articles of faith. In the empire, the most important of these were the Augsburg Confession adopted by dissident Protestant princes in 1530; the decrees of the Council of Trent 1545– 1563 with which the Catholic Church met the Protestant threat; and the Formula of Concord of 1577, through which the Lutheran church formalized its break with Calvinism. The crucial theological questions over which the churches separated and engaged in mutual heretication—questions pertaining to the relations between Christ's divine and human natures and his mode of presence at the Eucharist, the role of the sacraments and the priesthood in mediating salvation, and the relation between faith and works—were by no means purely abstract academic matters. They were central to the forms in which local communities participated in and were formed by sacramental religious rituals, in partic- ular Holy Communion through which one joined (or was excluded from) the circle of communicants. This link between confession and devotional practice is a pointer to the authentically religious roots of the phenomenon of confessionalization.

Confessionalization was characterized by the heightened training and disciplining of clergy in rival theologies, and by the intensification of preaching, religious devotions, and pastoral pedagogy for increasingly segregated congregations, leading to the emergence of distinct and mutually hostile religious cultures. This set of developments was dependent on and conditioned by a massive expansion of educational institutions, resulting in an unprecedented proliferation of grammar schools and universities across the empire from the mid-sixteenth to the mid-seventeenth century. In the expanding network of grammar schools, responsible for the training of school teachers and the preparation of candidates for matriculation, humanistic learning was tied to rival confessional theologies and pieties. At the same time, university philosophy and theology faculties grew in both num- ber and importance, owing to their key role in the training of clergy and theologians, the elaboration and refinement of rival theological doctrine, the determination of orthodoxy and heresy, and the publication of religious propaganda in raging confessional "culture wars." By the end of the sixteenth century, the role of Lutheran philosophy and theology faculties in explicating and teaching the metaphysical Christology embedded in the Formula of Concord had led to the appearance of a full-fledged Protestant scholasticism in those territories that had subscribed to the Formula, with the result that a modified Protestant metaphysical Aristotelianism dominated the universities there. In the empire's Catholic universities it was Jesuit Aristotelianism and Thomism that held sway; while Calvinist *Schulphilosophie* dominated the Reformed universities, giving rise in effect to three rival university systems across the empire. The confessionalization that led to intercommunal hatred, mutual heretication, and bloodletting was the result not of ignorance and superstition, but of an unprecedented expansion of educational provision led by some of the best minds in the empire.

It is the pedagogical and disciplinary character of confessionalizing religion that holds the key to its symbiosis with state-building dynastic enterprises within the empire. The building of new churches, schools and universities, the protection of breakaway congregations, and the juridical enforcement of confessional discipline were unthinkable without the financial, political, and military support provided by civil authorities of various kinds. At the same time, the confessionalizing churches provided civil authorities with an instrument of unprecedented scope and power for the disciplining of populations targeted by various programs of governmental and social reform. Particularly in the emerging princely territorial states—where the moral enclosure of the population within a formative religious culture was reinforced by its geopolitical enclosure within a governmentally administered political territory—the combination of confessionalization and state-building led to the superimposition of the religious and political communities, "frontiers of faith," and political borders.

Achieving a synoptic view of the interaction between confession and politics is rendered difficult in part by the sheer variety of political authorities and political interests operative within the juridical framework of the empire: bishoprics, free cities and urban corporations, imperial nobilities and knights circles, in addition to emerging princely territorial states. Such a view is also obscured by the lingering presence of several theoretical and historiographic paradigms that have outlived their usefulness. It is thus necessary to avoid the assumption that the political disposition of the churches might be read off from their theologies, as in earlier accounts of an antistatist rights-oriented Calvinism and an authoritarian statist Lutheranism. This assumption has been discredited by studies showing that Lutheranism was no less capable than Calvinism of galvanizing estate resistance to territorializing dynasties, some of the most important of which—the Hohenzollerns of Brandenburg for example—were Calvinist. No less unhelpful is the paradigm according to which theological cultures are read off from economic developments or processes of group formation. This paradigm has been called into question by accounts showing the historical autonomy of religious thought and practices of piety, particularly in establishing models of self and community that could be embodied in law and politics, and give shape to social and economic relations. More recent studies of the interaction of confession and politics have thus paid closer attention to the culture-forming character of confessional theologies and practices of piety, while tying the political consequences of religion to struggles between political groupings whose interests were in part theologically formed.

No less problematic for our present concerns is the long shadow cast by the nineteenth-century "Prussianist" historiography that saw the relation between confession and politics in terms of the postimperial sovereign territorial state, whose juridical and political structure were regarded as inherently secularizing. This historiography has been called into question by an array of studies showing the longevity of the juridically ordered imperial "society of estates" which, even after the Peace of Westphalia (1648), allowed the imperial estates and principalities to be considered as the *patria* or fatherland to which political loyalty was owed. It has also been undermined by studies showing the labile relations between confessionalism and juridification within the order of imperial public law, whose ambivalence has been a particular theme of Martin Heckel—Heckel has shown that, on the one hand, the juridification of relations between rival confessional estates led to an important degree of secularization at the level of the empire and its courts and parliaments. Here parity of treatment for the Protestant and Catholic estates resulted in a bi-confessional juridical modus vivendi, reflected in the *cuius regio eius religio* (whose the region, his the religion) formula associated with the Augsburg Religious Peace of 1555. This same juridical modus vivendi, though, unleashed the full force of confessionalization within the imperial cities and states. Here Augsburg's recognition of the Protestant princes' *ius reformandi* (right of reformation) facilitated the political enforcement of a particular confession, and the development of centralized and confessionalized judicial systems. The instability of this situation was revealed when confessionalizing princes and estates sought to use the formal parity of the empire's judicial system to pursue covert confessional goals—typically related to the alienation of church property and rights—which eventually paralyzed the *Reichskammergericht* (Imperial Chamber Court), opening the path to armed conflict.

If the impartial "rule of law" thus proved quite compatible with the enforcement of theocratically-oriented legal codes—replete with heresy and witchcraft statutes—then the first form of the sovereign territorial state was in fact the confessional state. This indicates the degree to which the secularization of politics—that we have identified in Pufendorf's differentiation of the man and the citizen—resulted not from a secularizing tendency inherent in law and the state, but from contingent struggles to secularize the juridical and political order of the confessional state. To explore this prospect, we should first turn to the confessional state, and indicate some of its characteristic forms of political and juridical thought.

Contours of the Confessional State (Saxony)

Under the state-building Wettin dynasty, Saxony became the most unified of the early modern Protestant confessional states, having been of course the birthplace and headquarters of the Lutheran Reformation. We can gain important insights into the intellectual architecture of the mid-sixteenth century Saxon confessional state by looking at the political testament of the Saxon chancellor, Melchior von Osse, presented to the Elector, Duke August, in 1555. In offering advice on the present condition and future development of the Saxon state, Osse draws on the genre of moral advice to princes—the "mirror for princes"—but combines it with a treatise on cameral government or *"Policey,"* and with a traditional natural law division of duties (to God, oneself, and others). The overarching genre of Osse's work is thus that of the patriarchalist literature of the "Christian commonwealth" and more specifically that of Lutheran Christian *Policey*. Here, the prince pursues the goals of a confessionalized state administration in a patronal–episcopal persona assisted by university-trained jurists and clergy. Osse's *Testament* belonged to the onset of the Wettin dynasty's program to transform Saxony into a centrally administered confessional state, even if Osse continued to regard Saxony as an electoral estate within the empire.

In the edition that Christian Thomasius prepared for his students at the beginning of the eighteenth century, Osse's *Testament* begins with general advice on the government of a Christian commonwealth and then, in its second part, proceeds to offer advice on the government of Saxony in particular. In outlining the contours of the Christian commonwealth Osse focuses on the figure of the godly patriarchal prince governing his subjects with the assistance of pious expert officials. In keeping with the mirror for princes' genre, the prince's political authority is understood to be morally grounded in his personal piety and virtue. The condition of the prince governing others is that he must first govern himself, conquering his own selfish passions, and cultivating the virtues of piety, liberality, magnanimity, fortitude, and mercy (8–12, 33–41). The prince cannot govern successfully, though, without officials to staff his court bureaucracy and judiciary, who must also combine their expertise with personal piety.

This picture of the Christian prince is then unfolded into a treatise on government via the three sets of natural law duties: to God, oneself, and others. In outlining the prince's duty to God, Osse enunciates the widely held central tenet of the confessional state: that political stability requires that the people should be taught a single religion by an orthodox clergy. Osse reminds Duke August that the just prince must wield the sword in order to curb the raw wildness of sinful men, and that he must also support the exercise of "ecclesial coercion" (bans and excommunication) by the clergy, in order to maintain order and discipline within the church (51–2). Above all, though, the prince must ensure that "in doctrine, the theologians, pastors and preachers are of one opinion and one meaning, and that all division, separation, aversion and bitterness is kept at bay" (53–4). In order to obtain the peace, calm, unity, and salvation of his subjects, the prince must thus have clergy and theologians who adhere to "one God, one Lord, one faith, one baptism, one Holy Scripture, one Holy Ghost" (56).

Under duties to oneself, Osse identifies three forms of governance, understood as management of the extended royal demesne and named as economic or household management (*oeconomica prudentia*) (57–92). The prince must thus master the arts of matrimonial governance (*regimen conjugale*, concerned with the marital alliance of royal persons), paternal governance (*regimen paternale*, focused on the education of the prince as future ruler), and household or court governance (*regimen dominativum*). The latter begins with moral management of the court and royal household, but extends to "'cameral'" administration of the treasury and *Rentkammer*, and thence to taxation and public revenue-raising seen as an extension of the prince's household finances.

Finally, Osse elaborates the prince's duties to others under the heading of the management of kingly rule (*prudentia regnativa*), as the third way in which a "'pious Christian magistrate'" pursues justice and good government. Here the chancellor is centrally concerned with advising the prince on managing his personal relations with his officials, nobles, estates, and subjects in a manner that will make him deserving of their esteem, loyalty, and acquiescence. As this can only be done by conducting himself in a just and moral manner, the longevity and stability of government is held to depend on the ruler's own righteousness. Osse thus approaches the exercise of government in terms of the regent's personal exercise of the "'governmental virtues'"—liberality, mercy, justice, fortitude, and so on—which are derived from Christian, Aristotelian, and Stoic sources

(115–50). Osse's advice on the appointment and management of officials is framed by the comment that he is concerned with justice and good government only as these are conducted by a "Christian authority," as opposed to the pagans. Osse reinforces this by citing Augustine to the effect that good government does not consist in the peace and stability of the state alone, but in ordering what is good and right in accordance with divine law, which means that only a Christian ruler can be a good and just prince (157–8). The detailed advice on the filling of offices—advisers, court officials, lesser magistrates—is informed by Osse's understanding of officialdom as the extension of the prince's personal rule, hence as requiring a similar combination of Christian piety and virtues. Osse thus does not regard the "state" as an impersonal instrumentality with its own defining ends and purposes—security, political order—but as an extension of the prince's personal rule for which he is qualified by the cultivation and enforcement of a piety whose form is determined by the territorial church.

In applying this general model of the pious prince governing a Christian commonwealth to the state of Saxony—in part two of the *Testament*—Osse advises the Wettin princes that they should focus their state-building activities on two things in particular: securing a supply of learned and pious clerical and judicial officials, and reforming the territory's educational institutions. With regard to officialdom, Osse's prime focus is on the need to replace "lay" noble advisers and judges with university-trained jurists expert in Romano-canon law. The clear implication is that only jurists with this training will possess the expertise, piety, and undivided loyalty making them fit to function as an extension of the prince's patriarchal-cameral rule. In a similar vein, Osse recommends the reform of the Leipzig *Schöffenstuhl*—one of several Saxon *Spruchkollegien*, or bodies responsible for rendering legal judgments—arguing that its lay members be replaced by legal doctors who would be capable of rendering speedy and uniform judgment on referred cases (489–95).

For the Saxon princes to acquire suitably trained clerical and judicial officials, however, they would first have to reform their educational institutions. In this regard Osse advises that the territory's three main grammar schools must all be equipped to teach Philip Melanchthon's curriculum in which the classical liberal arts are combined with Lutheran ethical and theological principles. The two universities—of Leipzig and Wittenberg—must also be thoroughly reformed. This is in part to ensure that they are financially capable of deploying appropriately trained lecturers and appropriately disciplined students. It is also to ensure that the law faculty is staffed by professors expert in Justinian and Canon law, taught according to the Italian glossators, who would be supported by an arts staff trained in the Melanchthonian curriculum (382–416). This reform was symptomatic of the transformation of the university from an independent urban corporation into an institution funded by and integral to princely territorial government. Osse's program is thus indicative of the reciprocal relations between law, religion, and government in the emerging confessional state, and of the crucial role played by the university in supplying the orthodox officialdom and "scholastic" intellectual architecture required for this reciprocity.

This was the historical setting in which the keystone of this architecture—Christian natural law—had been developed within the Saxon universities, initially in the form outlined by Melanchthon at Wittenberg in a series of writings from the early 1520s. In reactivating the view of natural law as the form in which human reason accedes to divine law and permits its embodiment in civil law, Melanchthon established an architecture in which the religious and civil authorities shared in the governance of a godly community. The norms of this Christian natural law were supplied by the "'spiritual sword" of the Ten Commandments and Christ's ethic of fraternal love—understood as supplying the model of an ideal moral community—while the Christian magistrate was empowered to punish the fallen man's deviations from these norms with the sword of the civil law. This construction of natural law provided a framework for the Protestant reception of Roman law—which Melanchthon argued was both harmonious with natural law and a model for civil law—and, more generally, a matrix for the relations between theology, law, politics, and (Aristotelian) moral philosophy characteristic of the early phases of Protestant scholasticism.

The mix of theological, juridical, and political purposes served by this natural law is reflected in the three uses that were assigned to it by Lutheran philosophical theologians: as a norm for disciplining sinners, heretics, and infidels (*usus politicus*); as a means for discerning sin and revealing God's judgment (*usus paedagogicus*); and as a norm of conduct for the religiously reborn (*usus in renatis*). These three uses are also a pointer to the key role played by Christian natural law in shaping a particular topography of personhood, as one might expect of a discipline responsible for combining religious discipline, legal obligation, and ethical duty. On the basis of a particular (Christian-Platonic, Christian-Aristotelian) philosophical anthropology, man is modeled as a creature whose rational soul permits him to participate in the divine intellection of norms—thereby restoring some of his lost integral condition—but whose sensuous passions lead him to sin and remind him of his fallen nature. By treating natural law itself as a discipline for the partial restoration of pure reason—understood as the *imago Dei* or image of God in man—"reborn" Lutheran theologians and philosophers claimed the moral qualification required to accede to divine law and mediate it in the form of natural law norms to the civil authorities. This conception of a prince whose civil laws find their legitimacy in the enforcement of Christian natural law norms against sinners, heretics, and infidels (the *usus politicus*) is central to Osse's model of the just and virtuous Christian magistrate.

The rationalist metaphysics implicit in the *imago Dei* doctrine became increasingly important in Saxon natural law following the adoption of the Formula of Concord in Saxon parishes and territories in the late 1570s. These were the circumstances in which the explication and defense of the Formula's speculative Christology and Eucharistic metaphysics impelled the installation of the Lutheran version of Christian-Aristotelian metaphysics at the universities of Wittenberg and Leipzig. The militant Wittenberg theologian and metaphysician Balthasar Meisner thus elaborated a sophisticated natural theology (metaphysics) designed to show how Christ's divine and human "natures" were united in his person, and how this permitted him to be simultaneously physically present at different celebrations of the Eucharist, as required by the Lutheran "ubiquity" doctrine. At the same time, Meisner also published a natural law treatise in which a rationalist anthropology holds the key to the theological derivation of natural law and its use as a justification for the civil punishment of sinners and heretics, Calvinists in particular. This kind of natural law was resurgent in the final third of the seventeenth century in the work of Valentin Veltheim (Jena), Johann Joachim Zentgrav (Strasbourg), and Valentin Alberti (Leipzig). All of these philosophers and theologians defended rational access to the natural law norms that governed man in his innocent condition (*status integritatis*), but now as a defense against Pufendorf's root and branch rejection of the rationalist anthropology underlying Christian natural law and the theocratic subordination of civil law entailed by this.

We can instantiate the relations between law, theology, and government in the Saxon confessional state by briefly looking at the career and works of the most important Protestant criminal jurist of the seventeenth century, Benedict Carpzov (1595–1666). Carpzov studied philosophy and law at Wittenberg before becoming a doctor of laws. In addition to his post as a law professor at Leipzig, he was a political adviser to the royal court, and Senior or presiding judge of Saxony's most important criminal court, the Leipzig *Schöffenstuhl*. Carpzov thus fully embodied the politically important role of academic jurists in the early modern German Empire and its emerging states. In his major juridical work—the *Practica nova imperialis saxonica rerum criminalium* (New Imperial Saxon Practice of Criminal Law) of 1635—Carpzov achieved a synthesis of Roman, canon, Saxon, and imperial public law in a practically-oriented criminal code that also served as a handbook for inquisitorial trial procedure. This reception and synthesis of positive law was framed by the Christian natural law conception of religious and civil authority. Carpzov construes the civil laws of the prince as grounded in divine and natural law, permitting civil infractions to be seen as instances of sinful conduct, and religious heterodoxy to be punished as a civil crime. The *Practica nova* thus specifies the elements of the crimes of witchcraft, blasphemy, and heresy; outlines the procedures for their inquisitorial determination, and assigns a schedule of punishments up to and including execution.

What made this confessionalized theocratic judicial code possible, however, was in fact the centralizing and unifying reform of the Saxon court system foreshadowed in Osse's *Testament*. In 1574, Elector August (1553–1586) had decreed that local judges must send the files for all criminal cases to the Leipzig *Schöffenstuhl* for processing and assessment. Here a panel of legal doctors, sitting as a central legal bureau, would render judgment on them before returning them to the local judges who would pronounce it, once the judgment had been cleared by the royal court at Dresden. The Leipzig *Schöffenstuhl* thus played a key role in the state-building program of the Saxon electoral princes. It permitted them to centralize jurisdiction in their own court system, and to establish uniformity of judgment via an institution that assimilated a variety of legal sources—local common law (the *Sachsenspiegel*), consistorial law, imperial public law, and Romano-canon law—in a single judicial practice. Nonetheless, even if the *Practica nova* was thus the product and instrument of a major centralization of jurisdiction in the Lutheran territorial state, Carpzov continued to conceive of political authority in imperial terms. Drawing on Althusius's conception of real and personal majesty, Carpzov viewed real majesty (sovereignty) as invested in the political body of the empire and shared by the imperial estates—especially the electoral princes—as a result of the historical public law enactments and capitulations determining the emperor's election by the estates. This gave the princes an imperial legal right against the (delegated) personal majesty of the emperor, a right, for example, to defend their religion.

This mix of imperial public law and "municipal" Saxon law can be seen in Carpzov's second major work, the *Jurisprudentia ecclesiastica seu consistorialis* (Ecclesial or Consistorial Jurisprudence) of 1649. Like other Protestant territories, Saxony had established a consistory—a mixed lay and theological body for the governance of the church and the exercise of ecclesial jurisdiction—in order to compensate for the loss of episcopal administration following the breach with Rome. This state of affairs was enshrined in imperial public law by the Religious Peace of Augsburg in 1555, which recognized the Protestant prince as both civil ruler and highest bishop in his own territory, thereby giving rise to one of the central doctrines of Protestant *Staatskirchenrecht* (constitutional church law), the *Zwei-Personen-Lehre* (doctrine of the two persons). In Carpzov's formulation: "By virtue of the Religious Peace, the episcopal rights of princes and the status of Protestant ruler coincide: by which they represent a double person and exercise a double power, ecclesial and political." Saxon consistorial jurisprudence was thus founded in the imperial public law modus vivendi that recognized two confessions in the empire, and yet facilitated the enforcement of Lutheran orthodoxy in the Saxon consistorial courts.

The *Zwei-Personen-Lehre* was accompanied by the *Drei-Stände-Lehre*, or doctrine of the three estates. This doctrine was initially elaborated by Melanchthon as a Lutheran social theory teaching that society consists of three estates: the political, clerical, and oeconomic (*Wehrstand, Lehrstand,* and *Nahrstand*). In the latter half of the sixteenth century, though, it was refashioned as a constitutional theory of the church, such that the three estates were renamed as the magistracy, clergy, and people, with the doctrine now being used to treat church governance as divided between the estates. Carpzov could thus use the dual civil–episcopal jurisdiction of the prince to defend the Saxon elector's episcopal right to enforce the Formula of Concord. This also served to justify the delegated competence of the clergy in the consistorial prosecution of religious law—in such areas as marriage, sexual misconduct, church attendance, and heresy—thereby adapting Catholic canon law to the actual practice of the Dresden Superior Consistory. At the same time, Carpzov could use the three-estate doctrine to defend the church against its political secularization, by arguing that the power of church government had to be divided between the secular magistracy, the clergy, and the people. The prince thus could be treated as a servant of the religious community to which he belonged and prevented from exercising civil authority in "internal" church matters—doctrine, liturgy, theological controversies—reserved for the clergy.

In overseeing the religious formation of the political nation, and in tying the state to the religiously formed nation, the interaction of confessionalization and state-building permanently transformed the political landscape of the Holy Roman–German Empire. It gave rise to the archipelagoes of confessional states and estates whose mutual enmity would exhaust the pacifying capacities of the imperial judicial order and tip the empire into the Thirty Years War, which quickly became international. Far from being innocent bystanders or unwilling conscripts to the process of a confessional state formation, the universities played a key role in it. As the prime source of theological doctrine, religious pedagogues, and confessional propaganda, theology and philosophy faculties were integral to the most powerful institutions of cultural pedagogy and community-building in early modernity: the rival churches and their associated schools and universities. For their part, the law faculties provided the legal doctrine and expert jurists required by the juridically ordered politics of the empire, and the judicial systems of its confessional states and cities.

In functioning as a theory program for the articulation of theology, law, and politics, Christian natural law provided the linkage between a formation of personhood deeply rooted in the anthropology and liturgy of salvation (the elect and sinners, Christians and infidels) and constructions of legal personality organized around the personae required by the exercise of political and juridical authority (prince and magistrate, subject and citizen). The thematic of the *imago Dei*—in which the purification of man's rational being permits reborn philosophers and theologians to mediate divine law to the prince via the discipline of natural law—is a typical instance of the manner in which Protestant *Schulphilosophie* effected this linkage of theology and law. If Christian natural law thus tied the persona of the citizen to that of the Christian or man, and if Benedict Carpzov could use this natural law to frame a positive jurisprudence in which the prince doubled as bishop, and in which deviations from the norms of Christian personhood were punished as crimes committed by citizens, this was not the result of some philosophical mistake. It was not indicative of some failure to establish the secular autonomy of philosophical reason and to build a secular, tolerant, and democratic modernity on this basis. Rather, it resulted from the articulation of confessionalization and state-building that had been effected by the most powerful intellectual instruments of early modernity—academic law and theology—and embodied in an institution that was itself distinctively modern: the confessional state. The undoing of this profound articulation—which remains contested and incomplete to this day—would be achieved not through the clean breakthrough to an autonomous philosophical reason, but through a grim hand-to-hand intellectual combat whose goal was to de-theologize law and politics and thereby destroy the intellectual infrastructure of the confessional state.

Political Secularization and the Pluralization of Civil Personae (Brandenburg-Prussia)

When, in March 1690, the political jurist and Pufendorf disciple Christian Thomasius (1655–1728) fled his Saxon homeland for exile in neighboring Brandenburg, he did so because a series of disputations and treatises—in which he attacked the foundations of Christian natural law and criticized the *Religionspolitik* of the Saxon state—had led to his banning from the University of Leipzig. The phalanx of philosophers and theologians who had engineered this ban included the Christian natural jurist Valentin Alberti, the theologian Johann Benedict Carpzov, and his brother the court pastor Samuel—nephews of Benedict—indicating the immediacy of Thomasius's engagement with the leading Saxon representatives of Lutheran scholasticism. The fact that Alberti and the Carpzov brothers were able to effect his banning and exile by laying a complaint before the Dresden Superior Consistory—leading to a condemnation of Thomasius's "indifferentism" and "irreligion" that would be converted into a ducal decree—shows the ease with which academic disputes in natural law could become religious and political conflicts to be resolved by the institutions of the confessional state. Philosophically speaking, the Christian natural law with which his opponents defended the Saxon confessional state was no less coherent than the Pufendorfian natural law with which Thomasius attacked it. This means that to understand this conflict we must do something more than just clarify the intellectual terms in which it was conducted. We must also clarify the play of political and religious interests that anchored these terms in political reality.

When Thomasius crossed the border into electoral Brandenburg, taking up residence in the town of Halle whose university he would help to found, he entered a religious and political landscape that differed significantly from that of Saxony. As part of a push to reform the religious and political order of Lutheran Brandenburg, the Hohenzollern dynasty had converted to Calvinism at the beginning of the seventeenth century. With an entirely characteristic mix of genuinely religious and ambitiously political motives, the elector Johann Sigismund turned to Calvinism in order to sweep away the "superstitious" practices of the Lutheran church—such things as baptismal exorcism, the Eucharistic "ubiquity" doctrine, the "papist" consecration of the communion host—but also as a means to incorporate his Lutheran estates (whose religious and juridical identity was attached to Lutheranism) within the emerging princely territorial state of Brandenburg-Prussia. In the event, despite the Hohenzollern's success in the territorial expansion and military consolidation of the new state, the planned religious reform ended in a stalemate, with the nobility successfully using their imperial estate rights to resist the Calvinization of the church, aided by a vehemently anti-Calvinist Lutheran clergy and a sometimes riotous populace.

As a result of this impasse, by the time that Thomasius arrived in 1690, Brandenburg was in effect a multiconfessional state in which a Calvinist dynasty ruled over a largely Lutheran nobility and population, in territories that also contained Calvinist and Catholic minorities. Unlike Saxony, the synchronization of confessionalization and state-building had misfired in Brandenburg-Prussia, leading to the emergence of an increasingly powerful and militarized state ruling over an array of religious communities none of whose churches could be endorsed and enforced by law and the state. It was the de facto and unplanned development of political secularization and religious toleration in Brandenburg—the result of political necessity rather than enlightenment aspiration—that provided political anchorage for Thomasius's campaign against the intellectual infrastructure of the Lutheran confessional state.

If the political conditions supporting Thomasius's campaign were distinctively local, then his main intellectual resources had a wider dissemination. In drawing on Pufendorf's anti-scholastic natural law working in tandem with a spiritualistic form of Protestant pietism and an antimetaphysical historiography of philosophy pioneered by his father Jacob, Thomasius availed himself of an intellectual culture with powerful resonances across Protestant Europe. Nonetheless, this intellectual array also had a regional character, finding its heartlands in the northern Protestant territories of the German Empire and in the adjacent Scandinavian and Baltic states. This is because it had been assembled to directly attack northern Protestant *Schulphilosophie* and, indirectly, the hinterland of southern Catholic scholasticism, both targeted for supplying the intellectual infrastructure for the confessional state. Not only does this setting provide the relevant context for Pufendorf's anti-scholastic natural law, it also contextualizes Thomasius's informed reception of Pufendorf's work, and the combative uses to which he put it in his war with the Protestant scholastics.

Pufendorf's Hobbesian natural law works of the 1670s attacked Christian natural law at its most fundamental level, by refusing its philosophical–theological anthropology and the forms of moral and civil personality informed by this anthropology. Pufendorf thus begins his massive *De jure naturae et gentium* by rejecting all doctrines that ground duties in an ontological moral nature, preeminently Christian-Platonic doctrines of man's "rational being," and Christian-Aristotelian doctrines of his "rational and sociable nature." He insists to the contrary that duties are vested in artificial "moral entities" (*entia moralia*)—a diversity of moral personae—that have been "imposed" or instituted for man, by God or by man himself, as a means of "governing his dangerous liberty." This axe blow to the roots of Christian natural law destroys the path of rational reflection through which philosophical theologians derive norms from man's own rational nature (the *imago Dei*), transferring the search for these norms to man's merely empirical nature and historical circumstances. In so doing, this blow also destroys natural rights of the kind that Christian natural jurists had derived from the rational nature that man is supposed to share with God and that gives him a capacity for rightful action independent of the prince's civil laws. For Pufendorf, man's capacities for rightful action depend upon the statuses or offices that have been instituted for his moral governance, which means that there is no singular or paramount moral personality at the basis of civil life, only a plurality of moral personae distributed as distinct regions of moral space.

It so happens that the empirical nature that God has instituted for man and that defines his natural condition (*status naturalis*) is that of a creature who needs to be sociable to flourish, but whose vicious passions overwhelm his knowledge of this need (154–78). This indicates that the fundamental natural law is that man must conduct himself in a sociable manner, but also that he is incapable of governing himself in this way, for example, on the basis of his "rational and sociable nature" (201–21). Obligation and duties therefore must be imposed on him from without by a superior (87–95). The superior is defined as an agent or agency possessing the power to coerce those subject to its command and a "just reason" for doing so (95–101). The superior's reasons for coercion are just in so far as individuals in a multitude have agreed to subject themselves to the superior in exchange for protection, from each other in the first instance, but also from foreign enemies. In subjecting themselves in this way, the individuals leave their *status naturalis* and enter the civil state (*status civilis*). They thereby acquire the persona of the subject or citizen, understood in terms of the duty of obedience to a sovereign in all matters pertaining to the preservation of social peace for which these civil personae have been instituted (949–66, 1000–09). Beginning with the rejection of Christian natural law's fundamental moral anthropology—the rational nature shared with God through which man might govern himself from within—Pufendorf's path of political secularization thus moves inexorably to a conception of natural law premised on security, rather than holiness or rationality. From thence it passes to a civil state in which there are no natural rights—because civil personae are artifacts of civil governance—and in which the determination of whether civil law enacts the (new) law of nature (social peace) is a right invested solely in the artificial persona of the civil sovereign. The intellectual architecture that was designed to preclude the political enforcement of religion was thus simultaneously intended to preclude religious intellectuals from subordinating civil laws to a higher tribunal of natural reason and natural right.

If Pufendorf's natural law provided Thomasius with a powerful weapon for undermining the relations between theology, law, and politics established in Christian natural law, then it was a second work by Pufendorf—his *De habitu religionis christianae ad vitam civilem* (On the Relation of the Christian Religion to Civil Life) of 1687—that showed him how to use this weapon in the domain of *Staatskirchenrecht* (constitutional church law), against the positive jurisprudence of the Lutheran confessional state. Written in the aftermath of Louis XIV's revocation of the Edict of Nantes (1685) and amid widespread Protestant concern that Catholic France aspired to a universal monarchy, the *De habitu* provides a fundamental architecture for the radical separation of religious and civil authority, church and state. If the civil state originates in the agreement of a multitude to subject themselves to a civil sovereign capable of preserving worldly peace through the exercise of coercive rule, then the church has a quite different origin and purpose. Churches arose independently of and prior to civil states from the gathering together of those seeking salvation through the free teaching of the gospels. Properly understood, churches do not form part of the state—their teachings are incapable of political enforcement and supply no justification for political authority—and must be regarded instead as "colleges" or voluntary associations existing within the security envelope provided by the state but disconnected from it (17–22).

Ultimately, the civil state and the church, politics and religion, constitute different spheres of moral duty inhabited by distinct moral personae. We have seen that the civil state is inhabited by the sovereign and the citizen, bound together by the reciprocal duties of protection and obedience that are in turn enforced by the exercise of coercive authority that defines the sovereign's persona. In the church, though, we find only the personae of the teacher and the learner, and they are bound together not by coercion but by the shared pursuit of the saving Word and the forceless relations of love and emulation (32–6, 67–73). If this fundamental restructuring of religious and political authority was designed to make it impossible for the prince to enforce a religion in the persona of bishop, then it was also intended to make the Christian immune from the kind of coercive sanction that properly attached to his civil persona as citizen. Someone who threatens social peace in the name of Christianity, however, is by definition acting in their civil persona and should of course be subject to civil punishment.

After encountering it while studying for his legal doctorate at the (Brandenburg) University of Frankfurt (Oder) in the late 1670s, Thomasius drew the lessons of Pufendorf's radical reconstruction of natural law with great acuity, applying them in a wide array of combative writings aimed at undermining the intellectual infrastructure of the confessional state. For our present concerns, it is his barrage of disputations in the area of *Staatskirchenrecht*, issued from the new University of Halle in the 1690s, that is of most immediate interest. In these disputations—dealing with heresy and witchcraft law, judicial torture and inquisitorial trial procedure, religious toleration and the prince's rights of religious supervision—Thomasius used Pufendorf's natural law to attack Carpzovian confessional jurisprudence and to frame a new reception of positive law, in keeping with the drive to secularize law and politics. Two of these disputations—one dealing with *adiaphora* or religiously indifferent matters, the other with the prince's right to settle religious controversies—will serve our purposes in exemplifying how the reordering of the relations between political and religious authority was reflected in and conditioned by a pluralization of civil personae.

The *adiaphora* controversy had its roots in the Augsburg Interim Formula of 1548 when, following their defeat by Catholic imperial forces in the Schmalkaldic War of 1546–47, the Protestant estates agreed to acquiesce in an array of Catholic ceremonies deemed indifferent with regard to salvation—that is, *adiaphora*—pending the reunification of the faith promised by a future church council. Lutheran orthodoxy as reflected in the Formula of Concord rejected this position, with the Formula stating that it is impermissible to change *adiaphora* simply to compromise with another confession or where this would "scandalise the weaker members" of the Lutheran congregation. The Formula denied secular princes the right to change or abrogate adiaphoristic ceremonies, which belonged to the internal order of the church. In Saxony, it was the redoubtable metaphysician Balthasar Meisner who updated the Formula's arguments at the beginning of the seventeenth century, defending the purity of Lutheran ritual against all "crypto-Calvinist" reforms, although similar arguments are to be found in Carpzov's *Jurisprudentia ecclesiastica* of 1649. From Thomasius's Pufendorfian standpoint, this view of the *adiaphora* was unacceptable as it failed to separate the religious and political communities—the Christian and the citizen—and represented an intolerable restriction of the secular prince's right to determine all matters impacting on social peace and not essential to salvation.

In his disputation *De jure principis circa adiaphora* (The Right of the Prince regarding Adiaphora) of 1695, Thomasius sought to demolish the orthodox Lutheran position on *adiaphora* and redeploy the concept within a politically secularized construction of *Staatskirchenrecht*. He did so by deploying arguments in both the theological and political–jurisprudential registers. Drawing deeply on the heritage of spiritualistic Protestantism, he sought to vastly expand the array of ceremonies that could be considered *adiaphora* by declaring that only the individual's inner relation to God counted for salvation: "The Christian religion would thus appear to be content with an internal worship, that is, with the true humility of a self-abnegating mind, which devotes itself entirely to God" (57). As a result, "Therefore I cannot help but conclude that all external worship in natural religion is an indifferent matter" (55). This allowed Thomasius to declare that the entire panoply of public sacramental ritual—not just "superstitions" such as baptismal exorcism, but baptism itself together with confirmation, holy communion, the last rites, and postmortem intercession—could all be regarded as indifferent with regard to salvation.

At the same time, Thomasius deploys Pufendorf's secularized conception of the state to place such ceremonies at the disposal of the prince, whenever and to the extent that they impact on civil peace. Departing radically from the constitutional foundations of the confessional state contained in the Treaty of Augsburg, Thomasius argues since "there is no sentence in the New Testament specifically directed at supreme secular rulers by which they are entrusted with a particular office concerning the church," then "all rights of Christian princes—regarded as princes—are to be learnt from the principles of natural law and the genuine nature of civil sovereignty" (68). These principles show that the authority of the sovereign comes not from divine law or natural right, but from the origins and purpose of the civil state itself, to provide malicious humans with mutual protection:

> The purpose of commonwealths in this corrupt state, however, is *for subjects to provide themselves with some protection against evils and attacks* with which their more powerful neighbors in the state of nature threaten them. For below God there is no more efficient instrument for coercing the malice of humans and for securing their safety than that ingenious invention whereby many humans by a mutual pact subject the direction of their will and their powers to the will of another, for the common benefit of the whole community of subjects. As a result, *it is undoubtedly true that a prince accrues as much power as is required for obtaining this purpose of the commonwealth, namely, for its internal and external peace.* (69)

This means that to extent they are capable of disturbing civil peace, external religious ceremonies are properly subject to the secular authority of the prince (69–70).

Through this dual spiritualization of religion and secularization of politics, Thomasius was seeking to reconfigure the relations between religion, law, and politics and to establish a new public law framework for civil governance of religion. This new framework permitted him to do away with the long-standing distinction between "internal" church matters (of doctrine, liturgy, and orthodoxy) reserved for the clerical estate, and "external" matters (of financing, political protection, and the disciplining of heretics and infidels) assigned to governmental estate or "secular branch." Commenting that this complex division was itself the source of innumerable disputes over the limits of the prince's rights of religious supervision, Thomasius proposed to replace it with the single threshold of decision. According to this criterion, any ecclesiastical matter—including doctrinal and liturgical issues—is subject to the sovereign's disposition to the extent that it has material consequences for civil peace, and to the extent that the sovereign exercises this disposition with complete disregard for religious truth and falsity. Thomasius was thus arguing that his attack on the use of civil power for religious purposes sets no limits on the exercise of this power over the church, as long as this exercise is for secular purposes. On this basis, in part II of the disputation, he argues that the prince has the right to introduce the Gregorian calendar in his territory (§ 6);[2] regulate the use of church music (§ 7) and church vestments (§ 8); and prevent abuses in the use of religious images associated with superstitious and idolatrous forms of worship (§ 9). Finally, the prince also has the right to abrogate baptismal exorcism, as this too is an indifferent matter subject to his authority; although, in reflecting on the disturbances arising on this account in both Saxony and Brandenburg, Thomasius urges that this right be exercised with prudence (§ 11).

The response that the *Adiaphora* disputation elicited from his old Leipzig enemy Johann Benedict Carpzov—in the latter's *De jure decidendi controversias theologicas* (On the Right of Deciding Theological Controversies)—shows the considerable intellectual power and political muscle retained by Protestant scholasticism, at least in electoral Saxony. Carpzov drew on Christian natural law to argue that the prince is responsible for mediating divine law in his civil commands, and is thus a "Christian magistrate" ruling over "Christian subjects." Further, he cited specific Saxon religious edicts in tandem with the *Zwei-Personen-Lehre* and the *Drei-Stände-Lehre* in order to show that, as an "internal" church matter, the determination of theological controversies rested with Lutheran theologians and clergy, with the secular prince restricted to an advisory and executive role: "The magistrate should thus attend to two things. First, he should acquiesce in his external power and not seek to infringe on the internal power of the ministers. . . . Second, even in external affairs he must consult the ministers of the church in difficult matters that concern the whole church" (63). To remind ourselves of the immediacy with which the confessional state permitted academic disputes to be transposed into the political and juridical register, we should observe that in addition to his counter-disputation, Carpzov preached against Thomasius's disputation from the Leipzig pulpit while his brother Samuel denounced it at the Saxon court. Meanwhile, the armed metaphysician, Alberti, again working through the Dresden Superior Consistory, succeeded in having the disputation confiscated by the Saxon Book Commissariat.

In his response to Carpzov's attack—launched in his *Das Recht evangelischer Fürsten in theologischen Streitigkeiten* (On the Right of Protestant Princes in Theological Controversies) of 1696, co-authored with Enno Rudolph Brenneisen—Thomasius showed the shattering consequences of Pufendorf's destruction of the philosophical anthropology underpinning Christian natural law. Thomasius's basic strategy in the *Recht in Streitigkeiten* is to use Pufendorf's multiple personae doctrine to consolidate and elaborate the reconstruction of the concepts of church and state that had been undertaken in the *Adiaphora* disputation, assigning these concepts to discrete juridico-moral personae. Beginning with the persona of the prince, Thomasius observes that just as private persons have different duties "because all men may be regarded in accordance with diverse purposes" so too the duties of the ruler differ "because he can be regarded as a man, as a Christian, and as a prince." As a man, "he is obliged to respect the general law of nature in relation to all men, no matter what their estate," practicing the general law of love, and pretending to no privilege "because he has human nature in common with all others." In his Christian persona, "he is obliged to observe the rules of Christianity and, through proper repentance and acknowledgement of the general misery of the human race, take flight to our Saviour, freeing himself from dead works through true living faith, and seeking his salvation with fear and trembling." In his persona as prince, however, the ruler's duties are quite different and arise from an entirely discrete normative purpose:

> As a prince, though, he is bound to preserve external peace and calm among his subjects through appropriate means of coercion. For this teaches him the ultimate purpose on account of which men relinquish their natural freedom in establishing states, subordinating themselves to a superior in those matters that have been deemed necessary for the preservation of the commonwealth. (27)

This disaggregation and restriction of the duties of the prince has the effect of lowering the moral threshold for participation in citizenship to a set of minimal duties concomitant with the state's purpose in preserving external peace: "And because for this final purpose it is not necessary that the subjects cultivate virtue with their whole hearts . . . it is enough for this if they refrain from external vices, to the extent that they disturb external calm" (27).

It is the separation of the ruler's Christian and political personae that most strikingly demonstrates the fundamental character of Thomasius's secularization of the juridical and political domain. Drawing on Pufendorf's separation of the persona of the prince (who exercises coercive power for the mutual protection of his subjects) from that of the Christian teacher (who establishes noncoercive relations of love and edification between the members of the invisible church), Thomasius argues that the ruler may not bear his princely persona in the church—where he is merely one teacher or listener among others—so that civil power may not be exercised for religious purposes (45–7). Carpzov's appeal to the *Zwei-Personen-Lehre* to defend the prince's duty in preserving the discipline and orthodoxy of the church through the punishment of heretics and the defense of the faith thus represents a fundamental misunderstanding regarding the relations between civil and religious authority. Similarly, Carpzov is wrong to claim that the church consists of the magistracy, clergy, and subjects, for, as Pufendorf has shown, the church is a community of believers consisting only of teachers and auditors bound together by love (43).

As there are no political subjects or citizens in the church, then no members of the church may be ascribed juridical rights qua church members. This allows Thomasius to deny that the congregation has a right not to be scandalized by the prince's modification or abrogation of *adiaphora*. Similarly, the clergy has no quasi-aristocratic right to settle such controversies over religion, as in the church their office is that of teacher who works through love not right, while in the secular state their status is that of subjects under the authority of the prince. As far as the prince is concerned, it is erroneous to regard him as a member of the church in part because this is to grant him some power there, and in part because this allows his power to be abused by the clergy for religious purposes. According to Thomasius, the confusions introduced by the *Drei-Stände-Lehre* have resulted in a widespread failure to understand that the church is an association within the state without being a part of the state. Above all, these confusions have supported the disastrous view that the prince has a duty to care for the salvation of his subjects, thereby failing to heed the restriction of civil sovereignty to the purposes of external peace, and opening the door to the coercion of consciences and the cruelest of persecutions and wars in the name of religion (33 ff).

Thomasius is now in a position to resolve the central question at issue between him and Carpzov: the prince's right in settling religious controversies. In the first place, he argues, we should cease seeking unity of religion in the form of a single body of theoretical doctrines such as those taught in public creeds like the Formula of Concord (1–7). True religion does not consist in the theoretical opinions of the understanding—which are quite incapable of grasping God's mysterious nature—but in the simple faith of the will conformed to the teachings of brotherly love. It is thus both vain and illegitimate for theologians and church councils to attempt to resolve conflicts between opposed theoretical opinions by imposing an orthodox doctrine or creed. This is in part because, as matters of the understanding, theoretical opinions about religion cannot be coerced. More importantly it is because true religion does not consist in theoretical opinions but in "simple active faith" and the demonstration of brotherly love.

At the level of the religious community, then, the resolution to long-standing and blood-soaked controversies—over the relation between Christ's two natures and one person, and the nature of his presence in the Eucharist—lies in the adoption of mutual toleration between those holding irreconcilable doctrinal viewpoints (12 ff). In this regard, in his persona as a Christian, the ruler is in the same position as all other members of the church, engaging in mutual toleration over doctrinal differences and pursuing his own inner salvation. He must on no account, though, seek to decide a religious dispute by issuing a legal judgment—as such judgments pertain only to his powers in maintaining civil peace—and he must eschew all use of his princely powers to enforce a particular confession: "If the prince is a Christian then he is bound to know the ground of his salvation and thus to familiarise himself with true theology. But with regards to what he holds to be true in religious controversies, he has no right to compel others to hold this for true, for this [right] does not belong to him either as a prince or as Christian. The former quality pertains to external peace to which these controversies do not belong, but the latter gives him no right to coerce others" (82).

At the same time, however, Thomasius argues that the entire history of the Reformation shows that ambitious and power-hungry clergy have indeed attempted to enforce particular confessional doctrines, enlisting princely support to do so, and giving rise to the dreadful catastrophe of the Thirty Years War. Notwithstanding the illicitness of a prince intervening in a theological controversy to compel the acceptance of a particular opinion, it is thus entirely proper for the prince to step in when such controversies threaten external peace—indeed it is his duty—as long as he does so without regard to theological truth: "With the emergence of theological controversies, the prudent prince takes care that he compels no-one to accept a particular opinion. If, though, the parties attempt to carry the day through force, then he sees to his duty and ensures that the external peace is not disturbed, in which case the truth will possess enough of its own power to come through, and to discredit the lies" (145–46). With this separation of peace from truth, the prince from the theologian and philosopher, Thomasius carries his secularization of politics and law to its highest point, articulating a conception of toleration not as a universal natural right, but as a political or constitutional right possessed by the prince or state to enforce religious peace. At the political level, then, it is the prince who exercises the right of toleration, which he does against intolerant religious communities.

Conclusion

Today we find it difficult to fit the thought of the great anti-scholastic natural law thinkers into our standard templates of moral and political philosophy. This is in part because the path that they followed—from the destruction of Christian rationalist anthropology, through the multiplication of civil personae, to the rejection of natural right as a condition of secularizing political authority—was a regional one, pioneered to outflank the intellectual bulwarks of the early modern confessional state. It is also because in the wake of Kant's moral and political philosophy, a different path was opened up, or perhaps an earlier one was resumed. This path leads from the reaffirmation of the anthropology of "rational being," through the unification of moral personality under a formal moral law, to the derivation of a universal natural right based on the exercise of moral freedom compatible with the like exercise of a community of rational beings. The fact that this new form of natural law has been aligned with the institutions of electoral democracy and democratic jurisprudence—in the normative philosophies of John Rawls and Jürgen Habermas—means that we are peculiarly blind to its regional character. Yet it too first emerged as a theory program for a particular grouping—the rationalist academic philosophers of late eighteenth-century Protestant northern Germany—and perhaps remains tied to similar groupings, albeit of a more cosmopolitan distribution and aspiration. In any case, the modern philosophical defense of popular sovereignty appears to have been achieved by restoring a political philosophy based on a rationalist anthropology and natural rights. What remains unclear is whether, under these intellectual circumstances, it is possible to maintain the secularization of politics that was based on the antimetaphysical pluralization of civil personae.

Notes

1. Research for this paper was made possible by the award of an Australian Professorial Fellowship. Thanks go to David Saunders for his incisive comments on the first draft and to participants in the Security, State, and Subject Formation workshop for their helpful feedback.
2. The Gregorian calendar, named after Pope Gregory XIII who proclaimed it in 1582, is now general in the Western world. It was religiously contentious as it modified the earlier Julian calendar, deleting ten days, in order to align the celebration of Easter with the time agreed to at the Council of Nicaea in 325. Many Protestant territories initially refused to adopt what they considered to be a Catholic invention, only gradually doing so during the course of the eighteenth century.

CHAPTER THREE

Reassembling Civilization: State-Formation, Subjectivity, Security, Power

Robert van Krieken

Soldiers! You are undertaking a conquest with incalculable consequences for civilization and world trade. You will inflict a decisive and significant blow on England...
        (June 22, 1798, Napoleon's speech to his soldiers en route to Egypt)

This struggle has been called a clash of civilizations. In truth, it is a struggle for civilization. We are fighting to maintain the way of life enjoyed by free nations. And we're fighting for the possibility that good and decent people across the Middle East can raise up societies based on freedom and tolerance and personal dignity.
        (September 11, 2006, President Bush's Address to the Nation)

Introduction

Security and civilization are generally thought of as close companions—an insecure existence is almost by definition uncivilized, and any conception of a civilized life will generally include peace, safety, and security. However, at the same time that "civilization" operates as a "black box" concept that people use almost casually, relatively firm in the belief that it has a solid, unambiguous meaning, it is also one of those essentially contested concepts, like "freedom" or "progress," carrying many different meanings with sometimes entirely contradictory implications. The combination of these two things is particularly potent and, for social and political theorists, problematic, which is just one of the reasons why there is an inclination to avoid it altogether. Most people are much happier talking about liberalism, democracy, modernization, globalization, rationalization, postmodernization, or cosmopolitanism. This is why there is a widespread view in social and political theory that the concept "should not only be 'deconstructed' but taken down" (Mazlish 2004:161).

The position I would like to take up here, in contrast, is that it is more important than ever that the meaning and application of civilization be scrutinized and developed. Its referent remains unavoidable and decisive, and the concept itself remains central to the public social and political discourse surrounding the state and security. The political myth of "the clash of civilizations" (Bottici and Challand 2006) has become an important part of the way in which symbolic power is exercised today, and much depends on the capacity to subject it to critical scrutiny. Like it or not, the civilization–barbarism distinction structures our thinking about most significant aspects of social and political life. The meanings attached to the concept, whether explicit or not, have decisive consequences for the way in which powerful state and non-state actors go about their business. The pursuit of a particular construction of "civilization" has been central to the processes, practices, and institutions of "empire," both as a central element of the modernization process in the past, and as part of the post-1989 "new world order."

The particular construction of "civilization" also organizes much of the critique of state action. Even the critique of "civilization as colonialism" is in many respects an internal critique, an attack on the treatment of indigenous populations from the standpoint of one's own standards of "civilization." The concept is a significant clue to the heterogeneity of liberal political thought, especially the exclusions, which operate alongside its claimed inclusiveness. Particular constructions of "civilization" tend to operate as a crucial "filter" for liberal citizenship (van Krieken 2002). Liberal political regimes thus appear as terrains across which the liberal concern for individual welfare and freedom is articulated with the exercise of power within more specific and ever-changing framings of civilization.

In terms of current developments in world politics, it is clear that a particular kind of "civilizing mission" is currently in train. We need not think only of US military adventures; they are in some sense a distraction from the broader "civilizing mission" taking place through what has been called the "new standard of civilization" in international law acting as a counter to domestic legal jurisdictions (Buchan 2006; Donnelly 1998; Bowden 2004a; Fidler 2001; Gong 1984; and Schwarzenberger 1955). Indeed, it is possible to say that the whole "project of modernity" has always been essentially about various kinds of civilizing missions, and that the current state of the world can be understood as the intersections and collisions of those civilizing projects.

My title is borrowed from Bruno Latour's *Reassembling the Social* (2005). Latour argues for the need to destabilize the idea of "the social" rather than treating it as a conceptual given, so that whatever "society" is becomes the endpoint of the analysis rather than its opening, and unquestioned premise (2005 :2). I believe that this argument also applies to a variety of other concepts in social and political analysis, including "civilization." Rather than reifying and naturalizing the concept, in relation to which we can adopt either an unquestioning or a critical stance, my argument is that much more can be gained from pulling the concept apart and then reassembling it, in order to be able to analyze and discuss real social and political relations and processes that get bundled up within it.

I will start by proposing that there are two central problems and instabilities characterizing the currently dominant usages of the term. The first is the conflation with "culture," and the second is its use as a noun, for a state or a condition, rather than as a verb, for a process of civilization.

Civilization versus Culture, Process versus State

The concept "civilization" seems to have always led a double life in Western social and political thought, at one and the same time an organizing principle and also an object of ongoing critique (Starobinski 1993). The critique of civilization was organized largely around the concept "culture," the distinction between profundity and shallowness, between moral and technical development. Civilization came to be equated, in this critique, with material, technological progress, and "manners" (seen as merely superficial), whereas "culture" referred to ethical maturity and cultivation, authenticity, and community (Kant 1970). The two terms themselves could still be unstable, often slipping and sliding across the boundary between what was being distinguished depending on the writer and the context.

The distinction overlapped with one between a clustering of universalism, cosmopolitanism, and rationalism (civilization) on the one hand, and particularism, national traditions, and spiritualism (culture) on the other (Coleridge 1830:42). As Brett Bowden puts it (2004b:38), the opposition overlaps with that between Enlightenment social and political thought (civilization) and that of the Counter-Enlightenment (culture). Or as Reinhold Niebuhr (1952) suggested, between Ancient Greece (culture) and the Roman Empire (civilization).

In the course of the twentieth century, the civilization/culture distinction lost much of its force, and by 1930 Lucien Febvre was observing that there are two main ways in which the concept "civilization" is used. It can have an "ethnographic" or primarily cultural meaning, collapsing the demarcation from culture altogether, referring simply to a way of life, a condition or a complex, a particular assembly of cultural, moral, political, and economic forms, and it allows for multiple "civilizations." In this sense it is pretty well interchangeable with "culture" or "society," and this is how it is being used when people talk about a "clash of civilizations," or "civilizational analysis" (Arjomand and Tiryakian 2004). Huntington, for example, makes it clear that he sees no need to distinguish between civilization and culture, declaring that any "civilization is thus the highest cultural grouping of people and the broadest level of cultural identity people have short of that which distinguishes humans from other species" (Huntington 1993:24).

The concept is also used to refer, in a more singular way, to a particular way of organizing social and political life, the operation of power, and the constitution of human subjectivity. In this sense, there is a linkage between civilization and the rule of law, operating through the embedding of the exercise of power in impersonal rules and structures, rather than in the unregulated will of dominant individuals and groups, a "government of laws, not of men." Here, the form taken by individual subjectivity plays a central role and the mechanisms by which this is "cultivated" is a core element of the ongoing production of governable citizens. This usage is also more closely tied to the distinction between civilization and "barbarism."

In practice, the two types of meaning are often conflated with each other, as culture and civilization become interchangeable, and civilization ends up referring to all and any type of "progress," material and moral. Particularly in the postwar American usage, it has come to refer not just to mechanization and technology, free trade and welfare, but also to individual liberty, democracy, and human rights, all of which were bound up with each other, in a universalistic conception with no cultural or national boundaries (Beard and Beard 1962:580–1). Since 1989, especially, civilization has come to function as "an over-arching indication of the inviolable basic rights of every individual regardless of sex, skin colour or religion, for a democratic political structure and for an independent legal system" (den Boer 2001:78). It has also become a static rather than processual conception, claiming to refer to a finished state of affairs, to which the rest of the (uncivilized) world

was meant to aspire, so that the only development taking places consists of approxima-
tion to the universal American ideal, captured with the concept "Western civilization."

However, the opposition between *Kultur* and *Zivilisation* is more than just a relic of
the nineteenth-century nationalism, a German reaction to Napoleonic imperialism. The
two concepts simply "work" differently in political discourse. It is possible to say that
genocides are a problem for "civilization" in a way that they are not for "culture." One
does not describe the slaughter of the Tutsis in Rwanda as "uncultured," but as "barbaric."
To say that the attack on the Twin Towers on September 11, 2001 was an attack on "civilization itself" makes sense in a way that an attack on "culture itself" would not.

Processes of Civilization: Power and Subjectivity

What, then, does a non-culturalist, processual conception of civilization look like?
In Norbert Elias's construction of the concept of "the civilizing process," it referred to the
linkages between particular transformations of subjectivity and the self on the one hand,
and the larger-scale institutional process of state-formation and its underlying mechanisms of power relations on the other. What we experience as "civilization" is founded on
a particular habitus, a particular psychic structure, sense of self and psychological identity, which changes over time, and, which can only be understood in connection with
transformations in the forms taken by broader social, political, and economic relationships—changes, which in the case of the West included state-formation, urbanization, and
the emergence of markets, bureaucracies, large-scale organizations, and legal systems.

The essential aspects of those ongoing changes, in the history of Western European
state-formation at least, and arguably characteristic of any society describable as "modern," include, first, an ongoing concentration of power and control over the "means of
violence" in a declining number of political "units"—either states or constellations of
states. Elias regarded any configuration of competing social units, such as states, towns,
or communities as characterized by a powerful "logic" pushing towards an increasing
monopolization of power and, correspondingly, of the means of violence by increasingly
centralized political authorities, eventually in the form of the sovereign nation-state with
its army, police, and legal apparatus. The dynamics of social, political, and economic
competition were organized, he suggested, around two "mechanisms": what Elias called
the "monopoly mechanism" and the "royal mechanism," which together tend to concentrate power in a decreasing number of larger political units.

The "monopoly mechanism" concerned the ways in which competition between
different "survival units" involves "elimination contests" in which some win and others
lose, and the number of units gradually decreases. Elias felt that, on the whole, competition would generally drive any human figuration towards "a state in which all opportunities are controlled by a single authority: a system with open opportunities will become a
system with closed opportunities" (2000:269). The concept of the "royal mechanism"
refers to a feature of the evenness or indecisiveness of any pattern of competition. Elias
observed that the position of a central authority is not based simply on some greater
power that they might have over any other social unit. But, it is based on their function as
a mediator or nodal point for the conflicts between the other groups in society, which can
neither individually overcome any of the others, nor stop competing to the degree
required to form an effective alliance with each other.

Second, one can see a steady increase in social differentiation and social density, what Elias referred to as the lengthening and increasingly multifaceted "chains of interdependence." Elias spoke of the "conveyor belts" running through individuals' lives growing "longer and more complex" (Elias 2000:364), making the requirement that we "attune" our conduct to the actions of an ever-expanding circle of others (2000:367), the dominant influence on our existence. In the process we gradually become less "prisoners of our passions," but correspondingly more captive to the requirements of an increasingly complex "web of actions" (2000:367), particularly a demand for "constant hindsight and foresight in interpreting the actions and intentions of others" (Elias 2000:378–9). Just as important as the sheer "length" of chains of interdependence was the increasing ambivalence of overlapping and multiple networks: as social relations became more complex and contradictory, the same people or groups could be "friends, allies or partners" in one context and "opponents, competitors or enemies" in another. "This fundamental ambivalence of interests," wrote Elias, is "one of the most important structural characteristics of more highly developed societies, and a chief factor moulding civilized conduct" (Elias 2000:318; see also Hirschman 1977; and Holmes 1995). The process begins at the centre of power relations, in court society and among the upper classes, but gradually spreads throughout society (much like the spread of "discipline" as understood by Weber (1948), Foucault (1977) and Oestreich (1982)—see van Krieken 1990a; 1990b). Therefore, the contrasts between different social strata gradually diminish in a process of "functional democratization," with increasing "pressure from below," from the broader population, on the conduct of social and political elites, at the same time that their own behavior is subjected to increasingly complex constraints and requirements.

For Elias all social life is characterized by a particular balance between external and internal compulsion (*Fremdzwang* and *Selbstzwang*), between social control imposed and enforced by individuals, groups, agencies, and institutions external to each individual, and internalized controls that operate even in the absence of such external constraints, under conditions of "freedom." He thought that what is experienced as a sense of being "civilized" is underpinned by this overall historical tendency for this balance to shift more and more towards internalized compulsion (as opposed to external control, hence, "freedom"). "The web of actions grows so complex and extensive," wrote Elias, and "the effort required to behave 'correctly' within it becomes so great, that beside the individual's conscious self-control an automatic, blindly functioning apparatus of self-control is firmly established" (2000:367–8).

Specifically Elias noted that in the course of European history, the standards applied to violence, sexual behavior, bodily functions, eating habits, table manners, and forms of speech became gradually more sophisticated, with an increasing threshold of shame, embarrassment, and repugnance. Gradually more and more aspects of human behavior were regarded as "distasteful." The exercise of violence, especially, is subjected to gradually increasing restraint, despite counter-tendencies and reversals of direction—of which the Holocaust is only the most obvious example—and for Elias the practical question was whether, and under what conditions, one can still speak over the longer term of a "master-trend" towards the gradual pacification of social and political life.

Elias referred to this increasing self-regulation as a process of "psychologization" and "rationalization," because it revolved around the growing reflexive understanding of our own actions, those of others, their interrelationships, and their consequences.

Later in his work (1991), Elias emphasized the importance of expanding networks of mutual identification (also raised in the 1930s by Harold Lasswell 1965 [1935]:37; 1934 [1930]:256–9; see de Swaan 1995) as part of increasing social interdependence. He also emphasized the issues surrounding the possible development of increasingly broad "we" identities, from the family and the village to the region, to the nation-state (see Anderson 1983), and in a shift to a cosmopolitan identity, to humanity as a whole (Beck 2006). To the extent that "circles of identification" widen (de Swaan 1995), one sees an increase in civility, in empathy, care, and concern for the well-being of others. Their contraction, or the widening of "circles of disidentification" (de Swaan 1997) on the other hand, appears to be an essential aspect of the emergence of intergroup hatred and violence and a general decline in security in social and political life.

A number of features of the debates around Elias's framing of the relationship between state-formation, security, and subjectivity draw out the ways in which his approach might be most useful for understanding contemporary issues. The first concerns the question of whether the formation of large-scale nation-states consisting of complex differentiated societies is necessary for the kind of internalized restraint regarding violence and emotions underpinning what we might want to call civilization. There are points where Elias does put what I have called the "strong" version of this argument, seeing a centralized state as essential to the formation of civilized self-restraint (2000: 369). This has tended to upset most anthropologists, because it is then difficult to avoid seeing those human groups existing outside the framework of the nation-state as lying at an "earlier" stage of the civilizing process, and suggesting some sort of hierarchical relationship between groups that are "more" or "less" civilized. In many respects, this ought to be beside the point, since it is always a conceptual error to mix historical and comparative analysis. However, there is also the simple empirical question of whether it is true that the kind of balance between external and internal compulsion that Elias sees as linked to large-scale, industrial, urbanized, and bureaucratized societies can only be found in a large-scale nation-state.

A number of anthropological commentators (van Velzen 1984; Duerr 1988, 1990, 1993, 1997, and 2002; Goody 2002, 2003) point out that one can often observe complex patterns of self-restraint in stateless human groups, and identify other aspects of social structure, such as particular forms of marriage and kinship relations, which can also produce a complex social interdependency. This social interdependency in turn generates the tight web of social expectations producing a "civilized" personality structure (van Velzen 1984). Hans-Peter Duerr suggests that there is far more, which we have in common both with our historical predecessors and with other cultures than Elias's perspective admits. And one central focus of Duerr's critique of "the myth of the civilizing process" is to draw attention to those features of human relations in all cultural and historical contexts, which produce roughly similar forms of behavior (van Krieken 1989). It may be preferable, then, to work with a "weaker" version of Elias's argument, in which there can be a variety of bases of complex social interdependency underpinning increased self-compulsion. State formation and increasing social differentiation are one possibility, but another can be particular forms of kinship-based social organization, which appear to produce very similar effects in a variety of settings.

A second, related issue is whether social differentiation, lengthening chains of interdependence, and state-formation are sufficient to underpin what Elias sees as processes of civilization, and indeed under what conditions they can produce exactly the opposite effect. Duerr, for example, questions whether greater social differentiation and lengthening chains of interdependence are necessarily linked to a restrained habitus and civilized emotional economy. Duerr suggests that Elias's account underestimates the extent to which, with urbanization and industrialization, "a certain degree of porosity also arose, which was unknown to the forms of social control in 'archaic' times and which gave people opportunities for freedom which they had never had before" (Duerr 1990:24). For Duerr, then, the same processes, which Elias saw as leading to greater internalization of social constraint can also be seen as underpinning the exact opposite, a relaxation of social regulation.

Stefan Breuer (1991) also draws attention to the "negative side of functional differentiation," the effects of the organization of capitalist societies around the logic of the market. Although longer chains of interdependence may demand greater foresight and calculation as Elias suggests, markets also display "a dimension of coincidence and anarchy, which undermines the calculability of individual action" (Breuer 1991:405). Market societies thus disintegrate and decompose social relations at the same time that they promote social integration and aggregation. Competition does not simply produce ever larger and better integrated "survival units," argues Breuer, it also generates "the atomization of the social, the increasing density and negation of all ties—asocial sociability" (1991:407; see also Burkitt 1996). To this, one could add the example of state socialism; characterized by the central feature of what Elias understood to be the civilizing process. This is the formation of a centralized state with a monopoly over the means of violence, but with its authoritarian political structure keeping the balance between external and internal compulsion firmly weighted toward the former, maintaining a higher level of violence at all levels of society (Engler 1991, 1992).

This last issue can be framed slightly differently, as connected with the question of the direction of processes of civilization to consider the following:

- whether there are times when one can observe developments in the opposite direction;
- when the balance between external and internal constraint shifts towards the former;
- large political units disintegrate into smaller sub-units;
- controls over emotions and violence become less stable and less differentiated;
- the levels of violence in everyday life increase, and;
- social life becomes "de-pacified."

This has always been one of the central critiques of Elias's concept of civilization, in that in practice it appears fairly consistently to encompass what is meant to be its opposite, barbarism (Gouldner 1981). The exercise of state sovereignty can often be a decivilizing force, the most obvious example being the waging of war, or genocide, in pursuit of cultural homogeneity. The monopolization of physical force by the State also allows it to use that force in an almost unrestricted way, and that is exactly what various States have done. For example, Rummel (1997) has observed that during the twentieth century, 170 million civilians have been killed by states alongside 34 million armed military.[1] Two questions are raised here: first, what does it mean to speak of decivilizing processes (Fletcher 1997; Mennell 1990), and how do they relate to processes of civilization? Second, are civilization and decivilization (or barbarism) always analytically distinct and mutually exclusive, even if they can occur simultaneously in the real world, or are they flip sides of each other, so that there is always a decivilizing or barbaric element to any process of civilization?

Decivilizing and Dyscivilizing Processes, and the Barbarism of Civilization

An important issue in understanding processes of civilization is the question of what kind of "container" one works with, or to put it differently, the question of what is the unit of civilization? How does such a container or unit "fit" within and between nation-states? Elias's own analysis tended to concentrate on France, England and Germany, with an emphasis on identifying the "master trends" they had in common. Only later, when he turned to the question of understanding the Holocaust in relation to civilizing processes, did he have more to say about what was specific and distinct about the German case, as well as considering the issue of relations between nation-states. Hans Haferkamp referred to this change of focus as "a shift of emphasis from intra-societal to inter-state-societal processes" (1987:546). One of the more important manifestations of this change in orientation is Elias's (1996) analysis of the "peculiarities of the Germans" which underlay the rise of German fascism and the Holocaust. His earlier emphasis in *The Civilizing Process* had been on identifying the "long-term trend," which would eventually override the changes in the direction of the civilizing process. In contrast, Elias described his later analysis of the rise of Hitler and the Nazi state's genocidal practices as "an attempt to tease out the developments in the German national habitus which made possible the decivilizing spurt of the Hitler epoch, and to work out the connections between them and the long-term process of state-formation in Germany" (1996:1).

The aggression and violence of the Nazi regime could be explained, argued Elias, in terms of four peculiarities of the German state-formation process. (1) The first was the particular position of the German territories within a larger figuration of nation-states, caught between Eastern and Western Europe. (2) The second was the exposure of the German territories to foreign invasion, which, Elias argued, "led to military bearing and warlike actions being highly regarded and often idealized" (1996:7). (3) The third was the larger number of breaks and discontinuities in the development of the German state. (4) The fourth was the ideological weakness of the bourgeoisie relative to the military aristocracy (1996:15).

The specifics of the case of Nazi Germany led Elias to argue for the reversibility of all social processes, and suggested that "shifts in one direction can make room for shifts in the opposite direction," so that "a dominant process directed at greater integration could go hand in hand with a partial disintegration" (Elias 1986:235). He remarked that the example of the Hitler regime showed "not only that processes of growth and decay can go hand in hand but that the latter can also predominate relative to the former" (1996).

Elias's view of the interstate civilizing process, until he developed his analysis of the German case, tended to be a relatively sanguine one, with the competition between states simply leading "eventually" to the formation of larger "survival units." In relation to the intrastate civilizing process and the formation of nation-states themselves, he (Elias 1972:278) spoke of a continuous development:

> ... from the multitude of relatively small, relatively loosely integrated dynastic states of the 11th and 12 centuries, by way of a great number of integration and disintegration spurts, gradually to larger, more populous and more closely integrated social units in the form of the larger dynastic states and then to the—so far—most highly integrated and interdependent large societies, the industrial nation states. . . .

Elias's view of the interstate civilizing process was largely an extension of this account, anticipating that nation-states would eventually—albeit over an indeterminate period and with many possible movements in the opposite direction—consolidate themselves into larger supranational entities. "One can see," he (Elias 2000:445–6) wrote in *The Civilizing Process*, "the first outlines of a worldwide system of tensions composed of alliances and supra-state units of various kinds, the prelude of struggles embracing the whole globe, which are the precondition for a worldwide monopoly of physical force, for a single central political institution and thus for the pacification of the earth."

Whether or not this is in fact the overall longer-term tendency, his own study of the German case shows that it can be a very long-term trend indeed. Further, it may be far more directly interesting and significant—indeed, crucial to exactly that "eventual" movement towards global pacification—to say a lot more about the "counter-trends" and their decivilizing effects.

There does not appear, then, to be anything to prevent any particular social formation (societies, ethnic groups, nations, and states) from displaying apparently contradictory combinations of civilized and decivilized modes of behavior. There is no, to put it in a postmodern way, "grand narrative" of civilization. Within any one society, culture, or political entity—there is no necessary or inherent unity in the way in which people treat different categories of "others." The torturer may also abhor domestic violence and refuse to eat meat because of cruelty to animals. In reality, the foundations of mutual identification appear to be contingent and volatile, in some contexts at least. Abram de Swaan's (1997; 2001) concept of a "dyscivilizing" process aims to capture this "partial" and selective civilizing process, addressing the ways in which people can compartmentalize their perception of their fellow human beings, engaging in a partial disidentification, which allows for potentially unrestrained violence, since its objects are perceived and experienced as not "really human."

De Swaan (2001:269) explains disidentification as constituting "the denial that the target population might be similar to oneself and the repression of emotions that result from identification, such as sympathy, pity, concern, jealousy, etc." This is generally linked to a certain set of "compartmentalizing" institutional forms and practices, including the separate conceptualization and treatment of the target population and "for the perpetrators the psychological separation of their psychic experiences from all other mental processes or social encounters" (2001:268). If enough people feel sufficiently vulnerable and threatened, whether because of competition between states and other political groups or for some other reason, this can and often does produce configurations of power relations, which bring about significant decivilizing effects. As Abram de Swaan (1997) points out in his analysis of the Rwandan genocide, one of the effects of interstate competition can be the destabilization of existing power relations, the erosion of the monopoly of violence, and the appeal by political entrepreneurs to whatever collective identities they find most strategically effective, whether along racial, ethnic, or religious lines.

In his analysis of the treatment of the Armenians in the Ottoman–Turkish Empire (1894–1922), the Jews in Germany before the war (1933–1939), and the "ethnic cleansing" accompanying the collapse of Yugoslavia (1985–1995), Ton Zwaan (2001) concludes that it is necessary to stress the sheer contingency of processes of civilization (2003:173–4). Zwaan says it is also necessary to identify those conditions and circumstances under which an inherently unstable balance between what we recognize as civilization and barbarism, or civilizing and decivilizing/dyscivilizing processes, can be tipped one way or the other.

This point can be made even stronger by bearing in mind the ways in which the mechanisms of processes of civilization—"pacification," homogenization, and so on—have very often had at their heart the exercise of particular forms of violence strangely invisible to contemporaries, often only becoming apparent in retrospect. Despite the increasing willingness to acknowledge the precariousness of civilizing processes and their potential accompaniment by processes of decivilization or dyscivilization, it is important to remain wary of the assumption that civilization and its opposite, barbarism, are mutually exclusive. There are traces of challenge to this assumption in Elias's own work, although they need further development, and run counter to his more central lines of argument. He pointed out, for example, that the monopolization of physical force by the state, through the military and the police, cuts in two directions and has a Janus-faced character (1996:175), because such monopolies of force can then be all the more effectively wielded by powerful groups within any given nation-state. It was possible, he suggested, to emphasize the integrative effect of social norms at the expense of their "dividing and excluding character," when they had an "inherently double-edged character," since in the very process of binding some people together, they turn those people against others (1996:159–60). The linkage between what has been understood as civilization and colonialism is a key example. The bringing of all the institutions of civilized society—private property, productive economic action, individual liberty, rational-legal organizational forms, and the rule of law—to indigenous populations appears to take place only through clearly barbaric mechanisms—dispossession, destruction of indigenous culture—which indigenous people themselves experience as "cultural genocide" (van Krieken 2008).

It also remains crucial to maintain a distinction that most of the literature on civilization tends persistently to lose sight of, between civilizing processes and civilizing offensives (van Krieken 1990b). Elias' overall theoretical orientation towards seeing social change as unplanned, rather than the product of rational, calculated action, puts his conception of civilizing processes at odds with most other observers, even when they themselves think they are drawing on his ideas. When Roger Chartier makes use of Elias to highlight the historicity of psychic makeup, for example, he speaks of self-discipline and mastery over the emotions as having been "instituted" by the state (Chartier 1989:116). But Elias himself says that "the 'circumstances' which change are not something which comes upon men from the 'outside': they are the relationships between people themselves" (Elias 2000:402). In looking at how everyday life, conduct and sensibility was transformed in Europe from around the sixteenth century onwards, Elias sees the compulsions acting on individuals at all levels of society as built into the structure of social relationships. He does not see these compulsions as coming upon peasants and workers from the "outside," in the shape of lawyers, judges, police officers, inquisitors, teachers, employers, and so on, all giving their own particular form to the civilizing "process" and turning it into a civilizing offensive (Kruithof 1980; Mitzman 1987; Franke 1988; and Verrips 1987).

There is an important difference, then, between what Elias saw as the civilizing process, and what is regarded by most other scholars as a project of social discipline, as "a conscious proselytizing crusade waged by men of knowledge and aimed at extirpating the vestiges of wild cultures—local, tradition-bound ways of life and patterns of cohabitation" (Bauman 1987:93). Clearly a great deal of planning did in fact go into the attempts to develop civilized social and interpersonal relations, on the part of the clergy, inquisitors, state educators, town councils issuing sumptuary legislation, founders of workhouses and systematic poor relief, employers, philosophers, political and legal theorists, and "advisors to the prince." As Bauman suggests, civilizing offensives have constituted ""above all else a novel, active stance towards social processes previously left to their own resources, and a presence of concentrated social powers sufficient to translate such a stance into effective social measures" (Bauman 1987:93). In addition, it is precisely at the point where civilization moves from being driven by broader processes of social, political, and economic transformation to being consciously pursued by human actors and institutions. It is in the arena of deliberate attempts to "bring about" civilization that most of the features of civilization's barbaric flip side, the exercise of power and violence in civilization's name, emerge.

Human Rights, the New "Standard of Civilization"?

Many of the more significant developments in relation to this question of the relationship between civilizing processes and civilizing offensive are currently taking place at the level of interstate dynamics, in the field of international relations. I would like to pull this discussion together, then, by looking at how these conceptual concerns relate to a central feature of those developments, the pursuit of human rights, which has become something of an umbrella concept for almost all types of offensives since the Holocaust and the dismantling of colonial regimes.

The term "civilization" plays a very particular role in international relations scholarship, where one speaks of differing "standards of civilization" (SOC) animating relations between sovereign states and a global regime of international law (Schwarzenberger 1955; Gong 1984). A conceptualization of a SOC emerged, explains Gong, in the nineteenth-century international law in response to two interrelated problems faced by Europe. These problems were (1) the practical one of how to protect European life and property in non-European countries, and; (2) the legal and philosophical one of how to make distinctions between which nation-states would be granted legal personality and standing in international law and which would not. One generally distinguishes between an "old" SOC, expressing a now discredited conception of civilization allied to imperialism and colonialism, and a "new" SOC defining civilization in terms of democracy, liberalism, tolerance and, above all, human rights. The "old" SOC was concerned with the maintenance of organized economic, social, political life; ensuring that sovereign states were able and willing to protect adequately the life, liberty, property; freedom of travel and religion of foreigners—especially, of course, Westerners in non-Western lands. The issues at stake have been the following:

- securing basic rights for foreign nationals;
- an organized political bureaucracy and military, systems of law, courts, written codes of law;
- fair administration of justice within bounded territory;
- diplomatic institutions able to engage in international relations, and;
- a willingness on the part of states to abide by international law and generally conform to customs, more of the Western societies (Gong 1984).

The dismantling of colonial regimes and the discredit brought upon a progressivist conception of civilization by the two World Wars made it difficult to sustain any claims based on civilization. However, as Donnelly (1998:13–4) remarks, the "death" of the old SOC produced new problems, in that its absence left only a pure Westphalian conception of national sovereignty, which left national governments more or less to do as they wished with their own populations. Almost immediately, the concept of human rights took the place of the SOC in order to remedy this problem (Donnelly 1998), so that it is possible to speak of a shift from "Westphalian" SOC to a globalized, liberal SOC (Fidler 2001). The globalized SOC is organized around concepts like: (1) human rights and the rule of law; (2) democracy in governance; (3) free-market economics, openness to international trade and investment; (4) efficacy of science and technology, and; (5) of course, recognition of a single global military power – the United States. The new conception of humanitarian intervention in international law exemplifies the human rights regime of civilization. As David Fidler (2001:147) observes:

> The new standard is more ambitious and intrusive . . . Under the new SOC, international law is a tool of political, economic and legal harmonization and homogenization on a scale that dwarfs what was seen in the 19th and early 20th centuries. The civilizational conquest started under the old SOC is now being carried deeper into the hearts of non-Western cultures through international law.

The organized pursuit of human rights through a variety of international legal and political instruments should, then, be understood as the latest, cosmopolitan stage of the global civilizing offensive that has always been the concern of international law, which is why Koskenniemi (2001) refers to it as the "gentle civilizer of nations."

The pursuit of human rights can best be understood in terms of broader civilizing and decivilizing processes—it does at times constitute the manifestation of a gradual pacification of social and political relations around the world, centered on a very gradual and uneven centralization of different forms of hard and soft power in the international society of states. This means that the pursuit of human rights need to be seen as continuous with those older civilizing offensives, and characterized by similar mechanisms and dynamics. This is as Elias outlined for processes of civilization and decivilization— linking the macro processes of formation of states and networks of states to the more micro processes of the formation of subjectivity, moral sensibility, and habitus (Linklater

2004:19). The implications of the analysis of decivilizing and dyscivilizing processes are crucial, highlighting the potential for times and conditions under which the expansion of human rights regimes might be reversed, especially in times of increasing fear and anxiety, such as post-September 11. The pursuit of security, if it compartmentalizes society and excludes particular categories of people from human rights entitlement (criminals, terrorists, etc.) can then in fact underpin dyscivilizing processes.

The "barbarism of civilization" problem (van Krieken 1999) is especially relevant for the politics of human rights, when wars are fought in their name and they are used to legitimize the exercise of varying forms of force on those who are seen as failing to accord the right kinds of rights, those recognized by the West. The ways in which different types of rights are to be prioritized and balances struck between competing rights are essentially contested and ultimately pose irresolvable normative questions. Also numerous commentators have outlined the various ways in which, in the world of *Realpolitik*, becoming a human rights gamekeeper appears to be the best way of continuing to be a poacher (Douzinas 2007).

To the extent that the human rights project is an extension of natural law since the Stoics and the Roman Empire, it is vulnerable to all the problems of "Romanization" and the pursuit of any universalizing moral, political, and social aims. One central issue is that the "other" of human rights is constructed as civilization's other, as irrational, unprincipled, tradition-bound, barbaric and thus fair game for just about any sort of "civilizing" intervention, no matter how barbaric the intervention itself may be. As Pagden (2000:4) has argued, if it may be going too far to characterize the cosmopolitan dream as "nothing more" than imperialism, "it is hard to see how cosmopolitanism can be entirely separated from some kind of 'civilizing' mission, or from the more humanizing aspects of the various imperial projects with which it has been so long associated." The human rights project reinvigorates the civilization/culture opposition, but with different valences attached to each term—so those who deny human rights are seen as doing so in the name of culture, and it is the job of human rights instruments to negate culture's power.

But the liberal pursuit of human rights, tolerance, and civilization does not, in fact, stand outside of culture or religion—what is understood as a legitimate natural human right, how it is to be balanced against competing concerns, and what action is justified in protecting such a right are all culture-bound issues. It remains useful to distinguish processes of civilization from the dynamics of culture and cultural change. However, civilizing offensives, in contrast, are irrevocably tied to particular normative constructions of the world, which are very difficult to detach from their embeddedness in a specific cultural setting (Brown 2006:188). Wendy Brown's (2006:204) comments on liberalism's politics of tolerance apply equally to the human rights ideal and to any form of civilizing mission. Brown says "Tolerance in a liberal idiom, both conferred and withheld, does not merely serve as the *sign* of the civilized and the free: it configures the *right* of the civilized against a barbaric opposite that is both internally oppressive and externally dangerous, neither tolerant nor tolerable."

The danger constantly snapping at the heels of the human rights project, most acute when it is at its most triumphalist and least reflective, is that of all forms of universalizing projects (Bowden 2004b). The danger is in the potential for the emergence of the decivilizing and dyscivilizing elements of processes of civilization that have continued so persistently to undermine the achievement of a genuinely peaceful and secure social and political life.

Note

1. . . . 62million in the Soviet Union 1917–1987; 10million in Nationalist China 1928-1949; 35million in Communist China 1949–1987; 21million in Nazi Germany.

CHAPTER FOUR

Without Exception: Democracy and Sovereignty after Carl Schmitt

Charles Barbour

Concrete Orders

In the "Preface to the Second Edition" of *Political Theology*, probably his most notorious work, and certainly the one that has received the most attention in recent years, Carl Schmitt references what appears to be an abrupt shift in his thinking—a shift that has been conspicuously overlooked by many of his contemporary readers. Revising the broad outline of legal theory he provided in the 1922 edition of the text, Schmitt's "Preface," dated "November 1933," claims to "distinguish not two but *three* types of legal thinking." To 'the normativist and the decisionist types' explored initially, Schmitt now adds a third: what he calls "the institutional one" (2005 [1934]:2). Whereas he had formerly proposed that all legal theories seek to root law in either impersonal norms or personal decisions, and had clearly indicated his preference for the latter, Schmitt now acknowledged the existence of a "institutional legal thinking" that "unfolds in institutions and organizations that transcend the personal sphere" and that "leads to the pluralism characteristic of a feudal-corporate growth that is devoid of sovereignty" (2005 [1934]:3). More accurately, if Schmitt had previously suggested that all norms rely on decisions that they must conceal, and that even the most objective legal order is ultimately founded on an exception that it can neither contain nor eliminate, he now admitted the possibility of an institutional "order" that was at least coextensive with decisions, or that decisions would have in some sense to negotiate. In the first edition of *Political Theology*, Schmitt had insisted that the sovereign decision has the qualities of a miracle, and that "[t]he exception [*Ausnahmezustand*] in jurisprudence is analogous to the miracle [*Wunder*] in theology" (2005 [1934]:36), meaning that it has no rational derivation, but seems to emanate from the void, utterly bereft of prior conditions. Now he proposed that decisions are structured by "institutions and organizations" that can exist independently, or even "devoid of sovereignty." Schmitt elaborated upon this new schematization of legal thinking in a work that was published the same year as the second edition of *Political Theology*, namely *On the Three Types of Juristic Thought*. "Every jurist who consciously or unconsciously bases his work on the concept of *Recht*," Schmitt begins there, "conceives of this *Recht* either as a rule [i.e. norm] or as a decision, or as a concrete order and formation [*Gestaltung*]" (Schmitt 2004 [1934]:43). He goes on to argue that, while these three types of juristic thought—rule/norm, decision, and order—invariably commingle in any actual legal system, every system nonetheless seeks to elevate one of them to a dominant position. And since, on Schmitt's account, it is clear that rules or norms cannot ground themselves—that "every norm presupposes a normal situation" and is "bound to concrete concepts of what is normal" which themselves "are not derived from general norms" (Schmitt 2004 [1934]:56)—the most significant question for legal theory is the exact relationship between decisions and institutions, or decisions and the "concrete order."

This small textual detail has, I would like to suggest, significant implications for the manner in which Schmitt is read today, and for the recent revival of interest in Schmitt's work. It also has important ramifications for contemporary theories of the relationship between the state, security, and subjectivity. There are, of course, many credible and valid interpretations of Schmitt's effort to include what he calls "concrete order" or "institutional thinking" among the possible types of juristic thought in the early 1930s, during the collapse of the Weimar Republic and the ascendance of National Socialism. Schmitt was closely associated with the Nazi party, but he may not simply have been *the* "crown jurist" of the Nazi regime. While *On the Three Types of Juristic Thought* is openly laudatory, and even enthusiastic, in its assessment of "the National Socialist movement" (Schmitt 2004 [1934]:89–99), some commentators have detected in the turn towards the "concrete order" a critique—however submerged—of Schmitt's own earlier "decisionism," or an effort to retract some of his more aggressive claims regarding the potential of the sovereign exception in favor of a deeply conservative, but not exactly fascist, understanding of a preconstitutional political order (Bendersky 2004 [1934]; McCormick 2004). Here the "concrete order" might be seen to represent an existential unity or community that, prior to any law, could mitigate the extreme possibilities of dictatorship, and blunt the notion that a sovereign decision can miraculously create a radically new political order *ex nihilo*. According to this interpretation, Schmitt's error had less to do with his commitment to the dictatorial force of sovereign decisions than it did with his characterization of the "concrete order" in relation to which such decisions emerged. As McCormick notes, Schmitt was certainly willing to call such an order "democratic," and even to treat "the people" as the source of a legitimacy that transcended mere legality. But, at the same time, Schmitt rejected all deliberative conceptions of democracy, and every notion of democratic participation. He treated the *demos*, not as a formal unity that would have to be forged, created, and repeatedly recreated through rational or rhetorically convincing argumentation, but as a substantial, "quasi-sacred preconstitutional will" (McCormick 2004:xxix). Because it had the status of an existential or ontological given, the question of how a popular will might be constructed in the first place was entirely foreclosed by Schmitt. Instead, at issue was how the popular will could be represented, or who possessed the capacity to act on its behalf. For Schmitt, only an executive authority could be invested with such power, and the only mechanism for installing such an authority was the plebiscite. Because, in Schmitt's words, "[t]he people can only respond yes or no," because they "cannot advise, deliberate, or discuss," it is obvious that "plebiscitary legitimacy is the single type of state justification that may be generally acknowledged today as valid" (2004 [1958]:93). The "concrete order" would thus directly acclaim, rather than participate in the composition of, the sovereign decision.

In this chapter, I am less interested in the strategy at stake in Schmitt's invocation of a "concrete order" in the early 1930s, or the historical significance of such a gesture (Balakrishnan 2000:155–208), than I am in the way this frequently overlooked aspect of his thought might inflect the theories of those who refer to his work today. Despite the "occasionalist" nature of his writings, and how the contingencies of events dictated the direction of his arguments, the element of Schmitt's work that has garnered the most attention in recent years is his strong version of decisionism, his consideration of states of exception, and his antagonistic concept of the political. For a range of thinkers broadly on "the left"—Giorgio Agamben, Chantal Mouffe, and, in a less explicit if no less important fashion, Alain Badiou—Schmitt is known for having treated politics as an irreducible condition of human social relations, and for defining the concept of the political in terms of an irreducible division or strife between friends and enemies. His work makes it possible to comprehend the vicissitudes of political difference, enmity, or struggle, without teleologically directing that struggle towards an ideal of humanity, and without presupposing a guaranteed end of history. Thus a cautious but still robust reference to Schmitt allows contemporary theorists to avoid two criticisms that have routinely been leveled at the left, and especially at those who accept a Marxist inheritance: (1) that it treats politics as an instrument or epiphenomenon of more fundamental social and material conditions, and thus has no conception of politics as an autonomous sphere of human experience; and (2) that, despite numerous qualifications, it relies on a metaphysics of history, and justifies every particular action by positing in advance a more or less predetermined goal. Although it is undoubtedly necessary to dismantle instrumentalist understandings of politics and teleological understandings of history, I would like to propose that drawing on Schmitt's work to do so is a more fraught adventure than some current theorists recognize or acknowledge. To torture a well-known phrase, here it may be a case of retrieving the bathwater while leaving the baby behind. For no matter how judiciously we navigate Schmitt's decisionism, there may be no way of evading the link he eventually posited between it and "concrete order" or "institutional thinking." Insofar as we accept his particular version of the sovereign decision and the sovereign exception, it becomes very difficult to avoid accepting also his particular characterization of the "quasi-sacred preconstitutional will" of the people, or the *demos* as an existential "given" that can neither discuss nor debate the conditions of its own unity, but only acclaim, in a plebiscitary manner, its representative. Indeed, this may be one unforeseen consequence of Schmitt's repudiation of all normative theories of the state, and of his famous—if enigmatic—claim that "[t]he concept of the state presupposes the concept of the political" (1996 [1958]:19).

Sovereign Exception

The most influential, if not the most thorough, contemporary interpretation of Schmitt is undoubtedly that of Giorgio Agamben, who credits Schmitt with revealing the "paradox of sovereignty," or the notion that "the sovereign is, at the same time, outside and inside the juridical order" (1998:15). According to this reading, Schmitt exposed a crucial, perennial contradiction in all western political and legal thought. In short, every order relies on an exception that it cannot contain, that it must seek to dissemble, but that nonetheless threatens or haunts that order. At the same time, Agamben maintains, Schmitt endeavored to cancel out the radical—and radically antinomial—implications of his own discovery. He did so by subordinating the exception to the figure of the sovereign. For Schmitt, Agamben proposes, "[t]he sovereign, who can decide on the state of exception, [also] guarantees its anchorage in the juridical order" (2005:35). In a sense, and with disastrous consequences, Schmitt offers with one hand what he withdraws with the other. He begins by recognizing the exception that conditions any order. But in an immediately subsequent move, he affords the sovereign, or an unchecked executive authority, the absolute right to decide upon that exception. Thus the exception is not so much a state of lawlessness or anomie. Rather, to use a phrase that Agamben borrows from Gerschom Scholem, in the state of exception, law is "in force without significance" (1998:51). All of the law's brute violence, but none of its normative protection, prevails. In such a situation, every individual subject is reduced to what Agamben calls "bare life" or "*homo sacer*" — the one who "*may be killed* and yet not sacrificed" (1998:9, 73), or the one whose death has no meaning. For Agamben, the paradigmatic example of such a state of exception is the concentration camp. But the logic of the camp is not specific to particular social or historical contexts. Instead, Agamben contends, due to a protracted, often arcane and secretive history of legal, political, and metaphysical thought, today "the state of exception has become the rule" (1998:9) and "we are all virtually *homines sacri*" (1998:115). The only solution to this quagmire is to "sever the nexus between violence and law" and to pursue instead what Agamben calls "'pure' law," or a law "that does not bind, that neither commands nor prohibits anything, but says only itself." Such a pure law would "correspond [to] an action as pure means [. . .] without any relation to an end" (2005:88). Law as a kind of instrument, or a means of achieving a future goal, would have to be replaced by law as a kind of game, or a pure potentiality without any direction or purpose. "One day humanity will play with law," Agamben prophesizes, "just as children play with disused objects, not in order to restore them to their canonical use but to free them from it for good" (2005:64).

The textual support for Agamben's reading of Schmitt comes largely from the first edition of *Political Theology*, the principle thesis of which is familiar but worth repeating nonetheless: "All significant [*prägnanten*] concepts of the modern theory of the state," Schmitt proposes, "are secularized theological concepts." In light of this thesis, and as noted above, Schmitt maintains that "[t]he exception [*Ausnahmezustand*] in jurisprudence is analogous to the miracle in theology" (2005 [1934]:36). He further asserts that "the modern constitutional state" is not entirely secular and objective, as its proponents like to claim, but tacitly or unconsciously relies on the theology and the metaphysics of "deism," or the conflation of God and nature that emerged along with "the rationalism of the Enlightenment." According to Schmitt, in banishing "the miracle from the world," in refusing the possibility of God's direct intervention into the natural order of things, the Enlightenment also, if rather surreptitiously, sought to exclude "the sovereign's direct intervention in a valid legal order" (2005 [1934]:36–7). Since, however, Schmitt believes that every legal or constitutional order is ultimately based on an exception, the modern constitutional state's effort to exclude the exception proved to be in vain. In concrete terms, it led directly to the tangled confusion of the Weimar constitution, which, in the infamous "Article 48," endeavored to contain within itself the conditions of its own dissolution. That is to say, for Schmitt, insofar as it captured the exception within the parameters of the law, or within the purview of objectively verifiable rules or norms, the modern constitutional state would invariably have to admit the possibility of an entirely legal dismantling of the law itself, a danger that Schmitt seems to have wanted to avoid. Paradoxically, then, the protection of the constitution relied on extralegal or extraconstitutional forces. More accurately, if more strangely still, for Schmitt an extraconstitutional force was required to protect the constitution from, precisely, extraconstitutional—Communist and fascist—forces (McCormick 2004:xiv–xxix). Schmitt therefore found it necessary to contend that "[t]he exception can be more important than the rule, not because of a romantic irony for the paradox, but because the seriousness of an insight goes deeper than the clear generalization inferred from what ordinarily repeats [*Wiederholenden*] itself," and that, in a state of exception, "the power of real life [*die Kraft des wirklichen Lebens*] breaks through the crust of a mechanism that has grown torpid by repetition [*Wiederholung*]." In these passages, the opposition between a vital, organic exception and a mechanical, repetitive norm or law is, perhaps, more than a little telling. So too is Schmitt's obvious taste for sharp, expressionistic contrasts. For now it is enough to quote another one of the pithy, polemical axioms for which Schmitt is renowned: "The exception [*Ausnahme*] is more interesting that the rule [*Normalfall*]," Schmitt declares. "The rule proves nothing; the exception proves everything [*Das Normale beweist nichts, die Ausnahme beweist alles*]" (Schmitt 2005 [1934]:15).

At the same time, and as Agamben is correct to notice that in the first edition of *Political Theology* Schmitt's depiction of the sovereign exception remains somewhat ambiguous. As Agamben puts it, the exception can be seen as a "topological" concept, operating by way of a confusion of inside and outside, thus constituting what Agamben likes to call a "zone of indistinction" or a "threshold." Or, in Schmitt's terms, it is a "borderline concept [*Grenzbegriff*]," not in the sense that it is "vague," but in the sense that it pertains to the "outermost sphere [*äußersten Sphäre*]" (2005 [1934]:5) of political and juridical life. The exception involves a "*[b]eing-outside, and yet belonging*," Agamben notes, or an "*ecstasy-belonging*" (Agamben 1998:35). Thus, and again in conformity with Agamben's interpretation, Schmitt seems to retreat from the potentially antinomial implications of his own thought when he insists that, "[a]lthough [the sovereign] stands outside [*steht außerhalb*] the normally valid legal system, he nonetheless belongs [*gehört*] to it, for it is he who must decide whether or not the constitution must be suspended in its entirety" (2005 [1934]:7). Or again, as he says a little later in the text, and a little more elaborately this time: "What characterizes the exception is principally unlimited authority, which means the suspension of the entire existing order. In such a situation, it is clear that the state [*der Staat*] remains, where law [*Recht*] recedes." Moreover, Schmitt continues, "[b]ecause the exception is different from anarchy and chaos, order in the juristic sense still prevails even if it is not the ordinary kind" (2005 [1934]:12). And finally: "Unlike the normal situation, where the autonomous moment of the decision recedes to a minimum, the norm is destroyed [*vernichtet*] in the exception. The exception remains, nevertheless, accessible to jurisprudence because both elements, the norm as well as the decision, remain within the framework of the juristic" (2005 [1934]:12–3). While Schmitt would appear to be negotiating a question of legal competence within a modern constitutional state, Agamben wants to propose his line of thought is as much metaphysical or ontological. As Schmitt describes it, the sovereign is not simply an individual, much less a political or administrative office, Agamben suggests. Instead, it is a kind of nothingness, or an ontological "pure Being (*on haplos*)" (1998:182) devoid of qualities, around which ontic beings take shape. Without getting bogged down in Agamben's more philosophical speculations, we can say that Schmitt rejects any simple personalism in his discussion of the sovereign exception, and suggests instead that crisis, decider, and decision all leap into existence in a single, compacted instant in time: "A distinctive determination of which individual person or which concrete body can assume such an authority cannot be derived from the mere legal quality of a maxim," Schmitt writes. Instead, once it is made, "the decision becomes instantly [*Augenblick*] independent of argumentative substantiation [. . .] Looked at normatively," Schmitt concludes, "the decision emanates from nothingness" (2005 [1934]:31–2).

While virtuoso and exhilarating, the difficulty with Agamben's reading of Schmitt is the way it overlooks his explicit references to "the people" as an authentic, preconstitutional source of legitimacy, and the sense in which, despite Schmitt's occasional proclamations to this effect, the sovereign decision does not quite emanate from the void, but is buttressed by a substance—or a "formation [*Gestaltung*]"—that precedes it. Even before introducing the "concrete order" as a third type of juristic thinking, Schmitt had already established his commitment to a populist foundation for law in his 1923 work *The Crisis in Parliamentary Democracy* and, more systematically, his 1928 study *Verfassungslehre*. In the second of these texts, which Agamben also cites, Schmitt proposes a distinction between "constitutional law [*Verfassungsgesetz*]" and the "constitution [*Verfassung*]" (1965 [1928]:18, 108), where the former refers to the norms of legal reasoning, and the latter to the prelegal community such rules are designed to protect (Preuss 1999:156–8). Despite the incredible latitude a sovereign authority might have to make decisions once it is acclaimed, for Schmitt, that authority is a fortiori answerable to those over whom it reigns, and from whom legitimacy derives. No matter how absolute the sovereign's monopoly on violence might be, in Schmitt's estimation, the possibility of resistance always abides with "the people" (although the exact legal content of "the people" must remain indistinct). In other words, political power is never power over a mute body or "bare life." It is always power over some consenting subject, or someone with at least the potential to act and to speak—even if, for Schmitt, consent is not established by way of active participation in governing, but only through a passive lack of resistance to those who govern (McCormick 2004:xxiv). Agamben argues that, insofar as it is organized around the sovereign exception, the law gradually transforms speaking subjects into sacrificial flesh. For example, the principle of habeas corpus, ostensibly designed to ensure the presence of the accused at the moment of accusation, and the right to defend oneself against spurious accusations, constitutes a trap that allows law more viciously than ever to take hold of the body in its silent physicality (Agamben 1998: 123–5). Agamben passes similar judgment on the concepts of democracy and human rights, for they too serve to politicize biological existence, and bring the human as a mere living being under the purview of law (1998:126–35). Along with the fact that law becomes here little more than an instrument of power, we must note that Agamben's prophetic vision of law as a game—as the immanence of a pure potentiality without purpose—has much in common with Schmitt's characterization of the *demos* as an existential "given." For if we suppose that every legal voice ultimately becomes the mute flesh of "bare life," then we also must ask what, save a capacity to acclaim, and to shout "yes" or "no," is left of the voice in the absence of law?

Radical Democracy

If Agamben's reading of Schmitt focuses on his conception of sovereignty and the state of exception, Chantal Mouffe offers a somewhat less dramatic interpretation, and attempts to appropriate Schmitt's attention to political enmity or antagonism for a pluralist understanding of radical democracy. The key texts in Mouffe's reading of Schmitt are

The Concept of the Political and *The Crisis of Parliamentary Democracy*. In the first, Schmitt holds that, apart from "the moral, aesthetic and economic [spheres of human existence], the political has its own criteria," and that "the specific political distinction to which all actions and motives can be reduced [. . .] is that between friend and enemy" (1996 [1958]:25–6). Against the liberal conflation of politics and ethics on the one hand, and the Marxist reduction of politics to economics on the other, Schmitt argues for the autonomy of the political, and proposes that, at its root, politics involves a mortal, existential decision that separates friends from enemies – a separation that, significantly, is always conditioned by the "real possibility [*reale Moglichkeit*] of physical killing" (1996 [1958]:33). *The Crisis in Parliamentary Democracy*, written a few years prior to *The Concept of the Political*, endeavors to prove that there is an "inescapable contradiction" between liberalism and democracy, or "liberal individualism and democratic homogeneity" (1985 [1923]:17). For Schmitt, liberalism is not a meaningful political category because it assumes the equality of all human individuals by virtue of their birth, and therefore cannot produce any distinction between friends and enemies. Democracy, on the other hand, does not suppose that "[e]very adult person, simply as a person, should *eo ipso* be politically equal to every other person" (1985 [1923]:11). Rather, "[e]very actual democracy rests on the principle that not only are equals equal but unequals will not be treated equally." In this sense, Schmitt continues, "[d]emocracy requires [. . .] first homogeneity and second —if the need arises—elimination or eradication of heterogeneity" (1985 [1923]:9). Democracy, then, is defined as a unity or a community that is both internally identical and separated out from humanity as a whole. "All democratic arguments rest logically on a series of identities," Schmitt insists, in a passage Mouffe will challenge. These include "the identity of the subject and the object of state authority, the identity of the people and their representative in parliament, the identity of the state and the current voting population, the identity of the state and the law" and the "identity of the quantitative (the numerical majority or unanimity) and the qualitative (the justice of the laws)" (1985 [1923]:26). In essence, Mouffe argues that Schmitt is half right. Schmitt is correct to claim that division is the condition of politics, and that politics is a condition of human existence. But he is incorrect to think that democracy requires homogeneity, or that the friend / enemy divide cannot be internal to a democratic order. Mouffe's goal, then, is to domesticate Schmittian antagonism or enmity within the structures of democracy.

Mouffe claims that what Schmitt represents as the contradiction or "paradox" of liberalism and democracy is less a damning criticism than it is a constituent feature of a modern pluralist political order. According to Mouffe, the political dynamic of a "radical democracy" relies on the "tension" between the abstract, unachievable universalism of the liberal concept of humanity, and the concrete, institutionalized freedoms of the democratic concept of a people. "The democratic logic of constituting the people, and inscribing rights and equalities into practices, is necessary to subvert the tendency towards abstract universalism inherent in liberal discourse," she writes. But at the same time, "the articulation [of democracy] with liberal logic allows us constantly to challenge—through reference to 'humanity' and the polemical use of 'human rights'—the forms of exclusion that are necessarily inscribed in the political practice of installing those rights and defining "the people" who is going to rule" (1999:43–4). Against Schmitt's ontological, existential, or substantialist conception of the *demos*, then, Mouffe proposes "focusing on the 'us' [or the 'friend' side of the 'friend / enemy' divide] and the nature of the social bond that unites its components." Instead of treating the *demos* as the original, self-identical foundation of politics and legitimacy, she would like to understand it as "the *result* of the political process of hegemonic articulation" or something that "can only exist through multiple forms of competing *identifications*" (1999:47). If it is true that political subjectivity can only be formed within a "conflictual field," and requires "the determination of a frontier" and "the definition of a 'them,'" it is equally true that, "in the case of liberal democratic politics this frontier is *an internal one*, and the 'them' is not a permanent outsider" (emphasis added, 1999:51). As in the case of Agamben's reading, however, Mouffe's appropriation of Schmitt is most interesting for what it ignores. For Schmitt, not only a democratic community, but any political community, and any division between friends and enemies, is established in conjunction with a "real possibility" of killing and being killed. Every political community is a community of fate, and it is this mortal condition of politics that renders politics prior to the state, and to any codified law. In fact, this is one clear reason why, in Schmitt's words, "[t]he concept of the state presupposes the concept of the political" (1996 [1958]:19). To be certain, Mouffe is not entirely forthcoming with respect to the exact status of the "conflictual field" of radical democratic politics, but given the organization of her argument, it seems difficult to distinguish it from what Claude Lefort calls "the institutionalization of conflict" (1988:18). And Schmitt's critique of parliamentary democracy is aimed at the institution of parliament as much as the ideals of liberalism. For Schmitt, "modern mass democracy has made argumentative public discussion an empty formality," and parliament "a gigantic antechamber in front of the bureaus and committees of invisible rulers" (1985 [1923]:6–7).

Schmitt is not typically thought of as critic of the state—indeed, he was one of its great proponents. But, following Max Weber, he was troubled by the emergence of a bureaucratic, mechanized "rational-legal authority" in the modern world, and believed it was necessary to couple such objective order with a "charismatic," personal form of authority (McCormick 2004:xiv). The issue is perhaps most extensively discussed in one of Schmitt's most unusual books – *The Leviathan in the State Theory of Thomas Hobbes: Meaning and Failure of a Political Symbol*. Prior to this 1938 work, Schmitt was a great champion of Hobbes, or at least of his own idiosyncratic reading of Hobbes, which hinged on the dictum *autoritas non veritas facit legem*. In Schmitt's book on Hobbes, however, the emphasis is placed on the "failure" of the Leviathan mentioned in the subtitle. Schmitt treats the Leviathan as a majestic political symbol, or a "mythical blending" of "god, man, animal, and machine" (1996 [1938]:19–20). Welding together an all-powerful sovereign and a colossal state apparatus, the Leviathan is a *homo artificialis* and a *materia ex artifex*. Man-made and thoroughly secular, it is a "mortal god who brings peace and security" (1996 [1938]:54) and "an irresistible instrument of quietude" that "has all objective and subjective rights on its side" (1996 [1938]:46). In short, no truth—divine or otherwise—transcends the commanding authority of the Leviathan. "Nothing here is true," Schmitt insists: "everything is command." Even the possibility of a miracle, which in *Political Theology* Schmitt had associated with the sovereign exception, is entirely internal to the Hobbesian state apparatus. "A miracle is what the sovereign state authority commands its subjects to believe to be a miracle" and, conversely, "[m]iracles cease when the state forbids them" (1996 [1938]:55). The text is ambiguous, and given the year of its publication, this might come as little surprise. But Schmitt seems to imply that the Leviathan "fails" because, in so thoroughly dominating public life, it relegates the exception to the individual conscience. "When political power wants to be only public," Schmitt writes, "when state and confession drive inner belief into a private domain, the soul of a people betakes itself on the 'secret road' that leads inward" (1996 [1938]:61). The subsequent "emergence of a distinction between inner and outer becomes for the mortal god a sickness unto death." While the personal sovereign of the Leviathan withered away, however, "his work, the state, survived him in the form of a well-organized executive, army, and police as well as administration and juridical apparatuses and a well-working, professionally trained bureaucracy" (1996 [1938]:65). The state thus became a "technically neutral instrument" that could be occupied by "the most varied political constellations" (1996 [1938]:42), or subjects who would "carry out their actions under the guise of something other than politics—namely, religion, culture, economy, and private-matters—and still derive the advantages of state" (1996 [1938]:74).

In his disdain for the "technically neutral" state, Schmitt finds an unlikely ally in Alain Badiou, who has forcibly revived a number of antistatist arguments that many believed to have been dead and buried. Countering the relativism and, in his estimation, nascent obscurantism of postmodern thought, Badiou characterizes the state as the realm of interests and opinions, and associates genuine politics with a militant commitment to disinterested truth. For Badiou, politics "is never the plurality of opinions regulated by a common norm." Instead, there are only "the plurality of instances of politics [. . .] which have *no* common norm, since the subjects they induce are different" (2005c:23). To be certain, the "truth" with which Badiou associates politics is neither objectively verifiable nor transcendentally guaranteed, but involves instead a subject's decisive fidelity to an event. This is not the place to pursue a detailed explication of the elaborate ontology of "being and event" Badiou develops to support this claim (Badiou 2005a). For now it is enough to note that, according to Badiou, "political truth" can only emerge in moments of crisis, or "rupture and disorder," and has nothing to do with the calculated negotiation of established interests and opinions. It generates, that is to say, a thoroughly "*disinterested* subjectivity," (2005b:55) which gripped by an event, prescribes unconditional axioms rather than composing convincing arguments. Badiou insists that such a militant subject must endeavor to operate at what he calls a "distance" (2005c:149) from the state, which cannot grapple with the unknown, exceptional event, but seeks only to formalize the recognized knowledge of a situation. In concrete terms, the state that Badiou castigates is the parliamentary state. Thus, in a telling passage, he insists that "a politics encompassing real decisions, I mean emancipatory decisions, is entirely foreign to the vote" and "hostile to established interests" (2006:91). Against the "technical rationality" (2006:92) of merely counting the votes of passive citizens, Badiou follows Rousseau in associating the "general will" of the people with the "active number," or those who engage directly in political struggle. "The active number must be untied from all correlation to the passive number," Badiou declares. "A meeting, a demonstration, an insurrection: all of them proclaim their right to existence outside any consideration that is not immanent to that existence" (2006:94). For Badiou, it is the "*active disciplined numbers*" and not the passive citizens endowed of a universal suffrage, who constitute the people when they are assembled together "in the heat of an event" (2006:95–6). Despite their many differences, the proximity between (1) Schmitt's preconstitutional will of the people and sovereign exception, and (2) Badiou's "active numbers" gripped by the "heat of an event," seems difficult to overlook. At any rate, they both appear to arrive at their respective concepts of the political by eliminating from the outset any normative theory of the state, and any notion that popular consent might be composed through broad-based participation in an ongoing, interminable discussion or debate.

Normative States

In this chapter, I have attempted to outline some of the limits of Schmitt's effort to think the political without any recourse to a normative understanding of the state. In seeking to clear away what I take to be a largely misguided reference to Schmitt among contemporary political theorists, I have, however, avoided providing any affirmative definition or defense of the kind of state and law Schmitt so ruthlessly attacked. While my own work will have to take up such a task in the future, I also believe that many of the essays collected in the present volume go a long way toward providing this project with points of departure. These would include, but obviously not be limited to: a detailed sociohistorical study of the early modern theorists of the civil state, and their attempt to dismantle the "confessional state" in all of its manifestations (Hunter, Chapter 2, this volume; Wickham, Chapter 9, this volume); a similarly detailed study of the still fraught and complex emergence of postcolonial states (Zachariah, Chapter 10, this volume); a careful assessment of the legal ramifications of government actions in actually existing states of exception (Saunders, Chapter 5, this volume); an exploration of the meaning of subjectivity, and of citizenship, from psychoanalytic and post-structural perspectives (Hoggett, Chapter 6, Zolkos, Chapter 7, this volume); and a related defense of the concepts of subjectivity and self-preservation that does not reduce such things to substantive identities (Yeatman, Chapter 8, this volume). In the case of Schmitt, we might even endeavor to salvage his warning, in a late work like his *Theory of the Partisan*, concerning the dangers of a stateless "international civil war" (2004 [1963]:68), and his attempt to reassert some element of what he calls "enmity in measured doses" against the possibility of an "absolute enmity" (2004 [1963]:38), where the other is not a potential combatant, but "the ultimate enemy of mankind as such" (2004 [1963]:66)—a danger that looms when, for example, an empire decides to wage war, not against an identifiable political entity that might have the capacity to surrender or make peace, but against a diffuse idea like "terrorism" or "evil." There is obviously no point in seeking to return to the types of state defined by the modern contract theorists, much less the *jus publicum Europaeum* of the Enlightenment—a false peace which, on Schmitt's account at least, was only made possible by virtually unlimited colonial expansion (Schmitt 2003 [1974]). At the same time, the retreat of such definitions of the state, and of their federalist cognates, need not lead immediately to international civil war, or a reinvention of the medieval notion of a "just war." Whatever else the stakes of academic intervention might be today, it seems to me that a consistent theoretical elaboration of a normative conception of law is at least one way to forestall such a catastrophe.

To challenge Schmitt's aggressive, bellicose concept of "decisionism," and his substantialist, often vitalist configuration of "the people," is also, it should be made very clear, not to exclude all formulations of the decision, of sovereignty, or of popular governance. On the contrary, all three types of juristic thinking identified by Schmitt—rule/norm, decision, and order—can remain operative within contemporary theories of the state and, arguably, the political more generally. Not only is it not necessary to reduce democratic participation to a moment of popular acclamation, or the event that affirms a sovereign, executive power. It is more than reasonable, and more than possible, to imagine new modes of democracy, even in the form of what Jacques Derrida often called a "democracy to come" and a "new Enlightenment for the century to come" (1994:90). For Derrida, democratic participation can be both oriented towards a future that never arrives, or that is never fully manifest in the present, and capable of undertaking the urgency of decision. In fact, and as Derrida again proposes, all genuine decisions take place amidst an "ordeal of undecidability" (1996:137). Neither aimed at a teleologically predetermined goal, nor founded on a quasi-sacred, preconstitutional will, political and legal decisions engage an uncertainty that rests at the heart of all law. They possess the capacity to rend open every established order, and even reformulate established norms, without ceasing to be, in broad terms, "normative." Only their enemies have ever depicted norms as inflexible rules or unquestionable absolutes, hovering over concrete situations and without any mooring in the complex world of political antagonism and affiliation. Their friends, on the other hand, are more than willing to allow norms to withdraw, even evaporate, when faced with the necessity of what Kant would call a "reflective judgment," or a judgment that proceeds without set concepts or criteria (Kant 2000:66–8). On this topic, Hannah Arendt's work—and perhaps especially her conceptions of politics and action—might be seen to have, not only continued relevance, but also untapped, under-appreciated possibilities. While she grapples with many of the same political puzzles or *aporia* as Schmitt, and is by no means a simple proponent of universal norms or humani-tarian politics, and while she engaged directly with the "dark times" that Schmitt at once sought to navigate and, arguably, rendered darker still, Arendt avoided succumbing to the romance of violence that often overtook the more radical political thought of the twenti-eth century. Indeed, Arendt remained steadfastly convinced that politics and speech are inseparable. Man, she maintained, "to the extent that he is a political being, is endowed with the power of speech," while "violence itself is incapable of speech" (1965:9). This is not to say that language is never violent, or that politics is necessarily pacific. It is only to demand that violence and politics justify themselves discursively, publicly, and convinc-ingly, before any exception is declared, and any law articulated with force.

CHAPTER FIVE

Antisecurity Personae: from David Dyzenhaus's Human Rights Lawyer to Giorgio Agamben's Illuminato

David Saunders

Emergencies

Because they have a circumstantial character, emergencies are multiform. This gives reason to pause before adopting a hyperbolic response, whether an urgent reassertion of fundamental rights or a nightmare warning against the state of things. David Dyzenhaus's hyper-legal appeal to common-law values as the safeguard against political executive overreach in times of emergency instances the first response. He invokes an "aspirational conception of law." The second response is exemplified by Giorgio Agamben's vision of a "killing-machine" security state where we had thought to find liberal constitutionalism and the rule of law . . . though this vision then promises a meta-legal glimpse of future life unloosed from law.

These are tempting normative flights. Yet, before embarking, it is worth anatomizing an actual state of emergency and considering the broader history of emergency powers invoked to preserve order, given that many liberal constitutions provide for exercise of such powers. I will begin, therefore, with an account of the French *état d'urgence* of 2005–06, and follow with a brief consideration of François Saint-Bonnet's history of the *état d'exception*. In this way, we'll be in a better position to consider Dyzenhaus and Agamben on emergency. Here the focus turns to distinctive features of the personae—the moral values of the human rights lawyer and the antinomian illuminations of the meta-physical philosopher—that these authors articulate. In the background floats a historical question: does an early modern clash of clerical and civil personae find some counterpart in today's critiques of state responses to civil disorder and public insecurity?

Emergency in France, 2005–06

In late 2005, 20 days of civil violence proved a serious test of public law in contemporary France. On the night of October 27, 2005 violence flared in the northern Paris suburb of Clichy-sous-Bois. It then spread to Aulnay-sous-Bois, Sevran, and other locales in the *département* of Seine-Saint-Denis. Arsonists' targets included a primary school and a police station, a pensioners' day centre and a fire station, a public bus depot and a used car business. Disruption of order proved limited in duration. So too did the "state of emergency" declared by a presidential decree as a necessary step toward quelling the unrest. In the "republican" words of Prime Minister de Villepin on November 8: France will "guarantee public order to all its citizens." The emergency decree remained in force until January 4, 2006 a total period of 58 days.

Formal declaration of the *état d'urgence* was preceded by reminders of the state's duty to restore public order. On November 2, 2005 recognizing a "dangerous situation," President Chirac confirmed that "there cannot be no-go areas in the Republic," underscoring the constitutional "unity and indivisibility" of France. On November 8, 2005 by Decree n. 1386, the President and Council of Ministers declared a "state of emergency" to exist in all or part of 25 of the 96 *départements* of France, including the whole of the Ile-de-France region of Paris and its surrounds. Under Article 16 of the 1958 Constitution, the President determines that a situation constitutes a crisis and the duration of that crisis. Legislation by decree is an established part of French constitutional normality, and not specifically related to emergency situations or periods of crisis.

This executive action rested on the authority of Articles 1 and 2 of the Law 55-385 of April 3, 1955, according to which an *état d'urgence* can be declared "in all or part of the metropolitan territory or in the overseas *départements*, whether in the case of imminent danger arising from serious threats to public order, or in the case of events having, by their nature and gravity, the character of a public disaster."[1] Declaration of the *état d'urgence* institutes a "state of exception." There are degrees of exception. Declaration of an *état de siège* would signal a higher degree of exception to the normal laws. Having assessed the "nature and gravity" of the circumstances, the French government did not take this step. The emergency measures available to Prefects and to the Minister of the Interior under a declared *état d'urgence* are nonetheless substantial: curfews, security zones, house arrests, closures of assembly places, and 24-hour searches without prior judicial warrant.

To remain valid, the originating decree required parliamentary approval within a limit of 12 days. On November 15, 2005 the Assemblée Nationale approved the emergency Bill adopted the day before by the Conseil des Ministres, voting 346 for, 148 against; the opposition being composed of the Greens and some Socialists. The Senate voted in support one day later. The *état d'urgence* was thus legislatively extended for a period of three months, commencing on November 20, 2005 even though the "disturbances" had by then subsided. The *état d'urgence* remained in force into 2006 in case of renewed violence over the New Year holiday. President Chirac then responded to his Prime Minister's suggestion and, on January 2, 2006 anticipated suspension of the state of emergency from January 4, 2006 following consideration by the Conseil des Ministres on the preceding day.

Despite apocalyptic images of photogenically combusting Renaults, the *état d'urgence* had not entailed implementation of the more severe measures available. Public meetings had not been banned; the media had not been subjected to censorship; nighttime searches without judicial warrant had not been undertaken; and curfews had been imposed in only 6 of the 96 administrative districts. The emergency powers had curtailed some normal legal rights in certain locales, but no new emergency legislation—*législation d'exception*—was enacted. No further executive decrees were issued. It is hard to believe that this *état d'urgence* entailed an abuse of powers.[2] A recent instance of legal parenthesis—when the normal legal rights are curtailed and then restored—this 2005–6 "state of exception" provides a concrete foil for current intellectual enthusiasms for proclaiming the "exception is now the norm."

François Saint-Bonnet: "State of Exception" and the Conservation of a Civil Order

In his history of the *état d'exception*, François Saint-Bonnet (2001:2–8) traces four configurations of "order" whose preservation has constituted an overriding directive (2001:27–8).[3] First, in the early medieval *res publica christiana* order was conceived as immutable because celestial, the overriding imperative being to ensure salvation through the *ecclesia christiana*. Second, in the emerging monarchical regimes of the thirteenth century—Saint-Bonnet instances the Capetian dynasty—order was conceived in terms of territory ruled, with the overriding imperative being to preserve a sacral dynasty. Third, in the absolutist regimes of the sixteenth and seventeenth centuries order was conceived as national-statist and the overriding imperative—following France's eight religious civil wars—was to establish stable government as guarantee of civil peace. Fourth, in the "citizen state" arising subsequent to the French Revolution order is conceived as grounded in an incontestable moral value identified as the inalienable rights of man.

Different orderings of life, then, but each in its context the privileged object of conservation. Given the fractured and disordered France of the religious civil wars, in the absolutist context legitimate order was that imposed by a state capable of providing security of life:

Facing the impossibility of finding a response to the religious crisis, the [absolutist] state appears as the only instance capable of guaranteeing order and peace. In the middle ages, order and peace were conceived as the reflection of the harmony willed by God; now, decades of war in the name of God could not but raise the deepest doubt as to this harmonic vision. (202)

Order was now political, not religious, hence Henri IV's notorious abjuration of his Calvinist faith and conversion to Gallican Catholicism. For Marcel Gauchet (1994:209): "Henri IV subordinates his own convictions to the imperatives of public peace and treats religion as a fact that—politically—the prince must take account of, before seeing this as a matter of conscience." The political "order" whose preservation was the overriding imperative presumed what we could term a security–secularity state.

A particular persona emerged with the new order of the security–secularity state: one that subordinates confessional conscience to the imperatives of public peace. As a figure of religious "disenchantment," Henri IV thus has certain exemplarity. The civil sovereign serves as prestigious model for emulation. In treating religion politically—as a fact to be addressed by the state, not as a truth to be enforced—Henri IV had the endorsement of the *politiques*. As Gauchet (1994:200) recounts, though, the *politiques* were denounced by counter-Reformation Catholic authorities as persons who "profess to prefer . . . the political state to the realm of God."[4] In our Christian moral culture, does this historical clash of offices—the civil and the clerical—find counterparts in today's responses to emergency and exception?

The exception arises when—to preserve the civil order in an emergency—the ordinary law is suspended. Saint-Bonnet (382) concludes that the exception rests neither in a principle of higher legality nor in a political decision on the exception. The legislator cannot inscribe prophylactic legal measures against every unforeseen emergency. No juridical schema can anticipate what might eventuate as "necessity." But nor is it a matter of political decision between respecting and suspending the legal norm: "the measure of necessity is not a decision because, precisely, no alternative exists." Rather, a state of exception rests in the "autonomous" evidence of an "irresistible force of necessity" that entails action because a crisis threatens to destroy the established order of living. Seen in this light, "the discourse in the state of exception appeals to sentiment, to submission to the irresistible force of necessity, to the impotence of the laws, to the finitude of [political] reasoning."

For Saint-Bonnet, then, approaches to the "state of exception" as resting ultimately in an ideal of law or in a political decision are both mistaken. Yet, these are the approaches to emergency, respectively, in Dyzenhaus and Agamben, to whom I now turn. The focus will remain on personae: respectively, the persona of the common lawyer as human rights advocate, and the persona of the metaphysical philosopher as political prophet.

The Hyper-Legality of the Human Rights Lawyer

The New York and Washington experience of September 11, 2001—and subsequent terrorist actions in other countries—have given edge to the issue of how liberal constitutional states respond to emergencies. Such attacks have raised seeming contradictions between politics as security and law as justice. They have provoked radical responses. Asserting that terrorism's threat has utterly altered the political situation, Oren Gross (2003) envisages permitting government officials to act in an extralegal manner to protect the security of the state in an emergency situation. This, with the proviso that actions committed while released from the bounds of the law would be susceptible to subsequent legal ratification or sanction.

By comparison with this endorsement of "official illegality," the view of Ferejohn and Pasquino (2005:239) appears quite calming. They envisage a "dual regime" as characterizing non-absolutist constitutional states. Thus, alongside the ordinary law and "regular government," an extraordinary law and "exceptional government" maintain a constitutional capacity to suspend the ordinary law in times of necessity.

But not everyone is calm. Challenging Gross's model of officially endorsed illegality as a valid response to present emergency, David Dyzenhaus (2005:77) argues to keep governmental actions within the compass of the rule of law, such that "legislative responses to emergencies can be controlled by the rule of law." The point of this "legality model" is to reduce to a minimum the "legally uncontrolled space" for extralegal action. It is a matter of terrorism. Civil unrest such as occurred in France in 2005 is a lesser issue.

In *The Constitution of Law: Legality in a Time of Emergency*, Dyzenhaus (2006) proposes an "aspirational conception of law," not only taking issue with Gross but also confronting that most resilient ghost in the field of the exception, Carl Schmitt.[5] The aim is both to establish a normative model for dealing with emergency and rebut Schmitt's challenge to liberal theories of the rule of law. That challenge was dual: first, for Schmitt, it is the sovereign power that decides if exceptional conditions obtain; second, it is the sovereign power that determines how to respond to such conditions. If the rule of law is a creature for governing in normal times, in the exceptional times of emergency, sovereign power acts outside the law. In Schmitt's (2005 [1934]:5) stark dictum: "Sovereign is he who decides on the state of exception."

Recognizing that for Anglophone common lawyers such talk risks seeming "over-blown," Dyzenhaus signals their unexpected complicity with Schmitt in their handling of emergency:

> However, . . . the [common-law] judicial record largely supports Schmitt's claims, albeit not through the idea that the rule of law has no place in an emergency, but through the idea that only a formal or wholly procedural conception of the rule of law is appropriate for emergencies (35).

Schmitt's claim that "liberals found unbearable the idea that the rule of law cannot constrain the political" is confirmed by judges who "prefer to pretend it constrains while recognising that in substance it does not" (35). Addressing the challenge of emergency in a "formal or wholly procedural" manner, common-law practice concedes the game.

The procedural and formalist disposition of certain common-law officials, Dyzenhaus argues, only cosmeticizes the morally unacceptable political reality of brute executive actions—detentions without trial, gross breaches of human rights, and acceptance of torture—by governments operating outside legality. Confronting such "legalisations of illegality," Dyzenhaus rejects any judicial justification that rests on a doctrinal separation of powers between judiciary and legislature or executive (9–10).

Interestingly, judges feted for "resisting" executive action—not least Lord Hoffman who in *Belmarsh* denied the UK Government's claim that a state of emergency existed—are found by Dyzenhaus falling short of the substantive rule of law. Thus Lord Hoffman (in *Rehman*) "accepted the second limb of Schmitt's challenge—that the executive is entitled to decide how to respond to an emergency, if in fact there is an emergency" (181). Given a state of emergency, there would be no derogation from the UK's human rights commitments under the Human Rights Act 1998, since the Act itself provides for an exceptional power to derogate. "Lord Hoffman is unperturbed by the existence of legal black holes, as long as they are properly created" (182).

One antidote to these displays of legal form without legal substance is publicity. True, for Dyzenhaus "to say that public opinion is the ultimate basis of the rule of law does not make its principles contingent on what the public thinks" (64). Yet he imagines that publicity—media reportage of judicial views that would prevent a government from claiming a legal basis for its extralegal action—will serve to sanction that government. What, though, of his reaction when there is popular support for such government action: "Unfortunately, in the present political climate, it is likely that the Australian people would accept a proposal for indefinite detention with enthusiasm" (99, n. 76)? Whatever the moral community might turn out to be; neither "the Australian people" nor the thinking public are it.

The primary antidote, however, is a "continuum of legality" (231) that goes, as it were, all the way down (or up). In a word, we might say, a "hyper-legality." Where Schmitt curtails law's reach in the face of the exception, the point of this hyper-legality is its sheer expansiveness. As a rebuke to judicial cosmeticizing of official illegalities, hyper-legality is undiscriminating:

> [I]t does not matter much from the perspective of the rule of law how the furniture is arranged: whether the legal orders are civil or common law, or have entrenched bills of rights or no written constitution at all. What places [different legal orders] on the continuum is their commitment to the constitutional project of realising the values of the rule of law. (231)

To rebut Schmitt's challenge and to rectify extralegal action by government, Dyzenhaus's incontrovertible "rule of law project" relies on a convergence of values between "common-law constitutionalism" and international human rights law. A remorseless accumulation of synonyms identifies the "values" and "principles" accompanying "a substantive conception of the rule of law that is appropriate at all times" (58). They include "fundamental legal values" (66), "fundamental or constitutional values" (87), "fundamental values of legal order" (98, 209), "rule-of-law principles developed by the common law" (116), and "fundamental constitutional values, whether written or unwritten" (147). When specified, though, these values turn out unsurprising: "presumptions about liberty and the principles of natural justice or fairness—the right to a hearing and the right to an unbiased adjudication" (103).

Dyzenhaus treats this value-based convergence of common-law constitutionalism and human rights doctrine as if it was in the nature of things. Viewed in a moral register as foundational of juridical order, this might be plausible, provided we accept that natural rights and natural law are the foundations of positive law and the political state.[6] Yet, this remarkable affiliating of common lawyers' constitutionalism and human rights law in a unified and universal "rule of law project" on behalf of "humanity" invites questions. What sort of legal persona is this common lawyer cum human rights advocate? Is this hybrid entirely or even primarily a legal persona or is it a quasi-sacerdotal office for moral admonition of the executive government?

Historically speaking, is granting common-law constitutionalism a universal value compatible with the common lawyers' reputation as a particular estate—if not a closed corporation—claiming particular offices and privileges? In the 1600s, as Thomas Hobbes observed, the common lawyers were an estate within the state, challenging certain uses of prerogative powers by the civil sovereign (Burgess 1999). If James I credited the office of monarch with divine agency, Sir Edward Coke in response celebrated the "artificial reason" of the common-law of England as a better manifestation of godliness.

Four centuries later, Coke's conviction seemed less persuasive. Attacked in the 1980s as a "closed-shop" labor union by the Thatcher Government, the English (common-law) profession had no ready discourse to persuade the British public as to its civic virtue, let alone its agency on behalf of all human rights. If judges have "gone a long way in developing the common law understanding of the rule of law in ways consistent with the post-war drive to protect human rights" (64), it might require a visionary genealogist to unearth a deep compatibility between this recent emergence of human-rights doctrine and the common lawyers' ancient stance as defenders of the natural rights of freeborn Englishmen.[7]

Conceptually speaking, there are two issues. First, Dyzenhaus rests his case for the aspirational "rule of law project" on reiterated pairings of contrasting terms setting law against law, formal against substantive. The model instance is "rule by law"/ "rule of law." Typical variants include: "justice at large"/ "justice of the rule of law" (206) or "positive law"/ "values of legality" (216). What are the relations between the contrasting terms? Negation? Opposition? Degree (relative placement on the "continuum of legality")? Second, as presented by Dyzenhaus, common-law constitutionalism stands alone, uncontested in the field. Might the picture alter if a rival was at hand to challenge common-law constitutionalism, for instance by resting the British Constitution not on common-law but on "republican" grounds (Tomkins 2005)?[8]

Politically speaking, the issue is sovereignty. Despite his aim of rebutting Schmitt's challenge—a challenge centered on the extralegality of sovereign decision and action—Dyzenhaus barely refers to "sovereignty." Instead, prerogative powers and executive action serve as proxy. This surprising lexical absence leaves Schmitt less scathed. For the "rule of law project," then, a common-law constitutionalism morally turbocharged with human rights doctrine is the crucial normative standard bearer against alleged illegality by executive powers. But does this project miss a key point concerning sovereignty and political history in liberal states? In emergency, no imperative outranks survival . . . and survival depends on a sovereign power capable of restoring order. In normal times, this power remains out of sight, like emergency repair crews in times of fair weather. Does this mean that the "rule of law project"—where the sovereign state's overriding duty "at all times" is to protect natural rights inherent in humanity—is itself a fair-weather project?

Agamben's Illumination: a Law That Is Not

Are we living in a "state of exception"? Giorgio Agamben's tract—*Stato di eccezione* (2003), now *State of Exception* (2005)—would leave no doubt: the exception is now the rule in liberal states.[9] As a result, we are a "man" reduced to "bare life." With this figure comes a thesis. By depicting the political and juridical ordering of life in today's liberal regimes as an exercise of "pure violence," Agamben proposes the "state of exception" as the paradigm of all modern government.

On this, we shall raise some questions. Is the philosopher's meditation on "life" an antipolitics? Is it an anti-juridism? But before turning to such questions—and to avoid caricaturing his views—we need a fuller exposition of Agamben's account of the exception as our permanent norm.

State of Exception, one of three volumes to follow Agamben's framing statement in *Homo sacer: Sovereign Power and Bare Life*, does not represent a conceptual advance on the earlier work. A thematic outline of *Homo sacer* is therefore in order:

1. A moral anthropology depicts "man" as "the living being who, in language, separates and opposes himself to his own bare life and, at the same time, maintains himself in relation to that bare life in an inclusive exclusion" (Agamben 1998: 8).[10] This anthropology opens a royal way to a chilling dialectic of "life" and "law": "human life is included in the juridical order solely in the form of its exclusion (that is, of its capacity to be killed)" (8). This concept mimics the condition of *homo sacer* or sacred man in Roman law, excluded from the city for breach of the law and thus reduced to a "bare life" at the mercy of the violence of the law.

2. A transhistorical vision levels historical differences but recognizes metaphysical conditions. Thus "if in our age all citizens can be said, in a specific but extremely real sense, to appear virtually as *homines sacri*, this is possible only because the relation of ban has constituted the essential structure of sovereign power from the beginning" (111). The "beginning" is that of Western civilization as a whole. The "state of exception" is "the permanent structure of juridico-political de-localisation and dis-location" (38).

3. This metaphysical vision reveals an "originary structure": "we will ask if this figure (the *homo sacer*) may allow us to uncover an originary political structure that is located in a zone prior to the distinction between sacred and profane, religious and juridical" (74). The claim is to recover nothing less than "the memory of the originary exclusion through which the political dimension was first constituted" (83).

4. These unbounded visions are nonetheless tied to a quite specialized philosophical-juridical debate in early twentieth-century Germany between Carl Schmitt and Walter Benjamin. The debate concerned contemporary issues: the relations of sovereign political power and law, the limits of law, and the relations of law and life.

5. The discourse is overtly antistatist in "thinking a politics freed from the form of the state" (109). In keeping with "the nihilism in which we are living" (51), the animus towards historical institutional orderings of life is manifestly anti-juridical: contemporary law is "all the more pervasive for its total lack of content" (52).

6. The shock follows: "the concentration camp" is raised to the status of "the hidden paradigm of the political space of modernity" (123). With this, the "hidden matrix and *nomos* of the political space in which we are still living" (166) revealed, a grim lesson is read: "The camp is the space that is opened when the state of exception begins to become the rule" (168).[11] The fear is instilled that we are all inmates of a political institution—the camp/state as "killing machine"—that reduces us to "bare life."

7. Yet this is not the final curtain. A gaze flickers towards a future light: "a new articulation of the relation of potentiality and actuality, which requires nothing less than a re-thinking of the ontological categories of modality in their totality. The problem is therefore moved from political philosophy to first philosophy" (44). At issue is something epochal: "an entirely new conjunction of possibility and reality, contingency and necessity" in which "the potentiality and actuality" relation must be thought "differently" so as to get beyond "the primacy of actuality" (44).

8. For those electing to be redeemed from their political history, a task of behavior is now set: "one must think the existence of potentiality without any relation to Being in the form of actuality" (47). This ascetic imperative to grasp "the potentiality of not to be" will not be an easy job. Such difficulty is precisely the point of this spiritual exercise: "it is this very task that many, today, refuse to assume at any cost" (47). The challenge for one wishing to glimpse the true legal order is sourced from Kafka: to think a law that "applies to him in no longer applying" (50). But if we dare accept this epochal challenge of a "task that our time imposes on thinking" (59), eschatological help might be at hand: the promise and prophecy—in Benjamin style—of a "new historical epoch" of "divine violence" (63).[12]

Each of these themes returns in *State of Exception*. Transhistorical perspectives remain in force in the sweep from the Roman constitution to the twenty-first century political circumstances, and in the "question that never ceases to reverberate in the history of Western politics: what does it mean to act politically?" (Agamben 2005:2).[13] To be sure, ahistorical essentialism is disclaimed: "it was obvious that there cannot be some sort of eternal human type periodically embodied in Augustus, Napoleon, or Hitler, and that there are only more or less similar legal apparatuses . . . that are put to use under more or less different circumstances" (84). But disclaimer comes late, after more than one easy reflex alignment of provisions in Roman law, the death camps of Nazi totalitarianism and the Presidency of George W. Bush. Characterization of *iustitium*—"suspension" in Roman law—as "the archetype of the modern *Ausnahmezuestand*" gives the game away (41).[14]

The long opening chapter on "The state of exception as a paradigm of government" contains substantial historical material surveying the "exception" in European and American contexts. There is nothing of particular originality here. The critique of executive powers as exercised by the current American administration echoes a familiar tune. More striking is the normative dimension of an investigation of "this no-man's-land between public law and political fact, and between the juridical order and life" (1). The "theorising" of the state of emergency in public law—"the juridical significance of a sphere of action that is in itself extrajuridical" (11)—poses the challenge of passing beyond "the primacy of actuality" into "potentiality." Two questions are raised: "How can an anomie be inscribed within the juridical order?" (23). How can there be "a zone in which application [of the law] is suspended, but the law [*la legge*], as such, remains in force" (31)? That such a zone—the "state of exception"—exists is a fact . . . but it is also the problem:

> [T]he state of exception separates the [juridical] norm from its application in order to make its application possible. It introduces a zone of anomie into the law in order to make the effective regulation [*normazione*] of the real possible. (36)

With this proposition in place, a crucial task is set: how to transcend "actuality" and the "effective regulation of the real" so as to approach the ever-deferred "potentiality" of life?

State of Exception lays down rules for rising beyond "actuality," beyond the law that merely is. Exception entails suspension of law, but there is a negative and a positive suspension. The negative version is predictably state skeptic in style: "The attempt of state power to annex anomie through the state of exception is unmasked by Benjamin for what it is: a *fictio iuris* [legal fiction] par excellence, which claims to maintain the law in its very suspension as force-of-law" (59). For Agamben, negative suspensions of law allow state horror—Auschwitz . . . Guantanamo—to "reinscribe violence within a juridical context" (59).

This "re-inscription" is sourced to Carl Schmitt, said to have attempted such a move "every time" (59). The aim is to raise "state horror" to a metaphysical level: "the strategy of the exception, which must ensure the relation between anomic violence and law, is the counterpart to the onto-theo-logical strategy aimed at capturing pure being in the meshes of the *logos*" (59–60). Lest thought of capture "in the meshes of the *logos*" is insufficiently chilling, the point is repeated in cruder references to "fascist and Nazi techniques of government" whose "power . . . attains its appearance of originality from the suspension or neutralization of the juridical order—that is, ultimately, from the state of exception" (85).

Agamben had already turned to the imagery of "the machine": "when the state of exception . . . becomes the rule, then the juridico-political system turns itself into a killing machine" (60) that reduces living to "bare life." The final pages announce that "the state of exception has today reached its maximum worldwide deployment." The vision, properly apocalyptic, is of "the working of the machine that is leading the West toward global civil war" (87).

This dramatic—if not melodramatic—utterance is not actually the conclusion. With a flick of the head, Agamben now reveals the positive side of the dialectic, the side of illumination and "potentiality." All along, it's been a two-faced play, a process of induction in two stages.

First, with Schmittian horror fully enrolled, there must be fear. To instill the desire to alienate ourselves from the existing political and legal ordering of life, the imagery must be deeply *anxiogène*. Only then will we see how impossible it is "to bring the state of exception back within its spatially and temporally defined boundaries in order to then reaffirm the primacy of a norm and of rights that are themselves ultimately grounded in it" (87). Talk of human rights offers no exodus. It is unclear how all Agamben's followers—not to mention jurists in the style of Dyzenhaus's common-law constitutionalists—could swallow such dismissal of their committed talk of human rights as paramount values.

But after the anxiety, a chance of illumination. In this post-anxiogenetic second stage of induction, we get a vital offer: to embrace the possibility "ceaselessly to try to interrupt the working of the machine" by laying bare its "central fiction." This "fiction" is that "life" can be lived within the "law." Were we released from its grip, we might at last see that between law and life "there is no substantial articulation" (87):

> Alongside the movement that seeks to keep [life and juridical norm] in relation at all costs, there is a countermovement that, working in an inverse direction in law and life, always seeks to loosen what has been artificially and violently linked. That is to say, in the field of tension of our culture, two opposite forces act, one that institutes and makes, and one that deactivates and deposes. (87)

This "inverse direction" loosens any grip of "law" on "life." By "deactivating and deposing" the institutions that are—and, in particular, the law that is—a space of "potentiality" is glimpsed. By grasping "the potentiality of not to be," we might just envision a law that is not existing.

True, for humans the pathway to "potentiality" has eternal dangers: "It is as if when faced with the opening of a wholly anomic space for human action both the ancients and moderns retreated in fright" (49). But an "opening" on to the pathway occurs where Agamben cites "the tradition of theological hermeneutics." The topic is precisely the "loosening" of legal norm and application: "Just as between language and the world, so between the norm and its application there is no internal nexus that allows one to be derived immediately from the other" (40). Breaking this nexus, an angelomorphic possibility appears. It is Benjamin's vision of a "pure violence" or "pure power" having an "existence outside of the law" (59):

> Here appears the topic—which flashes up in the text only for an instant, but is nevertheless sufficient to illuminate the entire piece—of violence as "pure medium," that is, as the figure of a paradoxical "mediality without ends"—a means that, though remaining as such, is considered independent of the ends that it pursues. (61–2)

Benjamin's meditation was on "pure language" as "that which is not an instrument for the purpose of communication, but communicates itself immediately, that is, a pure and simple communicability" (62). Is this not what angels do?

In fact, it is not to angels but to Kafka and Foucault that we are referred so as to picture the sort of "law" that corresponds to this "pure language." For Kafka, it is a "law that is studied but no longer practiced." For Foucault, "a 'new law' that has been freed from all discipline and all relation to sovereignty" (63). But do we not know this figure from theological visions of the vanishing of law after the coming of the messiah, or Marxian visions of the vanishing of law in the future classless society? In Agamben's own ecstatic prophecy, this law that is not a law is a law that will have been suspended . . . but suspended positively into "potentiality." It is a law so deactivated that it will have become an object of "play":

> One day humanity will play with law just as children play with disused objects, not in order to restore them to their canonical use but to free them from it for good. What is found after the law is not a more proper and original use value that precedes the law, but a new use that is born only after it. (64)

Where has this man been, watching children playing so contentedly with "disused objects" and not the most recent, must-have toy? What on earth has this vision of "law" to do with any actual declaration of a state of emergency, like the November 2005 *état d'urgence* in France?

Anti-Security and Its Personae

My focus in considering Dyzenhaus and Agamben has been, respectively, on two contemporary personae: that of the common lawyer as human rights advocate and that of the metaphysical philosopher as political prophet. Both have an evident moral appeal, though they share no consensus. Where Dyzenhaus appeals to human rights as fundamental common-law values that safeguard against executive overreach in times of emergency, Agamben coolly dismisses rights as a delusional liberty:

> [T]he spaces, the liberties, and the rights won by individuals in their conflicts with central powers always simultaneously prepared a tacit but increasing inscription of individuals' lives within the state order, thus offering a new and more dreadful foundation for the very sovereign power from which they wanted to liberate themselves. (Agamben 1993:86)

Such anti-statism—expressed as a demand for "thinking a politics freed from the form of the state" (Agamben 1998:109)—is as antipolitical as it is banal.

So where does Agamben's appeal lie? Perhaps—and here I conclude—it lies in a certain disposition and a certain discourse. The disposition is antinomian, that is, appropriate to "one for whom the law is not binding on Christians" (*OED*). The discourse—by happy alliteration—is apophatic, that is, one in which "knowledge of God [is] obtained by negation" (*OED*).

For two thousand years—as Anton Schutz argues in a recent essay on the genealogy of legal critique—the aim of Pauline Christianity has remained the subversion of the institutions of this world and, thereby, the unmaking of political and legal history. Stressing Christianity's history as "an anti-institutional, anti-legal and anti-religious campaign," Schutz (2005:71, 84–5) invites us to recognize "the exorbitant presence of Christian anti-institutionalism in the Western past and its necessary formative effects on the present." These include the allure of a Pauline "uncoupling from law." This uncoupling imagines itself as the prelude to entry into a coming "community of believers defined by their subjection not under law but faith, or in other words by their preparedness to deprive the law of its relevance."

If Schutz (2005:85) is correct, in company with Alain Badiou and Slavoj Zizek, Agamben is "looking in Saint Paul for the response to an event that has gravely affected the constituency to which each of them maintains a complicated and close relationship: the eclipse of the *Left*." In fact Zizek has offered his own reflection on the Paris unrest: "*C'est mon choix* . . . to burn cars." His article is illuminated by an image—a "torched car outside the Louvre"—but makes no reference to the *état d'urgence*. Instead, Zizek (2006:22) anticipates that the 2005 "event" will "survive in some kind of cultural registration, like the rise of a new suburban punk culture." Violence—*banlieuesarde* or punk—is elevated to the status and purity of "the real." In this romanticized *volkisch* light, "pure violence" becomes an unconditioned breakthrough moment to shatter the fantasy of legal order that underpins "our ideologico-political predicament."

But is it not a conditioned reflex of the antinomian disposition to favor allegedly unconditioned events . . . in order to interpret social violence as an occasion for us—finally—to "exist"? For such a disposition, the French emergency of late 2005 is not a 20-day civil unrest requiring a law-based restoration of public order. Indeed, civil unrest itself is of no concern . . . other than offering occasion to display the "anti-establishment potential of the New Testament." Only the spiritually pusillanimous—the unelect—stay with the legal ordering of life.

What style of persona bears such a disposition? At the end of *State of Exception* is announced "the possibility of reaching a new condition." It is a prophetic page, bearing the promise of a "politics" that is not "contaminated by law":

> And only beginning from the space thus opened will it be possible to pose the question of a possible use of law after the deactivation of the device that, in the state of exception, tied it to life. . . . To a word that does not bind, that neither commands nor prohibits anything, but says only itself, would correspond an action as pure means, which shows only itself, without any relation to an end. (Agamben 2005:88)

This mesmeric incantation of a law that "neither commands nor prohibits anything" launches a meta-legal flight beyond any sort of historical jurisdiction, common-law or civilian. We're invited to fly on an apophatic discourse of paradoxes in which "the rule applies to the exception in no longer applying," where "the original form of the law is . . . a commandment that commands nothing," and "the law is valid precisely insofar as it . . . has become unrealisable" (Agamben 1999:162, 166, 172). This is to be our "new condition" . . . provided we are sufficiently anxious and therefore graced with "the potential to not-be."

The proviso is serious. It is really quite hard to enter the habitus of the persona for whom "knowledge of God [is] obtained by negation." The question is posed: "What is the actuality of the potentiality to not-think?" (Agamben 1999:183). But an alluring answer is carried in the question. The challenge conceals a lure.

To achieve the "not-thought," a quite specialized literate task has to be mastered: "to read what was never written" (Agamben 1999:3). In this unscripted future, how will civil unrest—such as in France in 2005—be addressed? In the face of other public emergencies, what auspicious alternative will replace the existing juridical order? When there is serious public unrest or when a state's security is threatened, what action will be taken by this future law so "sacred" that it must not be spoken of, so "unrealisable" that it cannot be described?

Set against the apophatic figure of the judge whose "commandment commands nothing," the persona of the common lawyer as advocate of fundamental human rights begins to look less hyperbolic, modest even, bound as it is within a historically specific jurisdiction. Indeed, for all its air of open-ended futurity, is not Agamben's meta-legal conception somewhat archaic, a vindictive relay of historical clerical resentment towards the civil order? Is not it a philosopher's spiritual *coup d'état* against our political and legal history, a scholastic's imagined supersession of the political state and its secularized positive law? This assessment might seem mean . . . but it is quite in keeping with Walter Benjamin's (2003:393) observation in his tenth thesis on "history": "The themes which monastic discipline assigned to friars for meditation were designed to turn them away from the world and its affairs. The thoughts we are developing here have a similar aim." Quite so.

Notes

1. The Law of 1955 was enacted when France was at civil war with what was then part of itself. Aimed at restoring order in the Algerian territory, the 1955 *état d'urgence* remained in force for a year. In 1961, a subsequent Algeria-related crisis threatened public order in metropolitan France, endangering the stability of the French state (Ferejohn and Pasquino 2005).
2. Persons affected by the emergency measures may commence action in the administrative tribunal (*recours pour excès de pouvoir*) to have the measures annulled as illegal.
3. References to Saint-Bonnet (2001) in page numbers only.
4. See Bettinson (1989) on "*politique*" as the term of censure deployed by Catholic Leaguers to besmirch all those who would abandon religious truth and seek accommodation with heretics and schismatics.
5. Unless otherwise indicated, in the remainder of this section references to Dyzenhaus (2006) are in page numbers only.
6. Dyzenhaus (221) aligns his "rule of law project" with the jurisprudence of Lon Fuller and John Finnis.
7. These "ancient liberties" are not universal truths. They are historical arrangements between monarchs, lawyers, churches and other agencies. In this light, limitations on normal liberties in times of emergency appear less sacrilegious.
8. Though unconvinced himself, Martin Loughlin (Loughlin 2006:426, n. 6) finds a "reinvigoration" in Adam Tomkins' *Our Republican Constitution*, given that "the language of common law constitutionalism was spoken continuously throughout the 20th century . . . mostly with a soft inflection, since for many it conveys a reactionary message." For a recent critique of common law constitutionalism, see Poole (2005).

9. For Dyzenhaus (2006:38–9), Agamben "sides with Carl Schmitt" in envisaging dictatorship as operating "within a [legal] black hole." Schmitt is deemed the "more radical" in arguing that the "space beyond law is not so much produced by law as revealed when the mask of liberal legality is stripped away by the political." Lacking a response to the "legal void," Agamben offers only "dramatic and utterly opaque conclusions about not-law and pure violence" (Dyzenhaus 2006:61).

10. Unless otherwise indicated, in the remainder of this section references to Agamben (1998) are given in page numbers only.

11. Agamben reprises Benjamin's (2003:392) 1940 motif from *On the Concept of History*: "the 'state of emergency' in which we live is not the exception but the rule."

12. *State of Exception* channels Benjamin's (2003:404) message from the "messianic realm": "Only in the messianic realm does a universal history exist. Not as written history, but as festively enacted history. This festival is purified of all celebration. There are no festive songs. Its language is liberated prose—prose which has burst the fetters of script."

13. Unless otherwise indicated, in the remainder of this section references to Agamben (2005) are given in page numbers only.

14. Unlike Saint-Bonnet who begins the history of exception with medieval Christianity, Agamben begins with "dictatorship" in classical Roman law.

CHAPTER SIX

Doubt, Ambiguity, and Subject Formation

Paul Hoggett and Nigel Williams

Introduction

How do we deal with the danger within? This has been the essential question asked by Kleinian and post-Kleinian currents in psychoanalysis for whom the human subject is as much haunted by fear as guided by love. Using clinical examples in this chapter we will argue that if we can understand some of the ways in which the individual psyche places itself on a war footing and some of the ways in which it acquires the capacity for peaceful coexistence then this may also illuminate the problem of self-governance in the age of terror.

The Challenge of Ambivalence

Psychoanalysis sees conflict as constitutive of human existence. Moreover this is a particular kind of conflict, that is, a conflict born out of the tension between phenomena which exist in a relation of complementarity, that is, in which each constitutes the other. The central conflict upon which the whole edifice of psychoanalysis was built is a conflict between two fundamental forces, forces that Freud ultimately described in terms of Eros and Thanatos, a synthetic force of unity on the one hand and a fracturing and disintegrating force on the other. These forces require and partially constitute each other. For example, there can be no creation in art or politics or intellectual life, without destruction—to build the new we have to relinquish the hold of what was once loved but now constrains. For Freud, the individual and social body is the medium for the play of these opposing yet complementary forces, expressed in the earliest days of life in the infant's devouring affection for the breast.

For Freud and Klein such ambivalence extended to our relation to life itself, for Thanatos is antilife, and constituted the fundamental challenge facing all human beings. It also provides the key to understanding the decentered notion of subjectivity which emerges from the psychoanalytic tradition. For what is ambivalence if not to be in two minds? Indeed, but also, crucially, to be in these two minds at the same time, as when that baby pulls a little too hard on that nipple. This is a very different way of being in two minds to the baby that one day refuses to feed at all, turning away from the breast as if it were distasteful, and another day sucks contentedly and falls asleep. Now it is in two minds but not at the same time.

Melanie Klein, probably Freud's most influential successor, argued that our capacity to handle our ambivalent orientation to life is the single most important human capacity we develop. Klein's followers, particularly Wilfred Bion (1962) and Herbert Rosenfeld (1971), suggested that destructiveness first manifests itself at first as a silent deadly force at work within the psyche. This is the origin of psychotic anxiety, the kind of "fear of annihilation" (Rosenfeld 1971) people experience in breakdown, and one that others might glimpse during panic attacks. The Kleinians remind us that terror is our companion throughout life, from the night fears of the toddler to the monstrous realization of our own mortality in later life. We "manage" this inner terror by projecting it outwards so that the danger within becomes the danger without. Now we can name the fear, albeit incorrectly, and in naming the fear we name the threat and can mobilize our aggressive capacities to deal with it. Behind hatred one can always find fear.

Fear, hatred, love, these are the primary affects in the Kleinian vocabulary that mediate the relationship between human beings and those others they depend upon. Until our cognitive and moral resources have grown these affective impulses threaten to overwhelm us so we deal with them by splitting and other means.

On Having Mixed Feelings

T, a wealthy executive in the leisure industry, was a controlling and jealous man whose wife eventually decided she had had enough. He sought therapy and, in a short space of time, a number of significant changes began to occur in his personality even though some parts of him remained resolutely the same. Regarding the latter, at times, for example when an incident had occurred between his wife and himself that had hurt him, an icy and calculating man came to see me, one who was preoccupied with beating all his opponents and barely able to suppress his fury. But another part of him had also begun to emerge, one which was very much in touch with the depressed and vulnerable parts of himself which were subject to the same tyrannizing agency that he externalized upon his wife. Whilst the invulnerable part of him was incapable of empathy when he could escape the hold this had over him he could be a thoughtful and sincere man.

But the changes in him did not occur quickly enough to earn the trust of his wife who decided to separate from him not long before my summer break. On returning to therapy in the autumn T was full of hatred towards his partner and it felt like all the progress that had been made in therapy had been undone. T struggled to contain these feelings in the month preceding the moment when his wife moved into her new home at the beginning of October. The couple had managed to reach an amicable separation agreement in which responsibilities for the care of their children were shared but he feared that at any moment his rage would slip free and the cold but civil relationship with his wife would break down to be replaced by an open warfare in which their children would suffer terribly.

Eventually his anger broke loose and he snapped at one of his children. In the session immediately following he was full of remorse and this seemed to put him back in touch with more thoughtful parts of himself. Once more he was in touch with his own vulnerability and the terrifying feeling that the separation will reduce him to nothing. A few days later he snapped again, this time reducing his wife to tears. Once again he was full of remorse but this time he felt the remorse in the midst of his angry outburst rather than hours or days later—he realized what he was doing at the very moment of doing it and had made painstaking attempts to repair the damage with his wife in the period before our next session. In this session he oscillated dramatically between a split (him good, her bad) and more integrated view of himself and his world. In the next session he brought four widely differing emotional reactions which seemed to exist in separate fragments. When this was reflected back to him he commented that he had only ever been able to do one thing at a time, "I can't 'multi-task' he said. From this point on significant changes seemed to occur again. His loving and generous feelings towards his wife returned as did the pain at the coming loss. He recognized the "agony" his wife was also going through, for not only was the separation looming but her business was going badly. The sessions during this period were becoming filled with a multitude of conflicting feelings but now he was able to bear them and owned them as his own in a way which was often very moving.

Reflecting on this period in which he moved back towards an more integrated state of being he said, "it seems odd but the thing that seemed to change things was the realization that I could have two feelings at the same time . . . its taken me more than 40 years to realize such a simple thing."

We can see here the rapid movement between what Klein would have called a paranoid–schizoid and depressive state of mind (Klein 1935; Klein 1946). For T the crucial step seemed to have been the capacity to contain his ambivalence—his hatred and his love, his hurt and his hope. As he realized that he could have both, that is, mixed feelings, he became aware of his own complexity and the complexity of others. His wife became less one-dimensional, more of a tragic figure than either a heartless tyrant or a pathetic victim. The oscillation between idealization and denigration, both of self and other, was somehow transcended, even if only episodically. And as his ability to contain psychic complexity increased so did his curiosity about others.

We can see from this example how the depressive position is a vital accomplishment (albeit never a secure and once and for all accomplishment). In this state of mind the psychosocial complexity of the world can be grasped, multidimensionality replaces one-dimensionality. Inner conflict (the conflict between different parts of the personality and the different feelings associated with them) can be experienced and stayed with.

Freud saw that the psyche was based upon conflict. As he put it, the ego was not master in his own house but struggled to satisfy the conflicting demands of conscience and desire. But we can see now what a revolutionary contribution Klein has made by introducing the idea of these two positions. The depressive position describes the emergence, both phylogenetically and ontogenetically (in the development of a single child and in the development of society itself), of a new dimension to personhood, of a new civilized capacity—the capacity to contain conflict. Within contemporary psychoanalysis "containment" is a technical term, originating with Bion (1962), which describes the capacity to hold on to powerful feelings without suppressing them or getting rid of them by projection or enactment. To contain conflictual feelings one must be able to hold the tension and use this psychic energy for thought, "thinking under fire" as it is often described.

The above example also provides other insights. In the paranoid–schizoid position there is an oscillation between the different parts of the personality (the icy and calculating part of T, the tyrannical part, the victimized part, etc.) and therefore between different ways of apprehending the world. Moreover the destructive parts are expelled outwards and located in others. The subject switches between these part selves, which are kept very separate—tyrant/victim, winner/loser—there is no comprehension of a territory lying in between these polarities. Following Winnicott, "in between-ness" can be thought of as the third area (Winnicott 1971). Rather than being either a victim or a tyrant, in the space in between one can apprehend oneself as both victim and tyrant, winner and loser and, if the tension can be contained, then this antinomy may be transformed into a third position—neither victim nor tyrant. Crucially, for Klein, the depressive position is one in which good and bad can be integrated so that the bad can be discerned within the good and the good can be discerned within the bad. In contrast, through splitting, good and bad, virtue and vice, purity and danger are kept apart. Self, "us" are idealized whereas other, "them" are denigrated. But by locating all that is negative in the other the danger within becomes the danger without, hence the "paranoid" in the paranoid–schizoid position. T's hatred towards his partner was the complement to his fear of her, that is, his fear of her imaginary sexual power, a fear that was the basis of his jealousy. T's attempt to control his partner expressed his need to organize his intimate relations according to a set of fixed subject positions through which, paradoxically, T constituted himself as victim rather than perpetrator—the victim of his partner's powerful sexuality. In this way Melanie Klein adds a twist to our understanding of alienation by insisting that what we project into the world forever threatens to return and haunt us, we then frantically seek to control this return of the projected. David Bell develops this theme in his commentary on Mike Davis's (2001) reflections on 9/11 where Davis notes that the resort, following September 11, to increasingly pervasive forms of security and control within the USA actually contributed to the very anxiety these measures sought to address. Bell argues, "the grandiose demand for complete security creates ever more, in our minds, enemies endowed with our own omnipotence who are imagined as seeking to control us" (Bell 2003).

Breakdown

Such processes of idealization and denigration characterize the psychic reality of the group as well as the individual and are therefore a sociological as well as a psychological phenomenon. One common form of idealization finds expression in national "founding myths" or myths of origins. In his book *Chosen Peoples: Sacred Sources of National Identity* Anthony Smith (2006) argues strongly for the religious origins of nationalism, specifically in the Old Testament notion of ethnic election, that is, the idea of the "chosen people." Smith argues that for both Jewish and Christian peoples the idea of "chosenness" underlies popular nationalist mobilization. In this way the sacred and premodern is reaffirmed under conditions of secularized modernity. Smith also notes two forms that such mobilization takes. The first is inward looking and concerned with conformity to God's law. The second is missionary and therefore imperialist and concerned to convert the world to God's will. Smith's points out the paradox, that nationalism on the one hand bears all the marks of modernity and yet on the other is profoundly religious and premodern in form (i.e. in terms of its rituals, its symbols, its mass psychology, etc.).

"Exceptionalism" is a common feature of nationalism. The phenomenon of "American exceptionalism" can be understood in terms of the kind of idealized founding myth that

Smith describes (Fousek 2000; Bell 1975; Kammen 1993; McCrisken 2000, 2001). This concept refers to a tacit and often unarticulated ideology which implies that the USA is different to all other nations—both the exception and exceptional. According to McCrisken (2001) it informs both Republican and Democrat, isolationist (Smith's inward looking) and interventionist (Smith's missionary and imperialist) forms of US foreign policy. These exceptionalist beliefs can be traced back to the early settlers in New England who had left Britain in order to preserve their nonconformist brand of Puritanism. They therefore brought with them a particular kind of psyche; they were bearers of the earliest enlightenment but were also convinced that they had been chosen by God and that the New World had been given to them in order to bring redemption both to themselves and the world. Thus they were both harbingers of modernity and yet profoundly pre-modern. This idea of being uniquely blessed by God to undertake his work upon the earth has shaped American exceptionalism giving it three particular characteristics—benevolence, exemplariness, and finality. The assumption of benevolence has characterized American foreign policy from the war against Mexico in 1846 to interventions in Vietnam and Iraq in recent times, interventions which are seen not as acts of strategic self interest or impe-rial adventure but as acts designed to benefit the object of intervention. Exemplariness corresponds to the assumption that one is building a model society, exemplified by the early Pilgrim leader John Winthrop's metaphor of the "City on the Hill," which is so self-evidently better morally, politically, and economically that all others cannot but help be attracted to it. Third, finality has long been bound up with the idea that America is the engine of human progress and is therefore synonymous with the process of historical modernization. Modernization theory, exemplified by the neocons of the current Bush administration, assumes a teleology of history such that society is construed to pass through a number of preordained stages culminating in the endpoint of democracy and markets, exemplified by the United States—Fukuyama's "end of history" (1992). From this perspective, all other paths such as Communism or political Islam, are aberrations ,which will eventually be overcome (with assistance if necessary).

We can see how American exceptionalism provides the basis for group narcissism, the idealization of one's own group and the denigration of the other. But the narcissist is unable to grasp the possibility of other minds and other worlds, all that is properly "other" merely becomes an extension of self. McCrisken (2001) argues that Vietnam was the first shock to this narcissistic universe and 9/11 was a further shock (Clarke and Hoggett 2004). On each occasion the myth of American invulnerability was exposed, further, each event provoked the same incredulity that others could perceive evil in America's own benign interventions in the world. But of course "exceptionalism" is not just the pro-jection of a distorted identity in the international arena; first and foremost it is a distor-tion of self-identity, of how the nation projects itself to itself. In reality the United States, far from being exemplary, is riven by conflict and division, socially polarized, violent, fearful, and survivalist (Lasch 1985; Glassner 1999; Shapiro 2001). This has led some commentators, like the American psychoanalyst Ed Shapiro, to argue that the United States failure to understand the rage towards it that many peoples of the world feel is an expression of its own inability to face and think about the sharpness of its own inter-nal differences (Shapiro 2003). According to another of Klein's followers, Joan Riviere (1936), if we look deeper beneath narcissism we will find depression. For many Kleinians narcissism is a manic defense against the fear of self-annihilation, of inner destructive-ness. The internal wounds are covered up and disavowed, instead of guilt, concern and grieving towards the state of one's internal relations the manic response puts action in place of feeling or thought. But this is no ordinary action but what Freud called "repetition."

After the shock of Vietnam, which for a brief period in the 1970s did bring about reflection and reappraisal, the two invasions of Iraq correspond to the reassertion of traditional exceptionalist beliefs. Iraq becomes the melancholic repetition of Vietnam, another country to be liberated from tyranny. In *Beyond the Pleasure Principle* Freud noted how a child engages in the symbolic repetition of a traumatic experience in an attempt to overcome it. But this is not a simple repetition, rather it is a repetition in which the subject position of the child is reversed; from being the powerless object he becomes, in fantasy, the powerful agent. In his observations on the re-awakening of Serbian nationalism Vamik Volkan (1997) notes the same process. In this case the Serb, who had long imagined himself as the fantasized victim of a Turkish aggression immortalized in Serb folk history in the fifteenth century Battle of Blackbirds Field, becomes the scourge of the Muslims of Bosnia who are seen as a kind of Turkish fifth column. In similar fashion, 9/11 re-awakens the trauma of injured narcissism that was Vietnam. America once more goes in search of monsters to destroy and having bombed the Taliban into apparent submission it then goes in search of a more fulfilling target. In Iraq, Bush Jr. sets about "finishing the job" begun by Bush Sr. and achieving "closure," closing the narcissistic wound opened up by Vietnam and never properly healed.

But of course it takes two to make a conflict. These processes of idealization and denigration become considerably exaggerated when both parties to a conflict adopt the same way of seeing self and other. Benedict Anderson (1983) insisted that all communities are imagined, they vary however according to their style of imagining and this style is expressed in both the nature of the group's boundaries and the narratives that constitute the group imaginary. In situations of intercommunal conflict, which have economic, social, and/or political determinants, processes of identity construction take on a particular character because of the way in which they enlist the kinds of powerful group emotions described by Klein and others. In particular, we suggest, they become infused by a complex amalgam of love, hatred, and paranoia that give to such conflicts a dynamic and indeterminacy, which is irreducible to the material factors such as competing interests that first propels them. Such conflictual relations constitute, in Jessica Benjamin's (2004) schema, a "breakdown" in the relationship between self and other and in what follows we will examine the dynamics of breakdown in terms of what could be called the "paranoid style" of imagined community, a destructive dialectic of what Benjamin calls "doer/done to" relations. This is equivalent to a defensive and paranoid struggle in which each party experiences the existence of the other as a threat, and in which each seeks to obliterate the difference of the other.

Irrespective of whether it is the Somali community in Britain or the gay and lesbian community in Sydney all communities are defined by boundaries, which define who belongs and who does not. This is not necessarily an exclusionary strategy but simply a way of garnering the resources, including narrative resources, to sustain a group's sense of being. But where two groups cohabit the same space or compete for the same resources then boundary making processes can take on a different form (Olzak 1992). Boundaries take on a salience and sensitivity which in "normal times" they did not possess and the criteria—mores, dress, lifestyle, and behavior—that constitute these boundaries can become "policed" in order to make sure that group members adhere to them. In other words, the boundaries become brittle and inflexibly enacted and, as in Northern Ireland, transgression can be met with both moral and physical punishment. One of the worst forms of transgression is to have contact with the "other side"—by the 1990s it is estimated that less than three percent of Protestants married outside of their community (Ruane and Todd 1996). As external differences acquire increasing salience so internal differences become suppressed—it is not just that the other group becomes homogenized, lumped together under the denigrated term that comes to define them ("Taigs," "Yids"), but one's own group takes on a homogenized quality as well. As Shain (2002) notes, when Israel's Jewish population feels threatened the strong differences between, for example, secular and religious Jews recede into the background.

We saw earlier how the paranoid–schizoid state of mind lends itself to the cultivation of victimhood. The victim is always virtuous, unlike the other whose flaws and sins are seen to be the source of injustice. Victimhood therefore takes upon itself a moral quality; it becomes a kind of "moral narcissism." In situations of intercommunal conflict each side vies to constitute the other as the aggressor and perpetrator, and this dynamic of competitive victimhood in which each side rehearses its catalogue of injuries, traumas, and injustices can be very hard to break. Communication theorists construe this process in terms of what they term a "breakdown in the punctuation of the sequence of events" (Watzlawick, Beavin and Jackson 1968; Bateson 1972). Anticipating later concepts of complex systems these theorists argued that even in simply dyadic relationships parties try to manage the complexity by construing a chain of cause and effect relationships instead of the flow, circularity, multidetermination, and recursivity that actually consti-tute the reality in which they are immersed. In breakdown situations there is a discrep-ancy in the way in which the two parties punctuate the linear sequence, so that what one sees as the cause, the other sees as the effect. Specifically, each party sees its own behavior as a defensive reaction to the other's behavior which is interpreted as a provocation, but this defensive reaction will in turn be interpreted by the other as a provocation that they need to defend themselves against. In this manner each side construes it own aggressive behavior as a defensive reaction, that is, either as deterrence or as the legitimate attempt to defend oneself in light of the hostility of the other. In such situations spirals of "defensive provocations" can quickly escalate, a process the communication theorists conceptualized as symmetrical schismogenesis. A breakdown in the punctuation of the sequence of events also lies at the root of the self-fulfilling prophecy. Here action taken by party A which is designed to preempt or deter party B actually acts as a signal to party B to take the very action that A sees itself as preempting. In an earlier article Hoggett argued that the Bush/Blair invasion of Iraq had precisely this effect (Hoggett 2005), far from removing the resources ,which terrorism needed to thrive this intervention had the reverse effect, it strengthened the monster it sought to destroy.

While we prefer to think of conflict as something negative it is also important to understand the role of love and desire. We have tried to demonstrate the satisfactions to be derived from conflict—we enjoy our hatreds and the denigration of the other, we also enjoy the narcissistic pleasure of self-idealization, particularly the satisfactions to be derived from the identity of victimhood. Conflict builds group cohesion and strengthens social bonds but in a perverse way, something Richard Sennett referred to as "destructive gemeinschaft" (Sennett 1974). This is sustained by the selective use of historical memory and the construction of historical narratives and, on some occasions, the use of "chosen traumas," which lead to "time collapse" and the confusion of past and present. Breakdown is accompanied and reinforced by the destruction of reality testing fueled by rumor, paranoia, and the demonization of the other. There is a breakdown of trust—polarization leads to geographical segregation and the absence of communication between the conflictual parties, suspicions escalate regarding the nature of the other group's next move. Each group becomes blind to its own faults and mistakes and perceives its own aggressive actions as a defensive reaction to the behavior of the other. Some of the actions of each group lead to self-fulfilling prophecies and vicious circles emerge producing spirals of escalation and revenge characterized by forms of what Klein calls "talion morality" in which each group assumes for itself the right to retribution through a process of "tit for tat."

Repair

Jessica Benjamin (2004) construes self/other relations in terms of a dialectic of breakdown and repair. During phases of repair active efforts are made to reclaim what has been projected into the denigrated other, self is no longer construed in idealized terms and self's capacity for aggression and destructiveness is accepted and understood.

Unfrozen Grievance

X first came to therapy not long after his depressive breakdown and hospitalization in his late twenties. His parents were powerful and dominating figures who had long regarded X as a willful and difficult child. From what could be seen, neither parent was an emotionally sophisticated individual. They had planned to separate for a long time but had not told their children until one day they came to visit X at his boarding school and told him that they had decided to divorce. X was expected to take this news in his stride and when he didn't his behavior was seen as further proof of just what a difficult child he could be. Over the next fifteen years until his breakdown X's life took on the character of a catastrophe in slow motion. Unconsciously convinced that he was no good, someone who could not but help cause damage in his relationships to others, his hospitalization began a slow process of recovery as, for the first time, he began to encounter others who would actually listen to him.

The early stages of therapy were marked by X's recitation of the catalogue of grievances that he held towards his parents. It became clear that, paradoxically, he also derived satisfaction from these grievances, indeed that for him to begin to fully recover it was necessary for him to somehow give up these grievances. He had obtained a righteous satisfaction from being the wronged victim, a position from which he attacked his parents and successive female partners for the weaknesses and faults in their character.

Things began to really change when, through the therapy, he began to see how similar he was to the mother he so frequently berated. He found out that his father too had been seen as a failure by his parents and had labored under the shadow of his successful brother for most of his life. His father's sudden illness put him in touch with this man's vulnerability and a genuine compassion towards both of his parents began to develop. He didn't give up his grievance and nor should he have done. His parents had treated him poorly and were too insecure in themselves to ever make proper amends to him. But his grievance was no longer all consuming, it became something he could think and talk about rather than enact. He could accept that he probably had been a pretty difficult child because this idea no longer implied that "they" (his parents) had been right and he was wrong. Most importantly the possibility that others might show genuine affection and love towards him without suddenly withdrawing it (the legacy of the trauma of his parents' divorce) became glimpsed. He began to risk loving and being loved. Therapy ended after five years when he was in a stable loving relationship for the first time in his life and developing a successful career for himself.

Again in this example we can see the central role of loss. Whereas T feared "losing everything" if his wife left him, X confronted loss when facing the need to give up his grievances. In each case the potential loss of an external object is accompanied by the potential loss of a part of the self and the fear is that one will be left so denuded that one will lack the resources to recover and have a future. In *Mourning and Melancholia* Freud (1917) construes this loss of self in terms of "the shadow," left by the object, that falls upon the ego—a shadow which is not just a gap or absence but a wound resulting from reproaches made by one part of the self towards another. The melancholic (or today the person we would say is suffering from depression) is caught in an imaginary relation with another who is both the source of reproach (a stern internalized critic of the self) and the source of grievance.

We often use the phrase "nursing a grievance" and we think this reveals important insight into the perverse pleasure to be obtained by those who have been wronged and yet are unable or unwilling to abandon this subject position. It is interesting to note that not long after peace broke out in Northern Ireland there appeared to be a significant increase in the number of suicides, particularly in young men from both communities (McGowan, Hamilton, Miller and Kernohan 2005). Again, we think we have a sociological correlate in what Max Scheler, following Nietzsche, called ressentiment, a mass sentiment arising from the experience of injustice but where grievance is nursed, enacted, and projected rather than addressed towards the more powerful elites responsible for the injustice (Demertzis 2006). The boundary between resentment and ressentiment is a fine one. According to Andrew Schaap where we have been wronged "resentment involves a defiant assertion of one's value and . . . is oriented to the recovery and confirmation of one's moral status" (Schaap 2005:104). In this sense resentment can be the basis for a politics of recognition. However, Schaap also notes, this strategy risks entrenching resentment and fixating grievance. This may lend to a politics of victimhood in which grievance is nursed through what Schaap (Schaap 2005:105) describes as a "moralistic and unforgiving disposition" in which, like with T and X, oppression becomes synonymous with being in the right.

But the vignette of X also illustrates some of the processes by which projected hostility is reclaimed and feelings of compassion towards the other, even an unjust other, can be set in motion. Klein sees the emergence of the capacity for concern for the other and the feelings of guilt that one feels in relation to one's own aggression as the primary form of human love. Just as the psychologist Lawrence Kohlberg provided us with a theory of the development of moral thought in the child so the psychoanalyst Melanie Klein and her collaborators have provided us with a theory of moral feeling, evidenced, for example, by the title of one their most famous books *Love, Hate and Reparation* (Klein and Riviere 1964). For Klein, the feeling of guilt arises when we experience regret for damage we have caused to another and the desire to repair that damage. This seems straightforward enough. However Klein notes that in reality this is an achievement of human development. If guilt is to be felt the other must exist as a separate person who is real and can be hurt; they are not just a bundle of our projections. Only to the extent that the other is real can we, as in the case of X, suddenly be touched and altered by them. Indeed, in conflict between groups, movement sometimes only occurs when each party is willing to be altered by the other. In other words, for guilt to occur narcissism must be overcome and this is as true for the group as it is for the individual.

So, in contrast to the split and paranoid world of the narcissistic group Klein outlines another state of mind, more emotionally and ethically complex. Far from being idealized, in this state of mind (the "depressive position") the self can be apprehended as containing good and bad traits and impulses. And far from being denigrated, in this state of mind the other can be seen as having good and desirable as well as bad characteristics. This requires the reintegration of parts of the self which have been projected and located in the other, in this sense the self becomes less alienated from itself and what once seemed strange and foreign now becomes familiar. Black and white thinking is replaced by what Primo Levi (1988) called the "grey zone." The world now becomes more ambiguous, mixed up and messy. As Tony, one of the respondents in Kirsten Monroe's (1996) study of rescuers of Jews in the Second World War, put it, "the evil and the good can be in all of us." As we have seen, Klein calls this the "depressive position," it necessarily embodies a way of seeing the world, which is more sanguine, somber, and tragic. This then is the basis for the capacity for reparation—knowing what we are capable of mobilizes a reparative drive, a desire to make things better and the object of this drive can just as easily be the damaged and despoiled global environment in which we all live as the friend or loved one who we fear we have wronged in some way.

Drawing on the work of Hannah Arendt, Andrew Schaap suggests that there are in fact sound political grounds for forgiveness. Forgiveness presupposes plurality and recognizes the frailty and natality of the victim, "that those wronged were on the side of good as a matter of historical fact not as a matter of principle" (Schaap 2005:111), that is, not because they were necessarily better people. Similarly the perpetrators were on the side of wrong not because they were inherently bad people—who can say that any of us might not have done what the great mass of German citizens did during the Nazi regime, that is, turned a blind eye and given priority to the struggle of our loved ones and ourselves to survive? Schaap cites Arendt at this point who suggests that to forgive is therefore to see the other as "more than whatever he did or achieved" (Arendt 1968:248). Forgiveness is therefore to offer the other the benefit of the doubt, "this moment is hopeful because it is predicated on the potential inherent in the other to begin anew" (Schaap 2005). Forgiving does not necessarily entail forgetting, rather "it seeks to establish a provisional closure, one that acknowledges the persistent claims of the past over the present—and, therefore, the impossibility of any final reconciliation—but resists the power of the past to determine the possibilities of the present" (Schaap 2005:112). For Schaap, forgiveness can provide the grounds for the renewal of politics rather than the end to politics implied by some hypostatized consensus in which victims, perpetrators, and bystanders are all corralled into a false national unity.

However, because this reparative impulse is also partly a defense against our capacity for destructiveness then if this defensive aim should become primary the reparation we offer can be tainted by falseness, what the Kleinians call "manic reparation." It becomes driven less by a genuine concern for the other and more by a concern to free ourselves from moral anxiety through the act of offering apology. We can observe this double-edged nature to reparation at work in contemporary politics where, to some extent, it has become fashionable for political leaders to offer apologies (for slavery, the dispossession of indigenous peoples, etc) without real material reparation (Warner 2002).

While the reparative impulse is central to the process of repair, equally important is a change in the nature of anxiety. The paranoid and persecutory anxiety that so dominates the paranoid–schizoid position is replaced by depressive anxiety—fundamentally an anxiety about whether self possesses the inner resources (such as courage, resilience, and generosity) necessary to live with integrity in a tragic world. For Klein's followers, particularly those influenced by the work of Wilfred Bion (Anderson 1992), the persistence of paranoid anxiety also finds expression in what we might call the human subject's personal epistemology. Doubt, ambiguity and what Bion calls "not-knowing" lose their intolerable persecutory quality. In this group's favorite phrase (from Keats' correspondence to his brothers) this enables the subject to be "in doubts, mysteries, and uncertainties without irritable reaching after fact or reason," something they refer to as "negative capability." We are not far here from Iris Marion Young's notion of "wonderment"—an "openness to the newness and mystery of the other" (Young 1997:357).

A number of writers in political theory (Whitebrook 2002) and conflict resolution (Lederach 2005) have recently argued that the capacity for developing an awareness of the other as they really are (rather than as a bundle of projections) is equivalent to the development of a moral imagination—we cannot make any accurate assessment of the rights or wrongs, strengths or weaknesses of another if we constantly obscure our picture of them through our prejudices, fears, hopes, and jealousies. According to Lederach, "the moral imagination rises with the capacity to imagine ourselves in relationship, the ability to embrace complexity without reliance on dualistic polarity, the belief in the creative act, and acceptance of the inherent risk required to break violence and to venture on unknown paths that build constructive change" (Lederach 2005:29).

The perspective we have offered in this chapter is one, which stresses the centrality of internal conflict and destructiveness to the psyche. It is one, which also stresses the role of chance and accident in the constitution of the self and the way in which irresolvable contradictions inhere to our social relations, contradictions which confront us with irreconcilable dilemmas (Hoggett, Mayo and Miller 2007). It should therefore come as no surprise to find some analysts have gone so far as to rename Klein's depressive position "the tragic position" (Symington 2001). But this psychoanalytic tradition is also a hopeful one. It explores the ways in which conflicts and contradictions can be contained without being suppressed, the energy from the resulting tension being a resource for creative living. It examines the way in which the psyche develops the capacity to go beyond splitting and projection, accepting "in-betweeness," indeed not just accepting it but relishing it. In Bion's terms, contradiction, ambiguity, and otherness become food for thought rather than dangerous and foreign matter, which threaten to poison the mind. And so, paradoxically, tragedy, born from what the Italian Marxist Antonio Gramsci would have called "pessimism of the intellect," is also the foundation for a realistic hopefulness.

CHAPTER SEVEN

The Subject "At the Gates of the Polis": Theorizing Transitional Civic Order from the Site of Trauma

Magdalena Zolkos

Introducing Civic Order, Reconciliation and Trauma[1]

This chapter investigates the predicaments of transitional and reconciliatory politics from the perspective of a civic state order. In it, the expressions and practices of religious, nationalistic, and moralistic dogmatism are countered by the secular character of state institutions. "Secular" is broadly defined as pertaining to the matters of "common affairs" of women and men dwelling together (from Latin *sæculris*, "[of] this world"). The politics of transition and reconciliation are often conceptualized within the framework of "transitional justice," which structures them as coming to terms with and doing justice for the past (Ivison 2008:507–8). This means that dealing with the multidimensional consequences of historical violence and injustice becomes not only one of the key tasks and challenges of the newly (re)founded state, but also forms the context within which its civic character must be considered and practiced. In other words, my inquiry centers on the question of the implications of the imperative of historical justice and reconciliation for the transition to and/or (re)founding of a democratic state and, more specifically, for theorizing and practicing its civic character.

To complicate further the nexus of the civic state on the one hand and the project of transitional justice on the other, one needs to recognize two spatiotemporal dimensions of reconciliatory politics, namely: (1) the intricate ways in which "past" becomes conceptualized as onerous, even if (or, possibly, because) it is also seen as potentially politically manageable, and (2) the conceptualization of politics in terms of a movement beyond (the overcoming of or leaving behind) the historical violence and injustice that the political community in question has suffered (and possibly also perpetrated). In this chapter, the relation of the transitional moment of the political "now" to the violent past is conceptualized in reference to the idea of trauma.

The notion of trauma is understood here not in clinical terms, but rather as a collective "transformative event that is realized in a variety of historical, rhetorical, and cultural symptoms" (Ball 2000:2). As such, it captures the powerful constitutive legacy of the past in the present. Past traumatic events make themselves known, as it were, and overwhelm the present in a pattern of a repetitive and insistent return (Caruth 1995:4). Taking a departure point in the debates of the psychoanalytic trauma theory in 1990s (for an over-view of its various strands see for example Kilby 2002a, 2002b; Radstone 2007a), I use the notion "trauma" as a conjunction of: (1) a particular structure of psychic experience and (2) a catastrophic event, which is external to and affects the psychic. For instance Jacobus (1999:126) associates it with "an original inner catastrophe," which, in turn, connotes "an experience which cannot be experienced at the time, but none the less leaves traces of devastation in the psyche, like a shattered or ruined landscape to which the survivor returns again and again, or which returns in the form of recurrent dreams, unsolicited memories, and disturbances in [. . .] functioning." By claiming the centrality of trauma in theorizing transitional justice and civic order, I thus advocate a discussion of reconcilia-tory politics as a response to historically specific manifestations of the suffering and vulnerability of others. This does not mean that such manifestations need to be essential-ized as if they provided ultimate grounding for politics per se (and were thus vested with a metapolitical *ontos*). Rather, it is important to understand that (and how) the notion of trauma as a code word for historically specific manifestations of subjective precarious-ness gains momentary and contingent powers of political animation. It is, in other words, emblematic of an idea of political beginnings, that is, characteristic of a time when it has become a political imperative to respond to human suffering.

Not every traumatic experience lends itself to political consideration of this kind, but only ones that demonstrate collective dimensions. By "collective" I mean here not simply the cumulative effect of individual experiences of violence and atrocities, but, rather, a damage of the whole social fabric (Erikson 1995:188), which also points at the dynamics of "externalizing and objectifying" the traumatic experiences in the so-called "national narratives" (Olick 2007:32). While I view the subjective psychic formation and expression of trauma to be of primary importance for identifying and understanding traumagenic occurrences, I also highlight the ontological and epistemological specificity of what I term here "communal" trauma as irreducible to the "aggregated psychology of trauma" (Olick 2007:33). The work of Agnes Heller (2007) presents a productive possibility of working with the individual and collective dichotomy in the field of trauma studies. Heller differentiates between "individual" and "historical" trauma, not as separate typo-logies, but, rather, as distinct and yet interrelated dimensions of trauma (cf. also Green 2000). By "historical trauma" Heller (2007:104) means an occurrence of past injury, violence, or injustice experienced by a community as a whole: it is thus trauma that is intersubjective, relational and narrative in that it "always involves a story, or [. . .] several stories." This perspective creates a possibility for thinking of traumatic occurrences in terms of the complex modalities of political becoming that they facilitate: disrupting, modifying, but also forming communal existence and communal belonging (cf. Radstone 2007b:68–71). While Olick (2007:32) is right, I think, to criticize crude anthropomor-phizing of traumatized "collectivities [where] the collectivity itself [is presented as if it had] singular desires, needs, and will," it is also important to consider the conjunction of collectivity and subjectivity in collective trauma, as well as to investigate the logic that animates the figurative and synecdochic juxtapositions of "a damaged [human] body" and "a damaged social organism" (Erikson 1995:188).

I pursue the titular objective of theorizing civic order and transitional justice from the site of trauma with the following distinction in mind: between the "confessional" and "civic" concepts of reconciliation. The former describes a reconciliatory project that builds into its discourse quasi-religious imaginaries and practices of, inter alia, confes-sional speech and submission of the subject to the eschatological visions of social unity and moral restoration of the community (cf. Brudholm 2008). The latter critiques the confessional logic of reconciliation and investigates ways in which the civic act of (re)founding can combine (and facilitate) civic companionship and community with nonviolent practices of civic disagreement, conflict, and tension (what Yeatman in the Introduction to this volume names "the terms of pacification"). Furthermore, this chapter proposes that the distinction between "confessional" and "civic" reconciliation maps onto the philosophical notions of transcendence and immanence retrospectively. As regards their ontological status, the difference between the immanent and the transcendent translates into the question "whether the character of Being is considered as a being with reference only to itself and without reference to anything *beyond*, *higher than* or *superior to* being" (Berg-Sørensen 2004:12). More specifically, this difference points towards the problem of the communal possibility of reaching beyond its own (act of) founding and existence. As Berg-Sørensen argues (2004:12), the key question is thus whether "it [is] assumed that the being of the political community constitutes an order and has a common and united character including all members, or is it constituted by the singular being of the members without a final common character." LaCapra (2004:19), who has criticized the oppositional construction of immanence and transcendence in Holocaust studies and trauma studies as a "secular displacement of religious concepts," has coined the notion of "situational transcendence." It means that an "act [. . .], while being situated, or subject to contextual constraints and limited understanding, may also get beyond, or work through, its initial situation critically and transformatively, thereby giving rise to newer, more or less unpredictable, at times uncanny situations." Consequently, for LaCapra a traumatic event (extreme and limital) points into a direction of such "situational transcendence" by the very virtue of its elusiveness and unpredictability, or what Cathy Caruth (1996) called "unclaimed quality" of trauma. It is that impossibility of pacifying or neutralizing a traumatic experience that ultimately also blurs the distinction between working through trauma and acting it out. In what follows I will focus on that "unclaimed" experience of trauma, and on its disruption of the binary immanent–transcendent thinking, which informs the contemporary political theorizing of reconciliation.

The suggestion of this chapter is that as regards the distinction between "confessional" and "civic" reconciliation, the perspective of trauma becomes an insightful instrument of critique. Trauma is quite central for the "confessional" reconciliatory project, but it is primarily understood as: (1) an ontologically stable (metapolitical) pathologized condition of the subject and/or as (2) a desirable object of political activity. In contrast, it is puzzling that the existing attempts at "civic" redescription and reappropriation of reconciliation have remained relatively inattentive to the problem of trauma. The objective of this chapter is to consider and theorize the possibilities of situating the traumatized subject vis-à-vis the civic transitional order of a state that becomes engaged with its past through the pursuits of historical justice at the same time as it remains "haunted" by that past.

Reconciliatory Transcendence of the Communal Boundaries

The so-called "first wave" literature on transitional justice has centered upon advocacy and justification of the project of reconciliation, understood either in a strong sense of "cancellation of estrangement via [for instance] forgiveness in order to establish substantive agreement on moral issues" or in a weaker sense of the "cancellation of enmity with a help of a culture of reciprocity and mutual respect in order to have minimal disagreement on moral issues" (Bhargava 2000:63). Much of it was produced in response to the establishment of novel judicial and institutional solutions of transitional justice, such as the truth and reconciliation commissions, international tribunals, hybrid courts, reparations, initiatives of collective remembrance and mourning, and so on. Its focus was primarily empirical and socio-legal, rather than theoretical, but it has included critical and normative approaches, as exemplified by the work of Martha Minow (1998; 2000). While the "first wave" debate of transitional justice has been concerned with a variety of reconciliatory aspects, and is thus irreducible to a single polemical strand, this chapter stresses its one, arguably central, aspect, namely the conceptualization of justice as something exterior to and transcendent of the political boundaries of the transitional community.

In *Between Vengeance and Forgiveness* (1998), Minow argues that transitional situations, which raise questions of justice, bring into the picture diverse problems of political, legal, and ethical character, and hence that the politics of transitional justice should both be integrative of these diverse aspects and should focus on working out appropriate responses to the problems at hand. The objectives and strategies of reconciliation feature prominently among these responses as supplementary to the "hard law" solutions. As such, for Minow the process of transitional justice should not only aim at responding to trauma as a specific destruction of community, but should also facilitate institutional therapeutic responses to individual victimization and trauma. In fact, these two objectives are envisioned as complementary and mutually supportive to the extent that for Minow (1998:26) reconciliation means "reconstruction of a relationship, seeking to heal the accused, [and] healing the rest of the community." From the perspective of democratic politics, reconciliation is conceptualized as a strategy to "assist stability, and democracy," as it facilitates "restoring dignity to victims [and] dealing respectfully with those who assisted or were complicit with the violence" (Minow 1998:23).

It seems, at first, that this concept of reconciliation is not incompatible with, but in fact potentially supports civic modes of togetherness of the transitional community. However, I argue that Minow's conceptualization is positioned within the imaginary of both communal and subjective transcendence and that as such it posits certain risks for a transitional civic order. By "subjective transcendence" I mean that the subject of reconciliation gains a public appearance in the process of her/his practice of a confessional mode that is part of an external and foreign normative regime. It is telling that reconciliatory institutions such as truth commissions are, at least partly, justified by reference to their therapeutic effects on the subject and the collectivities to which the subject belongs. The way to achieve these effects of "healing" or "liberation" (from the violent past) is, inter alia, through confessional speech, or self-disclosure. The relation between trauma and reconciliation is conceptualized as conditional: reconciliation as a process is premised upon individual confessions of enduring, witnessing, or inflicting victimization in the past, and as such by the subject's liberation from the paralyzing grip of the traumatic past.

Referring to the existing research on treating post-traumatic stress disorder, Minow has concluded (Minow 2000:243, *emphasis mine*) that there is at least "anecdotal evidence [of] the healing power of speaking about trauma [and that] the trauma story is transformed as testimony from a telling about shame and humiliation to a portrayal of dignity and virtue; by speaking of trauma, *survivors regain lost worlds and lost selves.*" What is at stake here is a creation of a historically specific subject of reconciliation: one that speaks (rather than is silent) and who complies with the rules of reconciliatory engagement (rather than, for instance, remains resentful and disengaged). The aforementioned "transcendental imaginary" describes hence an almost theological idea on which the overcoming of trauma by the reconciling subject is premised, where what has been broken is made into whole again. Within that imaginary, while trauma is understood as damage experienced by the subject as loss of one's past and as self-estrangement, reconciliation becomes a historically unique moment of transcending the trauma, reversing the traumatic workings of the past, and carving out a possibility of a radically different subjective and communal life from now on.

To be fair, Minow's argument is not animated by a fantasy of theological ends or cathartic possibilities of transitional justice, or about the moral renewal of the national community as in some other, explicitly religiously motivated reconciliatory texts (e.g. Tutu 2000). At the same time, however, the nexus Minow envisions between reconciliation and human trauma is premised precisely upon a transcendent reach beyond the boundaries of political (civic) community. For Minow (1998:25–51), justice is constituted by an external intervention into community that is politically (but also morally) damaged, and as such lacks an immanent point of reference to understand and to judge itself. In more practical terms, this plays out through advocacy for instituting tribunals that have supra-state jurisdiction (Jarausch and Lindenberger 2007:31). From the epistemological perspective of transitional justice, this transcendent reach beyond the boundaries of political (civic) community is an act of acquiring knowledge about the past atrocities that is imagined as external to the forum at which it is revealed. It moves namely from the realm of the private, shameful, and tacit into the internationalized forum of recognition and vocalization of individual stories of trauma. Philipa Rothfield argues (2007) that in this process traumatized subjects are constructed as "citizen-survivors" by their willing participation in the reconciliatory process through acts of confessional and narrative speech.

Critical feminism has argued that confessional speech, rather than being "novel" and "emancipatory" is "always already" politically and ideologically situated and thus can be teleologically directed (Acorn 2004; Scott 1992; Butler 1997). The performative aspect of the confessional speech means that speaking out, while discursively positioned and disciplined, institutes reconciliation, rather than is just its contributive and/or resultant element. I argue that when confessional performatives attempt to capture in speech the experience of trauma, they often deny trauma's apophatic dimensions, that is trauma being "away from speech" (Franke 2007) or a signification of "what cannot be narrated" (Felman 2002:240). Felman argues (2002:240) that "[e]very trauma includes not only a traumatic story but a negative story element, an anti-story, [. . .] the unanticipated story of the impossibility of telling." Ruth Leys, for all her disagreement with Felman's perspective on trauma, makes a similar point when she writes that trauma is not "subject to the usual 'declarative' or 'explicit' and 'narrative' mechanisms of memory and recall [but] traumatic memory is [. . .] 'iconic' [. . .]. Traumatic memories are 'mute'" (2000:247). In other words, the confessional imperative is not able to accommodate that, which "threatens" to elude positive modes of description and to remain unsaid. As such, confessional performatives are also an attempt to pacify, or make harmless, the unsettling and subversive potential of trauma and to develop what Kristeva (1982) calls "counterphobic object," which, in contrast to the experience of trauma, can be contained and mastered by the subject.

What follows from that critique is a problematization of the confessional speech and its alleged nonideological space of articulation and therapeutic outcomes to the extent that it testifies to the possibility of violence in the process of reconciliatory subject formation. By labeling reconciliation as potentially "violent" I argue for investigation of whether and how the subject's becoming is linked to her/his subordination to the confessional regime of self-disclosure. The meaning of reconciliatory transcendence that this critiquing implicates is that of the collective crossing-of-a-boundary into the psychic life of a subject and, as if, "pulling it out" through measures of encouragement and/or coercion to participate in the confessional institutions and social spectacles. While the mainstream transitional justice literature (implicitly) endorses the idea that a traumatized person liberates herself/himself from the atrocious past experiences by the means of their public vocalization, I suggest that at stake is also a measure of the subject's dispossession and subordination. At the same time, however, I acknowledge that this critique of the reconciliatory subject formation concerns a specific type of institutionalized trauma vocalization, namely one that is animated by the logic of transcendence, such as in the case of bi-/multilateral initiatives (institutional or other) driven by interventionist, impositional, or imperial ambitions. These projects are thus radically different from the initiatives of public narrating of subjective trauma that build upon the subject's belonging to a specific political space, her communal togetherness and the political character of intersubjective mode of communication.[2]

Civic Reinterpretation of Reconciliation

In response to the work of the "first wave" literature on transitional justice there has been a development within the fields of legal and political theory that brought into critical light the idea of politics on which much of the "first wave" literature relied. Among others, Scott Veitch and Colin Perrin (1998; see also Veitch 1999) have suggested that many of the reconciliatory and restorative ideas have been animated by the fantasy of social unity and harmony. Others have suggested that the project of reconciliation after historical violence has been underpinned by hidden desires for the ultimate demise of politics (Schaap 2005; Christodoulidis and Veitch 2007). It is important to note that the response of the "first wave" transitional justice literature has not taken a singular or coherent trajectory, but has rather embodied a series of critical engagements with the dominant conceptualizations of reconciliation and transitional justice. In particular, I am interested in those attempts at critical and creative reinterpretations of reconciliation, which have aspired to make it congruous with (and facilitative of) transitional civic order. This section follows the civic theorizing of reconciliation in the work of Andrew Schaap (2005, 2006, 2007) who has advocated the facilitation of "civic friendship" in communities affected by historical violence.

Schaap's idea of civic reconciliation in *Political Reconciliation* (2005) resembles a philosophical patchwork quilt in bringing together the elements of political philosophy of Carl Schmitt, John Locke, Charles Taylor, and Hannah Arendt. This particular sequencing is important because each philosopher's work allows Schaap to come a step closer toward his civic redescription of reconciliation. Thus, these thinkers, positioned consecutively, are not situated as interlocutors. It is also that strategy of "sequencing" that allows Schaap to juxtapose Carl Schmitt's political theorizing with that of Hannah Arendt and, rather provocatively, labels their insights into the field of reconciliation as divergent, yet also cooperative.[3] Schaap envisions thus a synergetic model of theorizing reconciliation, which combines (for Schaap, only seemingly contradictory) Schmitt's "dissociative" political thinking and Arendt's "associative" vision of politics. At stake for Schaap is thus a way of theorizing reconciliation as a politics that provides both for a "space of power, conflict and antagonism" and for a "space of freedom and public deliberation" (Marchart 2007:38).

The centrality of Arendt's political thought for Schaap's civic redescription of reconciliation is because of her emphasis on "worldliness," which is associated with, inter alia, the idea of an immanent civic order. In other words, it means that politics requires the communal recognition of certain relational withinness of its members, or, in Deleuzian vernacular, of the radical "immersion" of the subject in this-worldly affairs. Accordingly, civic reconciliation means that the political community in question engages in meditative and propitiatory activities, which it directs, as it were, toward itself. Here, the main objective of transitional politics becomes the (re)constitution of the Arendtian "shared life of citizenship" (Dossa 1989:3). For Schaap, in order to make reconciliation compatible with (and useful for) the transitional civic order, one needs to "truncate" it of the assumed transcendent layout (i.e. either of the "stepping in" of extraneous justice or of a theological promise of societal unity and the end of violence).

Schaap argues that reconciliation should be redescribed in terms of a civic mediation and the moment of "coming together" in the political act of recognition of and engagement with the community's past violence and injustice. In this redescriptive strategy Schaap, interestingly, brings into light alternative (and largely downplayed) meanings of "reconciliation." In this context, tracing the etymology of the term "reconciliation" proves to be rather instructive. The Latin word from which the English "reconciliation" is derived is *reconcilitin-em*, a nominalization of the verb *reconcilire*. *Reconcilire* combines three related, but also different meanings: it can indicate action of the recurrence or restoration of: (1) unity; and/or (2) encounter or confrontation; and/or (3) agreement or friendship. In my view, the attempt at civic reinterpretation of reconciliation means that one becomes suspicious of the first meaning of reconciliation (of the restoration of unity) because of its politically problematic implications of organic social harmony. The attempt at civic reinterpretation of reconciliation focuses thus on the second and the third meanings (as reinstitution of the space of civic encounter and communication, and of civic fellowship). The emphasis is placed, in particular, on the fact that the outcome of the historical violence and injustice is a destruction of the aforementioned relational immanence of the community, namely the mutual "public encounters" of its subjects. The objective is precisely to show the "this-worldly," or immanent, and political possibilities of reconciliation.

Schaap does not stop there, however. His conceptualization seems to be hinting at something more politically radical to the extent that he does not only suggest the concurrence of reconciliation and the achievement of transitional civic order, but also portrays reconciliation as a quintessential political moment. Of course, the way in which reconciliation plays out empirically and historically is always only an imperfect embodiment of this moment, or, rather, a movement towards its horizon. I suggest that for Schaap reconciliation becomes the transitional moment at which politics is at its highest, so to say, because of its underlying *aporia* of a community that is, at the same time, "coming together" and "being apart." Reconciliation is thus imagined as a quintessential political event because of its close fusion of the associative and the dissociative moments.

To rephrase this apparent paradox of politics as an accretion of togetherness and dissocia-tion, which, this chapter argues, animates Schaap's civic redescription of reconciliation, it seems that here the transitional possibility of civic friendship is achieved precisely because of the real possibility of political enmity. To be clear, the latter is meant not simply as political separateness, but as something stronger and more radical, namely "political agonism" (cf. Mouffe 2000:105–6; Dryzek 2005:221–3). Since violence and injustice are always a possible alternate way of the conflict playing out, the legacy of atrocious communal past for contemporary political moment is the destruction of the associative ties of civic friendship, as well as, and potentially more importantly, the destruction of political enmity. Rather problematically, adversity is thus perceived as somewhat disruptive of the politics of transition and of transitional justice. The very idea of enmity and political antagonism is disconnected from (and depicted as incompatible with) civility: antagonism is acted out in violence of one kind or another. Also, at a more fundamental level, there is no permission for the coexistence of antagonists: the goal of adversary identification is precisely her/his elimination or submission.

The Pitfalls of Reconciliation

In mapping the conceptual trajectories of reconciliation one should consider the relation between the idea of "conciliation" (*concilire*) and "conciliar" institutions and practices (*concilium-ar*). In English the notion "council" was initially used to describe two separate institutional practices: (1) the secular assembly of advisory (as well as legislative) func-tions, such as the Athenian *boule* in the fifth century BC, and (2) the medieval *concilium*, an ecclesiastical institution that resolved doctrinal disagreements and/or settled aspects of the state–church relations. Consequently, the contemporary English usage integrates the sense of council and counsel, that is, the action of gathering for the purpose of articulating judgment and gathering for the purpose of giving advice.

While this equivocality is, admittedly, not paralleled in the origin and transition lan-guages of that term (Latin and French), it suggests three points, which problematize the notion of reconciliation. First, the (re)conciliatory moment is preceded by and condi-tioned upon the communal gathering. Second, the communal gathering corresponds to an opening of a communicative space where the actuality of deliberation proves its (trans)formative power in either the strong sense of achieving some form of unified social formation, or in the modest sense of creating civic ties among its participants. And third, there is a dark side of this etymological venture, which is that in its earlier historical usage (both religious and secular), there does not seem to be a necessary democratic dimension of the conciliatory practice. On the contrary, this communal gathering presupposes qualifying of the "communal" in exclusionary terms, which here are either religious or profession/class-related, that is, implicating those who are authorized to make legislative interventions into doctrinal disagreements through their sacral connection, or those who are authorized to give advice, administer, and legislate through their claim to knowledge. Consequently, the Foucauldian matrix of power/knowledge frames the conciliatory moment as a forceful intervention, where, rather controversially, not only the theological institution of (doctrinal, narrative, and other) uniformity, but also the civic project of forming friendship, manifests itself as potentially violent for the subject. I suggest that there is a threat of disciplining interventions and of covert possibilities of violence not only in the project of "transcendent" reconciliation, but also in the civic–political recon-ceptualization of reconciliation. It might be that the very conceptual (and political) framework of reconciliation hosts the potential for violent intervention, which is not eliminable through the strategies of critical redescription. The reconciliatory and confes-sional framework determines specific ways for the becoming of the subject as a "citizens-survivor," the "simultaneous fixing and unfixing of subjectivity" (Radstone 2007b:68), which I propose to conceptualize as potentially violent to the extent that reconciliation as a political idea and a political practice spurs conflicting impulses towards and away from democratization. The difficulty with political theorizing of reconciliation is related precisely to this observation: its theorizing is marked by a tension because the concept hosts (apparently) irreconcilable democratic and communal contradiction. As such, reconciliation creates prospects for both (1) the subject's empowerment through the logic of the coming together (deliberative, narrative, and retrospective-reflexive) and (2) the subject's violation because it is not merely deliberative, but also strongly purpose-driven and unifying.

In this context it is interesting that Schaap displays a particular caution when discuss-ing the deliberative aspects of reconciliation, namely reconciliation as a communicative public encounter. It seems that not only does he want to avoid problems of the Habermasian discourse ethics, from which the transformative moment brackets power positions from which the respective subjects speak (cf. Rostbøll 1998; Thomassen 2007), but also that he recognizes that the communal reconciliatory deliberation is working upon an already existing and non-problematized idea of democratic togetherness. To avoid the difficulties of such a non-problematized notion of the communal "we," Schaap (2006:257–61) gestures at, and mediates between, a dichotomous construction of the "agonistic" versus "deliberative" democratic togetherness. With reference to "agonistic" democracy, Schaap (2006:257–8) argues for the "the primacy of conflict [over deliberation]" in societies riven by historical violence, recognizing the dangerous temptations of political fantasizing about restoration of the organic social unity or achievement of narrative unity of the past. The emphasis on democratic agonism–and, in particular, its vindication of (incalculable and unquenchable) political conflict, and its democratic effects (cf. Mouffe 2005)—is meant to counter the coupling of reconciliation and restorative fantasies of unity, and instead reestablish the centrality of political antagonism in the lives of transitional com-munities. While rejecting the notions of reconciliation based on the assumed transcend-ence of justice and on the promise of social appeasement, Schaap (2006:257–71) imagines reconciliation as a utopian movement "towards a community that is 'not yet'" and as an "[always] contingent political possibility [of 'we']." It is therefore "[b]y constructing democracy in terms of a mode of being, as an *experience* that can be lost and needs to be recaptured, radical democracy keeps before it an awareness that the 'we' that a reconcilia-tory politics necessarily presupposes, exists as a potentiality of political action in the present" (Schaap 2006:272, emphasis in original). In other words, a given transitional community is democratically "radical" because its togetherness is formed, sustained and practiced vis-à-vis the demands of a justice-at-a-horizon (its realization is inadequate, and hence justice remains forever deferred). The infinite demands of justice (for the past) make the community be and act politically "here and now." However, it is a democratic community shaped and animated not by any form of social cohesiveness, but by disagree-ments and antagonisms concerning, inter alia, the meaning, the practice, and the politics of that justice (for the past).[4]

Subsequently, if rather surprisingly, Schaap brings Arendt's thinking about politics as a "particular and meaningful manner of living together" (Dossa 1989:4) into the redescription of reconciliation. Here, the importance of Arendt's theorizing is related to Schaap's redescriptive attempt to think about reconciliation not only in terms of its civic possibilities of dissociation, but as an immanent political act. Also, it is thanks to Arendt that the event of reconciliation can be theorized as a moment of beginning anew (Schaap 2005:90–3). Through Arendt's concept of natality (1998 [1958]:247), as the "miracle that saves the world," Schaap hopes to illuminate the radical novelty of the current (i.e. transitional) political temporality as, simultaneously, separation of and the connection between the violent past and hopeful future. Arendt's natality, "the condition through which we immerse ourselves in the world" (Benhabib 2000:81) and thus become the constitutive participants of its immanent withinness, is also evocative of the "human capacity to begin, [. . .] the power to think and act in ways that are new, contingent and unpredictable" (Canovan 2000:25).

The nexus that Schaap constructs between Arendt's politics as a possibility of freedom realized in the public performance of one's unique being and Schmitt's politically constitutive notion of enmity is based on the linkage between antagonism and plurality. While for Arendt "political antagonism entails the clash between a plurality of perspectives that are brought to bear on the world by individuals," for Schmitt antagonism "necessarily refers to the conflict between two opposing groups" (Schaap 2007:70). It is precisely this centrality of plurality and antagonism that allows Schaap to imagine reconciliation as political and as an immanent gesture through which the transitional community reaches towards and within itself (its-plural-self) in a concurrent act of constitution and de constitution. What that (transitional) communal "we" has in common is, so to say, its lack of any organic or pre-political commonality.

Finally, it follows from the conceptualization of reconciliation as both the manifestation of civic association and dissociation moment that for Schaap the political moment remains a fragile and uncertain event. The unpredictability of transitional situations means that the difficulty of practicing "ordinary politics," or what Mouffe (2000:101) calls "the ensemble of practices, discourses and institutions which seek to establish a certain order and organize human coexistence," is framed in relation to that ephemeral possibility of the political reconciliatory moment. It is the "extraordinary moment [of] the *intensification* of association or disassociation between groups that is conditioned by the possibility of violent confrontation" (Schaap 2006:268, emphasis in original). The fragility of politics is thus linked not only to the temporal proximity of the past violence and injustice as such, but, also, to the ubiquitous possibility of breakdown, or self-destruction, that is coded within the very occurrence of the political. This possibility of self-destruction is thus conceptualized as one that also opens the "potentially world-disclosing or integrative function [of politics]" (Schaap 2007:60). Here, it is important to recognize that while Schaap writes about the fragility and uncertainty of politics in transitional contexts, he also brings that observation onto a more abstract and theoretical level, and thus suggests that the fragility and uncertainty as a generic features of the political, which is revealed in moments of violence when politics breaks down, or implodes. This chapter suggests that this "dark side" of transitional civic politics, that is, its imminent possibility of collapse (and the temporal proximity of violence) is thought of as not necessarily destructive, but as potentially formative and productive.

There is thus a difficult, yet potentially productive, tension between enmity and friendship upon which the civic redescription of reconciliation is founded, as well as this redescription's acknowledgement that there is nothing easy or obvious in the transitional (re)founding of the civic order. Where this chapter becomes critical of the redescriptive project is in regard to the framing of the traumatized human subjectivity in the situations of reconciliation and transitional justice. To put it in rather simple terms, does it have any particular significance or consequences that the community of civic friends/enemies remains traumatized by its violent past? Why does the issue of trauma remain unseen in the civic redescription of reconciliation, and what would be the consequences if it were placed at a more central position in the transitional civic order? This chapter argues that the fragility of that order needs to be related not only to the ephemeral moment of its occurrence or to the proximity of violence, but also, and more importantly, to human vulnerability revealed in the traumatic experience. It also argues that the category of trauma be given more central placement in theorizing of the transitional civic order. This would potentially (1) tighten up the conceptual linkage between the question of the fragility and uncertainty of the political (transitional and civic) moment on the one hand and human fragility on the other and (2) problematize the initial distinction made in this chapter between the immanent or transcendent transition. This could potentially unlock alternative thinking about reconciliation as a framework for considering historical injustice and historical violence.

In Lieu of Conclusions: Trauma, Periphery, and the Community's "Closest Outside"

This chapter has suggested that the distinction between: (1) the dominant or "first wave" discussions of transitional justice and (2) their subsequent critique, self-identified as a project of political re-description of reconciliation, is a distinction between (1) the theological or confessional notion of the reconciling community on the one hand, and (2) the communal conceptualizations, which are firmly positioned within the imaginaries of immanent political togetherness on the other hand. It has also suggested that it is only the second project that makes a connection between civic order and the community's "fragmentation." Here it is useful to refer to the conceptualization of "fragmentation" in the work of Marcel Blanchot (1995:60) as "the mark of coherence all the firmer in that it has to come undone in order to be reached, and reached through a [dispersion], [. . .] for fragmentation is the pulling to pieces (to tearing) of that which never has preexisted (really or ideally) as a whole, nor can it ever be reassembled in any future presence whatever." Subsequently, Blanchot also helps to draw the connection between the lack of recognition of society as "fragmentary" and the articulation of the confessional vision of transitional order. Namely, Blanchot (1995:64, 'emphasis mine') refers to Levinas' point on the etymology of "religion" as "that which binds, [and] that which holds together," and poses the question: "what of the non-bond which disjoints beyond unity—which escapes the synchrony of "holding together," yet does so without breaking all relations or without ceasing, in this break or in this absence of relation, to open yet another relation?" Taking a point of reference in Blanchot's consideration of the fragmentary, this chapter suggests that theorizing civic transitional order requires radicalization of the political being in common as nonunitary modes of living together, but rather as the equivocal event of "breaking," as connotative both of some separation, rupture, and destruction (of completeness or continuity) at play and of some creation, initiation, or liberation (as in breaking the habit, breaking the siege, or breaking bounds).

Furthermore, as Rothfield has argued (2007), the ambivalence of reconciliation (theorized as either "transcendent" or "immanent"), marked by its teleology of closure, activates the tension between the collective aspects of the community on the one hand and the subject's singularity on the other. Rothfield (2007:3) discusses reconciliation in reference to the Derridian notion of "pharmakon," as both remedy and poison, to suggests that reconciliation is a Janus-faced project, which, through its liberating promise of closure and remedy, "normalizes a pathway of healing and closure to which the survivor of violence must conform." Reconciliation promises to take its willing participants (the traumatized subjects who speak out) to a different form of political order and the embodiment of civic subjectivity. The transitional vernacular suggests that we think of the reconciliatory political moment in terms of the "span" between the irreversible (the violence of the past) and what manifests itself as (the possibility of) a hopeful future. Even in Schaap's civic–political reinterpretation, reconciliation comes to signify "the way in which the nation is to move on, beyond the trauma of the past, towards a horizon of peaceful coexistence" (Rothfield 2007:9). The past is declared "[to be] 'overdetermined' [as] it lends itself to the overcoming of a conflict for the purpose of achieving a common future" (Christodoulidis and Veitch 2007:2). An alternative way of thinking about "transition" would be through emphasis of the meaning of its prefix trans- as "across," or "on the farther side of." Here, the meaning of the word "transition" opens itself to a potentially richer interpretation than as a temporal in-betweenness, where the moment of the political "now" is imagined as a meeting point of the past and the future. Rather, that political and transitional moment becomes a gesture towards what is beyond (or, "on the further side"), that is, as a gesture towards the peripheral. This phrase hints at the distinction between the "marginal" and the "peripheral" as theorized by Noel Parker (2008). Parker's work is an attempt at delineating geometries of marginality understood as being on the edge or at the boundary of a political entity and of its area of impact. Contrary to Parker, however, who focuses in on the concept and the constructive possibilities of the marginal, as the "furthest inside," I am preoccupied with the peripheral as the "closest outside," the one who is almost, but never quite in, or the one who is right at the gate of the-polis. In other words, while Parker is interested in the formative potential of marginality, I am interested in disempowerments and impasses of peripherality. The notion of peripherality resonates with what Louise du Toit (2007:185, emphasis mine) defines as "borderline" (Jasper's *Grenzsituation*), which she calls "not a marginality, but *delineation*." Importantly, transition as a gesture towards "the further side" is not synonymous with a transcending reach, which actually opens the gates of the polis in order to draw the peripheral inside (and, subsequently domesticates it, makes the peripheral "feel at home in the polis"). Rather, the gesture towards, but never the complete grasp of, the peripheral testifies to its dark presence right at the gates of the polis, and intimates that in the transitional situations, one might be pointing at something more complicated than passage from one form of political organization to another.

The suggestion is that the communal/subjective trauma after historical violence and injustice is conceptualized in relation to the transitional civic order precisely as such peripherality. This peripherality might indicate that some (traumatized) subjects become vested with a status of abject bodies (objects of simultaneous desire and repulsion) vis-à-vis the transitional community. However, peripherality denotes not solely subjective or bodily abjection, but also a certain spectral quality and reemergence of the traumatic past; a past that insists on manifesting itself in the present, and thus announcing the threat of the recurrent disclosure of violence. Referring to Shoshana Felman's recent work on law, trauma, and testimony (2002), I suggest that if one looks beyond the imperative of reconciliation and recognizes that transitional justice requires acknowledging the community's peripheries, one notices that what lurks at the "further side" of the polis and manifests itself in human trauma is an abysmal experience. For Felman (2002:88), an abyss is "an experience of a break [a loss] of contact and of ground; [it is] a fissure, a dividing gulf, a bottomless ocean, a gaping wound." Here, it is useful to consider some of the archaic and mythological meaning of the notion of "abysm" as the "bottomless pit" or the "infernal region." For instance, in the New Testament the Greek word αβυσσος ("having no bottom") is used primarily in apocalyptical and infernal contexts. In Tanakh, however, the Hebrew word תהום is used in Genesis to designate chaos (the "no-being of the world," prior to the moment of the divine creation). Some cabbalistic literature, for example, gives description of a secret passage under the Jerusalem temple, which led to an abysmal space, which was placed below the foundations of the world, and where the foundation stone of the earth was placed. An important motif in those imaginaries is that of relating the world within and upon that, which has no positive spatial identification and no foundation in and of itself (the foundationless/the bottomless). It is, thus, the story of foundation of that, which symbolizes the visible, the material, and the actual established within and upon that, which is invisible and vacuous.

Felman (2002:94–5) writes that an abyss is "what cannot be totalized, what a closing argument will of necessity fail to contain, to close or to enclose. [It is] what escapes legal summation, what eludes reflective or conceptual totalization." In contrast to the civic and confessional theorizing of reconciliation, where transitional justice becomes a totalizing project, which premises its inclusiveness and achievements upon the declarations of its own possibility, the perspective of communal/subjective trauma both speaks of the inadequate politics of doing justice for the past and radicalizes justice as justice-at-a-horizon. The failures of justice, "have their own necessity and their own [. . .] speaking power" Felman (2002:166, paraphrase). Placing trauma in a close relation to the civic order that emerges after historical violence animates the following point: rather than declare violence to be a closed episode in the communal history, it requires acknowledgement of its continuing powers. This is not to say that the past has any absolute determining effect on the politics of the present, but rather that it remains in existence (at the peripheries of the community), thus contributing to the intricacy, difficulty, as well as insecurity of instituting transitional civic order. The perspective of trauma also suggests that we think of politics of transitional justice as coextensively "transcendent" and "immanent," and thus avoid the temptation to dichotomize these two categories in our contemporary political imaginary. On the one hand, instituting transitional civic order requires that politics is practiced by communal subjects who are "standing face to face to each other" and with their backs turned against, inter alia, the theological promises of collective unity. On the other hand, the human frailty and vulnerability coded within the experience of trauma point to certain "beyond-ness" of that civic order; both (1) the horizon of possibility and desirability of politics to respond to human suffering and (2) the unceasing threat of the impending possibility of collapse, without the necessity of its actualization.

Notes

1. Many thanks to the participants of the workshop on state, security, and subject formation at the University of Alberta in October 2007 for their comments and criticisms, Joanne Faulkner, George Pavlich, Kamila Stullerova, and Charles Barbour. A particular thanks goes to Anna Yeatman for her careful engagement with this text, and the contribution she has made into my thinking about reconciliation and collective trauma.

2. I acknowledge Anna Yeatman's authorship of this phrase and thank her for bringing up this point in her comments on my chapter.

3. This juxtaposition of Schmitt and Arendt in Schaap's *Political Reconciliation* (2005) remains highly problematic. While more in-depth discussion of that strategy exceeds the scope of this text, three such problematic areas need to be indicated. First, there is the general question about bringing together such diverse, and one could also argue incompatible, theoretical projects as Arendt's and Schmitt's, without elaborating and validating such a reading strategy in a more explicit manner. Is not the reading of Arendt and Schmitt as (almost) "symmetrical" theorists a misdirection, if not an imposition? Second, there is a problem of selectiveness and contextual reading strategies: what are the consequences of, for instance, separating Schmitt's identification of the political moment with dissociation from other aspects of his theorizing, such as decisionism or the state of exception? And third, and possibly most importantly, this strategy represents a somewhat reductive reading of Arendt as a theorist of civic association in that it does not consider Arendt's own theorizing of public antagonism and dissociation.

4. Anna Yeatman has raised here an important point about the viability of the transitional and reconciling "we," as theorized from a radical democratic (or agonist) perspective. In that perspective, the democratic "we" is infinitely deferred, a sliding signifier of a community to come, rather than practiced within its current spatial and temporal specificity. My reading of Schaap, and the way he employs the radical democratic perspective for a theorizing of reconciliation, is, however, that for him it is the achievement of justice, rather than of the democratic "we," that is infinitely deferred. That means, also, that "deferral" has a very precise meaning in that theorizing of reconciliation: it is synonymous to the radicalization of justice (not an agreement or a settlement, not a calculation, and not a retaliation), as a formative principle of the transitional and reconciliatory civic order.

CHAPTER EIGHT

Self-Preservation and the Idea of the State

Anna Yeatman

Introduction

In this chapter I explore the relationship between two ideas: first the idea of self-preservation considered as a right of the human subject to assume existence as a centre of subjective experience, to enjoy freedom to be and become a self; and second the idea of the sovereign state as the only possible basis of peaceful coexistence between subjects considered as selves.

The idea that the subject has a right to exist as a self is the basis of the modern idea of right. Of course the subject is necessarily plural, and so to say that the subject has a right to exist as a self is to propose that this is true of all subjects. A demanding challenge for the subject follows from its plural nature: how are subjects as selves to peacefully coexist where peaceful coexistence refers to a condition in which their integrity as selves is secure (or as secure as it is possible to be) from the potential violence of other selves?

The idea of the individual (or self) as a unique centre of subjective experience makes sense only so far as subjective life itself is valued and understood to be the phenomenological terrain of social life. When social life—its shape, nature, and dynamics—is understood as driven by the dynamics of subjective life, we have entered a world where self-consciousness and the functioning of social life have a co-determining relationship. Against this backdrop, we may ask two questions: Firstly, what is the role of government in providing an authoritative institutional design for the conduct of this relationship? And, secondly, how does government have to be conceived if it is to provide such design?

In this chapter I suggest that in the early modern civil philosophy of Hobbes and Locke we find two thinkers who work with these questions. We do not have to regard their conceptions of the self, subjective life, and self-consciousness as sophisticated, for surely they are not by today's psychoanalytically informed standards, although it is in fact possible to read Hobbes as a precursor of Melanie Klein's insights into the phenomenology of self-consciousness. Sophisticated or not, in their thinking we find as clear and true a statement as there can be of how and why it is that the sovereign state is necessary to securing the terms of peaceful coexistence for subjects considered as selves.

Valuing Individuality

Individuality is a way of being that becomes available to the human subject when she is invited to be present in her social world and relationships as a unique center of subjective experience. Individuality as a way of being implicates the whole being of the human subject, both body and mind as together constitutive of an integrated whole; thus it makes no sense at all to speak of securing the individual's life as though it referred only to her being alive in a physical sense. Secondly, individuality is a relationship. When subjects are invited to become present to each other as individuals, they are also challenged to work out how to relate to each other and to themselves as individuals, or as distinct centers of subjective experience. Let me elaborate on each of these two points.

Subjective experience is not just "embodied" as though the body were a mere container for subjective experience. Rather, subjective experience, or mind so understood, implies that the individual is able to experience herself as an intentional centre of animation where it makes no sense at all to set off one aspect of animation (sensing, feeling, thinking, and moving) from any other;[1] these are integrated aspects of this subject's unique way of being alive. In subjective experience, mind is embodied, and embodiment is endowed with the quality of mind.[2] Because the phenomenon of mind-embodiment is instantiated only in the singularity of the subject as an individual living being, mind-embodiment is present only as a unique order of being. In its elementary sense, self-consciousness refers to the individual's awareness of herself as a distinct center of somatic/subjective experience.

When the human being is valued as an individual center of subjective life, it is the individual as a whole person who is valued and who is accorded integrity as such. Put differently, it is the "empirical individual" who is the touchstone for the idea of right and for how this idea supplies the basis of legitimacy for government. In other words, if individuality is valued, a legitimate government is one that secures the right of human beings as subjects free to live their lives as individuals. In securing this right, government actually imposes the conditions of the right on those who come under its jurisdiction.

Yet such a government is possible only if the self-consciousness of individuals functions so as to make this role of government seem intelligible because it is seen as necessary to their integrity. The nature of the link between government so understood and selves is phenomenological in character. The challenge for self-consciousness is for the self as the unit of subjective life to come to understand that its existence is relational in character: it involves internal intrapsychic /subjective relationships that are dynamically and dialectically related to interpsychic /subjective relationships with its others.

In this chapter I examine the political conditions that are necessary for securing the existence of the subject valued as an individual with reference to the idea of self-preservation as it is offered to us by Hobbes and Locke. I focus on two such conditions. The first is the construction of the sovereign constitutional state (government as I have been calling it to this point), which imposes a lawful order of coexistence between selves—this is the judicial pacification of which Hunter (2001) speaks, and the social pacification to which Elias (1988) refers. The second is implied in the first: this is the state's provision and specification of the status right to be recognized as a self or individual in the conduct of one's life. Both conditions take on sense and significance only as they etch out the idea of the state as the institutional design, which secures the plural existence of selves—that is, their self-preservation.[3]

The idea of self-preservation is a modern republican idea I claim. At first sight it may appear to be a premise that also anchors liberal political thought. Liberalism, however, takes as its premise the freedom of the individual, which is a starting point that bypasses the question of the self and how it might be preserved. Thus liberal thinkers refuse to give such freedom any specification lest they should interfere with the freedom of any empirical individual (Berlin 2002 is exemplary of this refusal). Freedom is a central value in modern republican thought but it concerns the freedom of the self to be a self, and thus freedom can be specified in terms of what it means to be a self. For this reason it is possible for a modern republican conception of freedom to show why it makes sense to value freedom if we value individuality and proceed to confer the status of the person on each human being. Liberal thought, on the other hand, simply posits the nexus between freedom and being an individual, naturalizing the nature of being an individual, so that both of these terms, and the nature of the relationship between them, remain shrouded in opacity.

In order to secure the principle of noninterference in relation to the freedom of the individual, liberalism cannot supply an account of how the state as both body politic and public authority is necessary to securing the plural existence of selves. Modern republican thought in working with the issue of the integrity of the self is able to show how the specifications of selfhood lead in the direction of an account of the sovereign state.

Here my intention is to examine the idea of self-preservation in early modern civil philosophy with reference specifically to the thought of Hobbes and Locke. In so doing, I am claiming that they are better appreciated as early modern republican thinkers than as anything else, as exponents of "liberty before liberalism," as Skinner (1998) puts it. We can see what these two seventeenth-century thinkers have to offer a contemporary concern with the nature of subjective life in both its public and private dimensions only if we notice the role the idea of self-preservation plays in their account of right and of the state as public authority by which right is secured.

The Idea of Self-Preservation

Self-preservation as an idea assumes a critical role in the conception of the right or law of nature in the seventeenth-century civil philosophy. I contend that this idea provides the ground of the conception of the person as the subject of right whose integrity it is the business of the state to secure. In seventeenth-century philosophy the discovery of the sovereign state as a state under law as this conception follows from the idea of self-preservation is there for us to see and seek to understand. This discovery is presupposed by Montesquieu and Hegel (in *The Philosophy of Right*) but it is never again represented with the classical purity of first discovery.

Strangely enough, however, the idea of self-preservation has attracted very little curiosity on the part of those who are specialists in seventeenth-century civil philosophy. The interest of the individual in survival is taken for granted rather than interrogated, and the notion of the subject as a self is completely neglected in commentaries on this body of political thought. Such commentaries equate self-preservation with, simply, the interest of "each man" (seventeenth-century language for the subject of political life, a subject that in my work I term the patrimonial individual) in survival, as though this interest spoke for itself.

Even Vickie Sullivan (2004:94) who sees clearly that for Hobbes, "human life itself is desire," at the crucial point in her discussion of how it is that self-preservation becomes the ground of government, reduces self-preservation to "the desire for life" (Sullivan 2004:108). Here she makes an important discovery but she cannot see it: if human life itself is desire, then the desire to live, and go on living, as a unique desiring being is a more complex proposition than simply proposing that it is an interest in survival that provides the basis for Hobbes's conception of government. It is more like Hegel's conception of self-consciousness as "desire in general" (see the section on "the Truth of Self-Certainty" in the *Phenomenology of Spirit,* my specific reference being to Rauch and Sherman's edited text, 1999).

Commentators' lack of curiosity seems warranted perhaps by the terms in which Hobbes casts self-preservation. Yet consider the complexity already suggested in this passage, the beginning of chapter 14 in the *Leviathan*:

> The Right of Nature, which Writers commonly call Jus Naturale, is the Liberty each man hath, to use his own power, as he will himselfe, for the preservation of his own Nature; that is to say, of his own Life; and consequently of doing any thing, which in his own Judgement and Reason, hee shall conceive to be the aptest means thereunto. (Hobbes 1996:91)

In its simplistic nature the equation of self-preservation with an interest in survival misses what is so interesting about the emergence of this idea in seventeenth-century civil philosophy. Namely, the survival in question refers to the nature of being that is a self.

Thus when the individual uses his own powers to do what he judges best to secure his "own Nature," he is judging how best to act so as to secure his integrity as a self. This is why the idea of the self opens up in seventeenth-century political philosophy to become the idea of "propriety," that which belongs to each individual as distinctively his "own," where this is taken to include both his life and his liberty. Locke uses the phrase "the Preservation of the Life, the Liberty, Health, Limb or Goods" of a Man; and, as Quentin Skinner (1998:21) says of the "neo-Roman" seventeenth-century political writers he considers, they, in Nedham's words, speak of "security of life and estate, liberty and property." It is this individualistic attachment to the security of the self that for both Blandine Kriegel (1995) and Vickie Sullivan (2004) distinguishes modern republicanism from its ancient Roman counterpart as a liberal republicanism. Sullivan proposes that it is Montesquieu who clearly sets off the virtue of self-renunciation associated with ancient republicanism from the modern republican orientation to individual security: "Individual security, not selfless dedication to the polity, is the focus of the modern republic, he claims" (Sullivan 2004:4). Sullivan (2004:4) remarks further:

> Not only ancient practice but prominent elements of ancient philosophy, of course, furnish a stark contrast to liberalism's emphasis on individuals and their desires. Aristotle, after all, declares both that the city is prior to the individual and that it is natural. (Sullivan 2004:4)

Life and liberty are two terms that together demarcate what it is to be a self. Thus life is not "bare life" (Agamben's phrase) but life as it is lived by a free subject. Understood thus, it is possible to see why Agamben's (1998:1) use of the Aristotelian distinction between *zoē*, designating "the simple fact of living" and *bios*, "the form or way of living proper to an individual or a group," cannot be applied to the idea of self-preservation. Here it makes no sense to set off the animal quality of being alive from the *bios* of freedom for these are two aspects of being a self where one inheres in the other. As I have argued elsewhere (Yeatman 2007), the integrity of the self is focused on the question of what it is to be alive as a self who can enjoy a freedom of exploration of its potential and of its various possibilities of being. Here *bios* and *zoē* interpenetrate to become the way of life of the subject as a self who is free to engage in living his life in his own way.

For this reason in my view it is misleading, if not simply erroneous, to read Hobbes, as both Carl Schmitt (discussed by Schwab 1996:xix) and Carole Pateman (1979) do, as offering a conception of government based in the exchange of obedience for protection. To be sure, Schmitt's state is authoritarian rather than totalitarian since its legitimacy resides in the effective protection of the lives of those who come under its authority (see Schwab 1996:xviii–xix). However, it is not security for the subject's "physical existence" (Schmitt cited in Schwab 1996:xix) that is at issue. As Joanna Penglase (2005) shows of orphanages in Australia, generally speaking, those who ran these institutions attended carefully to the "physical existence" of the children in them—they were clothed, sheltered, fed, and educated. However these were institutions of endemic neglect, abandonment, frequent humiliation, and abuse in relation to these children considered as distinct centers of subjective life. If it is the integrity of the existence of the individual subject that government is designed to protect, then the subject's obligation to obey government cannot be understood in an authoritarian way;[4] discharge of this obligation has to be congruent with the subject's integrity. Both Hobbes and Locke argue that it is important that acceptance of the state's authority be achieved at the level of the individual subject, where each uses her capacity to think about the conditions of her existence to understand why she must obey a government designed to function on behalf of her preservation and that of other selves. In offering a thoughtful acceptance of the authority of government, subjects obey government but they do so in a way that expresses their attachment to freedom. Their obedience is of a kind as to continually iterate the ongoing legitimacy of government through their acceptance of how government functions to secure their existence. Without such continued iteration of its legitimacy, which is simultaneously a set of expectations as to how it should conduct its business, government could not function in the way that it is designed to do. Let me turn now to the terms of Hobbes's and Locke's arguments concerning self-preservation to show how they concern the *bios* of the living being that is a self.

Hobbes's Account of the Idea of the Self as the Subject of Self-Preservation

Turning first to Hobbes, his idea of the self refers to man as a living being who is constantly in motion as his passions direct him now towards this, then away from that. Hobbes does not privilege one passion in relation to the other; he accepts the empirical reality of the variety of human passions: "The Desires, and other Passions of man, are in themselves no Sin" (Hobbes 1996:89). He allows that different kinds of desire open up different kinds of ways of living for men; in particular Hobbes contrasts the kinds of desire that disposes the subject to value peace as distinct from war as in this passage:

> Desire of Ease, and sensuall Delight, disposeth men to obey a common Power: Because by such Desires, a man doth abandon the protection might be hoped for from his own Industry and labour. Fear of Death, and Wounds, disposeth to the same; and for the same reason. On the contrary, needy men and hardy, not contented with their present condition; as also, all men that are ambitious of Military command, are enclined to

continue the causes of warre; and to stirre up trouble and sedition: for there is no honour Military but by warre; nor any such hope to mend an ill game, as by causing a new shuffle. (Hobbes 1996:70–1)

Sullivan (2004, especially 90–8) rightly emphasizes how Hobbes's individualistic conception of each man as a desiring being is tied to an emphatic insistence on the equality of men as desiring beings. Hobbes rejects a view of reason that sets it apart from the passions and has it rule the passions; his is an embodied conception of mind. Mind both serves and articulates the passions in Hobbes's thought, and, on this count, there is nothing that distinguishes one man from another.

While individuals, then, may differ in the kinds of passion that are uppermost in motivating them, it is Hobbes's emphasis on how the self constitutes its own way of being through its constant motion to which I want to draw attention. To be alive for Hobbes is to be in constant motion. Motion is always voluntary, that is, it is directed by the imagination of the individual (so far Hobbes makes no distinction between human beings and animals as individual living beings): "because going, speaking, and the like Voluntary motions, depend always upon a precedent thought of whither, which way, and what; it is evident that the Imagination is the first internall beginning of all Voluntary Motion" (Hobbes 1996:38). Thus freedom for Hobbes refers to the absence of impediment to such voluntary motion; and "the Felicity of this life" refers to the capacity of each individual to life his life freely understood as "continuall successe in obtaining those things" which he desires:

Continuall successe in obtaining those things which a man from time to time desireth, that is to say, continuall prospering, is that men call FELICITY; I mean the Felicity of this life. For there is no such thing as perpetuall Tranquility of mind, while we live here; because Life itselfe is but Motion, and can never be without Desire, nor without Feare, no more than without Sense. (Hobbes 1996:46)

The constant dynamic of motion of the individual as a living being is driven by his appetites and aversions in relation to what it is that presents in his environment. Because the individual is in constant motion, a dialectical relationship opens up between his desires (appetites and aversions) and, what we may call (after psychoanalysis), the object world, including as this does both things and other people: "it is impossible that all the same things should always cause in him the same Appetites and Aversions" (Hobbes 1996:39). Each individual is a distinctive centre of animation (Sheets-Johnstone 1999) so that the subjective attachment of each to the object world will be unlike anyone else's.

It is the intentional or desiring quality of action that brings the self into existence as the unique living being that it is. The human individual as a distinctive centre of animation shares with other living beings this quality of intentional life. However, human intentionality becomes more elaborate and more complex because it is subject to what Hobbes sees as the kind of sequential thinking that the use of speech makes possible. It is in speech that human curiosity about how one event produces another is constituted:

. . . whereas there is no other Felicity of Beasts, but the enjoyment of their quotidian Food, Ease, and Lusts; as having little, or no foresight of the time to come, for want of observation, and memory of the order, consequence and dependence of the things they see; Man observeth how one Event has been produced by another; and remembreth in them Antecedence and Consequence; And when he cannot assure himselfe of the true causes of things (for the causes of good and evill fortune for the most part are invisible,) he supposes causes of them, either such as his own fancy suggesteth; or trusteth to the Authority of other men, such as he thinks to be his friends, and wiser than himself. (Hobbes 1996:76)

When awareness of how one event is produced by another enters into subjective experience, Hobbes (1996:76) argues that the subject develops "anxiety" about its fate in the future, especially knowing that it can affect how one event follows another and determine its future through its own action. A desire to control what happens in the future becomes central to how individuals orient their action in the present.

It is, then, of considerable consequence whether individuals are knowing or ignorant of causes. If their "sense of causality" (Nietzsche 1982) is sound, then they will be confident in judging for themselves and will not give up their power of judgment in a credulous dependence on the judgment of another. Such an act of trusting to the authority of other men must be for Hobbes deeply problematic for other men are oriented in terms of their own desires, from which it follows that their representations of causality are colored by their desires not those of the credulous. Moreover, if an individual is unable to think well, then he is liable to being driven by fear of "some Power, or Agent invisible" to whom he attributes the power to make his life miserable or felicitous:

This perpetually feare, alwayes accompanying mankind in the ignorance of causes, as it were in the Dark, must needs have for object something. And therefore when there is nothing to be seen, there is nothing to accuse, either of their good, or evil fortune, but some Power, or Agent Invisible. (Hobbes 1996:76)

It is all too likely that self-appointed prophets of one kind or another will seek to exploit such fear in order to advance their own cause.

Hobbes emphasizes the dependence of thinking on speech. Geometry as a set of propositions is not as dependent on an intelligent use of speech as is "the constitution of Right, Equity, Law, and Justice." Here it is not just a matter of individuals being able to think well about the relationship between antecedence and consequence, it is also a matter of their being able to understand "the signification of words," to use their capacity to think to subject the rhetorical use of words by others to their own independent scrutiny:

Ignorance of the signification of words; which is, want of understanding, disposeth men to take on trust, not onely the truth they know not; but also the errors; and which is more, the non-sense of them they trust: For neither Error nor non-sense, can without a perfect understanding of words, be detected. (Hobbes 1996:73)

It is on individuals' sense of causality that their security depends. They can learn from their experience so that they become aware of how the state of war leads to chronic insecurity and/or they can develop a scientific knowledge of consequences that is cultivated through study and industry (Hobbes 1996:35; discussed by Sullivan 2004:97).

Hobbes presents the science of human coexistence in terms of the first and second laws of nature:

That every man, ought to endeavour Peace, as farre as he has hope of obtaining it; and when he cannot obtain it, that he may seek and use, all helps, and advantages of Warre.

From this Fundamental Law of Nature, by which men are commanded to endeavour Peace, is derived this second Law; That a man be willing, when others are so too, as farre-forth, as for Peace, and defence of himselfe he shall think it necessary, to lay down this right to all things; and be contented with so much liberty against other men, as he would allow other men against himselfe. (Hobbes 1996:92)

In these two laws of nature, we can see Hobbes engaged in a normative enquiry of how must we think if we are to reconcile the three terms—uniqueness or selfhood, the equality of subjects as selves, and what Arendt (1998 [1958]) aptly terms the paradoxi-cal plurality of unique beings—that together constitute a sociality of selves. Hobbes does not consider his civil science to be arcane. While most men "are too busie in getting food and the rest too negligent to understand" the laws of nature, they "have been contracted into one easie sum, intelligible, even to the meanest capacity; and that is, Do not that to another, which thou wouldest not have done to they selfe" (Hobbes 1996:109).

It is not incapacity to think that explains why some prefer war to peace but rather passions that incline them to war rather than to peace. Sullivan (2004:98–101) discusses, as she sees it, Hobbes's radical "assertion of human equality" in the face of "centuries of custom" that associated the most valued virtues with an aristocratic way of life. For Hobbes, this way of life nourishes warlike passions of pride, a heightened sensi-tivity to apparent slights to one's honor, vainglory, as well as a martial orientation to the practice of war. Hobbes is especially alert to how pride can lead people to compete with and fight each other in order to demonstrate their superiority or to vindicate their sense of wounded honor (Sullivan 2004:99), and to how pride can nourish rage. It is clear that Hobbes thought that passions that habitually orient the subject come to structure his self-organization:

Pride, subjecteth a man to Anger, the excesse whereof is the Madnesse called RAGE, and FURY. And thus it comes to passe that excessive desire of Revenge, when it becomes habituall, hurteth the organs, and becomes Rage: That excessive love, with jealousie, becomes also Rage: Excessive opinion of a mans own selfe, for divine inspiration, for wisdome, learning, forme and the like, becomes Distraction and Giddinesse: The same, joyned with Envy, Rage: Vehement opinion of the truth of any thing, contra-dicted by others, Rage. (Hobbes 1996:54)

What is fascinating about Hobbes's account of the passions that lead to war (the destruc-tion of others and self) is that these passions, like all others, are driven by the subject's desire to preserve itself (this could be Melanie Klein at work). In this case, its desire to survive as a self is expressed in ways that make war rather than peace the modality of how one subject relates to another. For this reason he has to find a way of containing those whose sense of self is organized in this way. Sullivan argues, rightly I think, this is why Hobbes is antipathetic to classical republican thought, for he sees the "assemblies that characterize republics" as affording plentiful opportunity for "the desires of the vain and ambitious to be ignited to the detriment of the state and the individuals who compose it" (Sullivan 2004:101). It is also she suggests one reason he so clearly insists on individuals giving up their natural right to all things to the state; it is thus that the state becomes an absolute sovereign endowed with unlimited right (Sullivan 2004:99). Sullivan (2004:100) sees Hobbes as especially concerned to withdraw legitimacy from a superior sense of self that licenses it to assume the law "cannot apply to them, but rather to their inferiors."[5] Here we see Hobbes refusing to allow the state to be at the mercy of the vicissitudes of desire.

Let us now gather together the components of the idea of the self that we find in Hobbes. Firstly, we have a self that is constituted through and in the process of its desiring relationship to the object world (including as this does both things and other selves). It is a self in constant motion, changing through the course of its dynamic and dialectical desiring engagement with the object world. It is as this desiring subject that the self seeks to be alive. The self's desires acquire a complexity through how the self's ability to imagine is elaborated in both speech and thought. In speech, the self imbues its desires with meaning. Here we are close to the territory of the followers of Melanie Klein who investigate the mental aspects of desire (Isaacs 1989; see also Segal 1988). Since use of speech implicates thinking, it is not just meaning but also thinking that give desire a complex and dynamic mental existence. Just how the subject engages with meaning, and how the subject thinks, determines how their desire becomes actual in the world that they share with other subjects. This is of great importance when we remember that self-awareness has a distinctive temporality: its awareness of the relationship between antecedence and consequence leads it to be deeply invested in seeking to use his "present means, to obtain some future apparent Good" (Hobbes 1996:62). Thus he will do all he can to increase his present power to secure his future:

> That the object of mans desire, is not to enjoy once onely . . . but to assure for ever, the way of his future desire. And therefore the voluntary actions and inclinations of all men, tend, not only to the procuring, but also to the assuring of a contented life; and differ onely in the way: which ariseth partly from the diversity of passions, in divers men; and partly from the difference of the knowledge, or the opinion each one has of the causes, which produce the effect desired.

> So that in the first place, I put for a generall inclination of all mankind, a perpetually and restlesse desire of Power after power, that ceaseth onely in Death. And the cause of this, is not alwayes that a man hopes for a more intensive delight, than he has already attained to; or that he cannot be content with a moderate power: but because he cannot assure the power and means to live well, which he hath present, without the acquisition of more. (Hobbes 1996:70)

Now we are in a position to understand the complexity of the idea of self-preservation as it is expressed in Hobbes's construction of the right of nature: this being "the Liberty each man hath to use his own power, as he will himselfe, for the preservation of his own Nature; that is to say, of his own Life; and consequently, of doing anything, which in his own Judgement, and Reason, hee shall conceive to be the aptest means thereunto" (Hobbes 1996:91). It is the object of Hobbes's political philosophy to secure the right of self-preservation. For this to happen the individual has to give up his right to use anything and any one to advance his own power, "and be contented with so much liberty against other men, as he would allow other men himself." For Hobbes it is of little consequence whether the individual voluntarily accedes to the power of the sovereign state in its role of judicial pacification (Hunter's 2001 phrase) or whether it is the individual's fear of punishment by the state that accounts for their acceptance of the law that is imposed by the state. In either case, the law is constitutive of the freedom of the subject to be and act as a self in the company of other selves (see Skinner 1990 for his appreciation of this conception of "the compatibility of law and liberty" in Hobbes's thought). We can take Hobbes to be demonstrating how an individualistic type of relationship between subjects must lead in the direction of an ethic of individualism if, first, their equality as individuals is valued, and, second, science ("knowledge of consequences") is brought to bear on how their shared situation is structured—whether it is left in a state of war of all against all, or brought under the public authority of government as the sovereign power.[6]

Locke's Account of the Idea of the Self as the Subject of Self-Preservation

Locke's account of the self is less interesting than that of Hobbes for it lacks any concern with the dynamics of the self. The virtue of Locke's account is that it, more than Hobbes's, draws our attention to the status condition of being a self in the company of other selves. While Hobbes may be seen as drawing our attention to the basic dynamics of what it is to assert one's being as a self in the company of other selves, Locke draws our attention to a basic condition of selfhood: the subject has to be legitimately constituted as a unique centre of social action. This is a status issue (my argument here is similar to that of Pettit 2002).

Locke advances a version of the seventeenth-century doctrine of natural right that posits God as the creator of men, and where it is as though God endows men with the status of a freeman. This status is expressed in the obligation of each man to preserve himself and "so by the like reason when his own Preservation comes not in competition, ought he, as much as he can, to preserve the rest of Mankind, and may not unless it be to do Justice on an Offender, take away, or impair the life, or what tends to the Preservation of the Life, Liberty, Health, Limb or Goods of another" (Locke 1967:271). Let us enquire more closely into the connection that Locke sees between the status of being a freeman and the idea of an obligation to preserve oneself, and so far as this is possible, the self of others.

Locke shares with the neo-Roman theorists that Quentin Skinner considers (Nedham, Harrington, Sidney, Milton, and others) a method of specifying "the idea of civil liberty" (Skinner 1998:36) in terms of its opposite status condition: slavery. Skinner says of these neo-Roman theorists that for their understanding of slavery they relied on Roman moralists and historians who, in turn, based their views on "Roman legal tradition, eventually enshrined in the Digest of Roman law" (Skinner 1998:38). Accordingly, Skinner refers to how the Digest dealt with the concept of slavery. There "we are told that the most fundamental distinction within the law of persons is between those who are free and those who are slaves" (Skinner 1998:39). What is it that makes the slave unfree? Skinner suggests it is not so much that the slave is oppressed by his owner as that the slave is "*obnoxius*, perpetually subject or liable to harm or punishment" (Skinner 1998:42) because the slave is subject to the jurisdiction of his owner, and thus remains at all times in *potestate domini*, within the power of their masters (Skinner 1998:41). So if the condition of being a slave is to be the property of someone else, then this is best understood if we understand "the distinction between those who are, and those who are not, *sui iuris*, within their own jurisdiction or right" (Skinner 1998:40–1). Skinner continues with reference to the law of persons in the Digest: "A slave is one example—the child of a Roman citizen is another—of someone whose lack of freedom derives from the fact that they are "subject to the jurisdiction of someone else" and are consequently "within the power" of another person" (Skinner 1998:41).

Armed with such knowledge of the Roman distinction between the status of the freeman and the status of the slave, we are in a position to discern the status component of Locke's argument that men are naturally free—the following passage is how Locke begins his chapter on "Slavery" in *The Second Treatise of Government*:

> The Natural Liberty of Man is to be free from any Superior Power on Earth, and not to be under the Will or Legislative Authority of Man, but to have only the Law of Nature for his Rule. The Liberty of Man, in Society, is to be under no Legislative Power, but that established by consent, in the Commonwealth, nor under the Dominion of any Will or Restraint of any Law, but what the Legislature shall enact, according to the Trust put in it. (Locke 1967:283)

For men to continue to enjoy their natural freedom in society, government has to be so constituted that it is the public authority subject to the impartial administration of law.[7] In other words, government has to be so constituted that it cannot be directed by the arbitrary will of someone, a faction, or party, for this would be to wrongfully place freemen under the jurisdiction of the will of another man:

> To understand Political Power right, and derive it from its Original, we must consider what State all Men are naturally in, and that is, a State of perfect Freedom, to order their Actions, and dispose of their Possessions and Persons as they see fit, within the bounds of the Law of Nature, without asking leave, or depending upon the will of any other Man. (Locke 1967:269)

It is the role of Government to instantiate the law of nature in a positive legal order that is designed to secure the status of those who come under its jurisdiction as freemen.

Locke explains how the status of enjoying natural liberty is tied to the right of self-preservation. He argues that subjection to the arbitrary will of another necessarily means that one is subject to the power of another; and what is to stop this other from using, abusing, or destroying me as he pleases? The passage I have in mind here reads: "I have reason to conclude, that he who would get me into his Power without my consent, would use me as he pleased, when he had got me there, and destroy me too when he had a fancy to it: for no body can desire to have me in his Absolute Power, unless it be to compel me by force to that, which is against the Right of my Freedom, i.e. make me a Slave" (Locke 1967:279). Later Locke clarifies that the issue concerns the condition of slavery as one that contravenes the obligation of the individual to secure his own preservation and, as far as this is compatible, to secure the preservation of others. Accordingly, on this basis, he reasons that the individual cannot consent to enslave himself to another since this would be to contravene his (divinely imposed) obligation to preserve himself: "This Freedom from Absolute, Arbitrary Power, is so necessary to, and closely joined with a Man's Preservation, that he cannot part with it, but by what forfeits his Preservation and Life together" (Locke 1967:284).

The final comment in this section that I would make concerning Locke's use of the idea of self-preservation is to emphasize again that bare life is not what is at issue, but the capacity of the individual to live as a freeman. This divinely-given status is one that all men (members of humanity) enjoy on an equal basis. Thus even though Locke thinks in terms of the patrimonial household social organization of his time so that the modal individual is a male head of household, he is consistent in extending the obligation of self-preservation within the patrimonial household. The male householder cannot exercise the power of the master (*potestate domini*) over his wife, children, or servants, and, indeed, his wife and servants have to consent to join his household.

The Argument from the Right of Self-Preservation to the Rationale for the Sovereign State

Like other liberal republican thinkers (see Sullivan 2004) both Hobbes and Locke offer an account of the sovereign state as the only possible vehicle by which self-preservation can be secured for all individuals. As individuals, all persons are equal in their entitlement to live their lives as free beings. It is this entitlement that Hegel (in *The Philosophy of Right*) terms the status of the person referring to the individual as the subject of right. The only basis of legitimacy for the state resides in the provision of security that it provides for this right. This is "the republic or the state ruled by law" discussed by Blandine Kriegel:

> The early modern doctrine of power can be summed up in a word: sovereignty. Since the Renaissance, the law of the sovereign state has served as a foundation stone for every development in the law of modern states. The republic, or the state ruled by law—we could also define it as a state whose legitimacy derives from society organized for the good life, the general interest of the common good—confers a decisive role on law. (Kriegel 2002:4)

In this instance the common good refers to the shared interest that all men have in security for their ability to enjoy their lives as free beings, as individuals.

In each case, Hobbes and Locke argue that the state of nature is inadequate to the provision of such security. They emphasize somewhat distinct disadvantages. For both it is the disadvantage that follows from each individual having unconstrained discretion to follow their private judgment as to what they need to do to preserve themselves. For Hobbes this means that each individual seeks power after power even "farther than their security requires" (Hobbes 1996:88). Hobbes's argues that when individuals have a right to all things, conflict must ensue when "two men desire the same thing" (Hobbes 1996:87). His emphasis falls on the preemptive offensive action men are prompted to make in order to defend themselves in anticipation of attack or appropriation from others: "there is no way for any man to secure himselfe, as Anticipation; that is, by force or wiles, to master the persons of all men he can, so long, till he see no other power great enough to endanger him" (Hobbes 1996:88). But this situation cannot remain stable; he will remain in perpetual fear of his enemies:

> Whatsoever therefore is consequent to a time of Warre, where every man is Enemy to every man; the same is consequent to the time, wherein men live without other security, than what their own strength, and their own invention shall furnish them withal. In such condition, there is no place for Industry; because the fruit thereof is uncertain: and consequently no Culture of the Earth; no Navigation, nor use of the commodities that may be imported by Sea; no commodious Building; no Instruments of moving, and removing such things as require much force; no Knowledge of the face of the Earth; no account of Time; no Arts; no Letters; no Society; and which is worst of all, continuall feare and danger of violent death . . . (Hobbes 1996:89)

Hobbes offers an account of the logic of a competitive management of uncertainty (this is Peter Marris' concept) that follows from an individualistic social structure where there is no "common Power to keep them all in awe" (Hobbes 1996:88). He relies on men's capacity to anticipate the future when he assumes that after they have experienced what it is to be in "continuall feare and danger of violent death," enough of them anyway may be willing to think about what is necessary to establish the conditions of peace and to proceed to establish the sovereign state: "The finall Cause, End, or Designe of men (who naturally love Liberty, and Dominion over others), in the introduction of that restraint upon themselves (in which wee see them live in Commonwealths) is the foresight of their own preservation and of a more contented life thereby" (Hobbes 1996:117). Were this to occur, on a reciprocal basis, each would surrender his right to all things "and be contented with so much liberty against other men, as he would allow other men against himselfe" (Hobbes 1996:92). The only way this new relationship can be positively instituted is through the agency of the sovereign state, which imposes peace on those who come under its jurisdiction. It does this in two ways. Firstly, those who create/accept the authority of the state agree to submit their wills to the will of the sovereign in all matters concerning their common peace and safety (Hobbes 1996:120). Hobbes proposes that this is the surrender of the right of self-government to the sovereign in such matters. Thus when the state as sovereign power acts on behalf of peace and security, they are to accept the legitimacy of its action and do what is required of them to obey the state. There can be no legitimate difference of will between the sovereign power and the individual subject in these matters; as Hobbes constructs the relationship, "every particular man is Author of all the Soveraigne doth" in these matters (Hobbes 1996:124).

Secondly, the state as sovereign power institutes the right of self-preservation in positive law, but does so now, as the law of reciprocal right. It is by means of the sovereign agency of the state and its embodiment in law that the "propriety" or sphere of freedom of action for each individual subject to pursue its self-preservation as he sees fit is specified in such a way that the propriety of one cannot interfere with the propriety another: "These Rules of Propriety (or *Meum* and *Tuum*) and of *Good, Evill, Lawfull,* and *Unlawful* in the actions of Subjects, are the Civill Laws; that is to say, the Lawes of each Commonwealth in particular" (Hobbes 1996:125, emphases in the original). It is in the rules of propriety that the status of the subject as a self is positively constituted.

In both cases, sovereign power is imposed as the condition of ensuring a reciprocal right to self-preservation. It is important to see that Hobbes is offering a public conception of sovereign power. Its legitimacy resides in it doing what it was set up to do. If it is to secure peace on the basis of reciprocal right, thus respecting the equal right of individuals to "propriety," and to offer effective protection of their respective right to self-preservation, then this is the sovereign understood as the public authority. Should the sovereign no longer meet the end that gives it legitimacy, then those who have come under its jurisdiction are no longer obliged to obey the sovereign (to authorize its actions): "The Obligations of Subjects to the Soveraign, is understood to last as long, and no longer, than the power lasteth, by which he is able to protect them" (Hobbes 1996:153). If the sovereign power should act in such a way as to bring about either internal discord or a state of war between states such as to imperil rather than to protect its subjects, they are released from obligation to it for they cannot relinquish their right "by Nature to protect themselves, when none else can protect them" (Hobbes 1996:153).

Locke's account of the establishment of the state as sovereign authority is also an account of how men use their capacity to reason to discern the conditions under, which their natural right may be secure after they have experienced the radical insecurity to which the state of war exposes them. While Locke clearly accepts the logic of Hobbes's conception of the state of war, he emphasizes how impossible it is for men in the state of nature to be impartial for their wills are particular and too liable to arbitrariness in judging the justice of one's action in relation to another. He has in mind especially the mistakes in fact and errors in judgment that the private prosecution of justice readily entails especially if one is judge in one's own cause. Essentially, in the state of nature, men are chronically exposed to the problem of being made subject to the arbitrary will of another. So Locke's conception of the state is that of a public authority that makes and implements law in an impartial and nonarbitrary fashion. Locke argues that men have to give up their natural power to judge and punish breaches of the law of nature—the obligation to respect the right of each to self- preservation as far as is conformable with one's own obligation to preserve oneself—to "the Community" (Locke 1967:324). In this surrender of natural right, they unite into "one Body, and have a common establish'd Law and Judicature to appeal to, with Authority to decide Controversies between them, and punish Offenders" (Locke 1967:324). As with Hobbes, the state as public authority has indivisible power to impose and administer the law (Skinner 1990:135 emphasizes this point of congruence between Hobbes and Locke). As also with Hobbes, it is the state that establishes the "Rules set as Guards and Fences to the Properties of all the members of the Society" (Locke 1967:412). "The Reason why Men enter into Society, is the preservation of their Property; and the end why they chuse and authorize a Legislative, is, that there may be Laws made, and Rules set as Guards and Fences to the Properties of all the Members of the Society, to limit the Power, and moderate the Dominion of every Part and Member of the Society."

Again as with Hobbes, for Locke, should those who act on behalf of the authority of the state use its power to "take away and destroy the Property of the People, or to reduce them to Slavery under Arbitrary Power, they put themselves into a state of War with the People, who are thereupon absolved from any farther Obedience" (Locke 1967:412). In the essentials of the argument there is nothing that distinguishes Locke's account from Hobbes's. This may seem an odd claim given that Hobbes offered a nontraditionalist defense of monarchy, Locke a defense of representative government (for some discussion of Hobbes's "republicanism" see Tuck 1996; also Sullivan 2004). Yet the account of the sovereign state under law is remarkably similar, and it becomes more obviously so, when we start from where they based the legitimacy of the state: its public authority is derived from its lawful imposition of the reciprocal right to self-preservation.

Conclusion

Finally, I would suggest that this is only a beginning. Were we to build on the inheritance that these thinkers give us we would develop their conception of the individual subject especially in relation to insights that psychoanalytic thought permits us. We would ask such questions as the following: What responsibility does the state as public authority have for the cultivation of subjects as selves? What responsibility does the state as the public authority have for facilitating the development of passions for peace as distinct from passions for war? How can the state sustain its legitimate monopoly of force but not exercise it in such a way that violates the subjective integrity of those subject to it?

Notes

1. These four aspects of animation are Moshe Feldenkrais's (1980) four components of action in the waking state.
2. This way of thinking characterizes "the new sciences of mind" (Varela, Thompson and Rosch 1993:xv) that bring together insights from cognitive science, phenomenology, attachment theory, and, sometimes, psychoanalysis. (See for example Varela, Thompson and Rosch 1993; Wallin 2007; Siegel 1999; Fonagy, Gergely, Jurist and Target 2004.)
3. The structure of my argument is essentially the same as Blandine Kriegel's (1995) but, where she is content to work with an unrevised early modern conception of the self, I am working with a contemporary, postpsychoanalytic idea of the self in this chapter to flesh out the idea of self-preservation and make it a more robust foundation for the idea of the sovereign state.
4. "The state . . . guarantees me the security of my physical existence [and] in return it demands unconditional obedience" (Schmitt cited in Schwab 1996:xix).
5. The relevant passage from Hobbes (1996:205) reads: "Of the Passions that most frequently are the causes of Crime, one, is Vain-glory, or a foolish over-rating of their own worth. . . . From whence proceedeth a Presumption that the punishments ordained by the Lawes, and extended generally to all Subjects, ought not to be inflicted on them, with the same rigour they are inflicted on poore, obscure, and simple men, comprehended under the name of Vulgar." And further: "And that such as have a great, and false opinion of their own Wisedome, take upon them to reprehend the actions, and call in question the Authority of them that govern, and so to unsettle the Lawes with their publique discourse, as that nothing shall be a Crime, but what their own designes should be so."
6. Sullivan (2004:105) who sees Hobbes, along with Machiavelli, as supplying the constituents of a liberal–republican synthesis, proposes: "although Hobbes is not a liberal himself, elements of his thought point in a liberal direction.'" She also comments "it is not difficult to see how others, who accept Hobbes's notion that government is a construct to satisfy human desires and to promote the general improvement

of human life, would be tempted to create a wider sphere of inviolable rights around the individual."

7. "And thus all private judgment of every Member being excluded, the Community comes to be Umpire, by settled standing Rules, indifferent, and the same to all Parties; and by Men having Authority from the Community, for the execution of those Rules, decides all the differences that may happen between any Members of that Society, with such penalties as the Law has established: Whereby it is easie to discern who are, and who are not, in Political Society together. Those who are united into one Body, and have a common establish'd Law and Judicature to appeal to, with Authority to decide Controversies between them, and punish Offenders, are in Civil Society one with another: but those who have no such common Appeal . . . are still in the State of Nature, each being, where there is no other, Judge for himself, and Executioner . . . " (Locke 1967:324).

CHAPTER NINE

Society, State, Security, and Subject Formation: the Emergence of Modern Neutrality Society and the Formation of the Types of Subjects It Requires

Gary Wickham and Barbara Evers

Introduction[1]

Modern neutrality society is defined by the formal neutrality of the state and the judiciary regarding religion and ideology. It developed from the de-confessionalization of politics and law in early modern Europe, as part of the fragile civil peace put in place by the Treaty of Westphalia and similar instruments, whereby religion became a private matter, formally beyond the reach of the law, though only so long as the proponents of the different faiths did not seek to disturb the aforementioned civil peace. This technique for dealing with the explosive violence all too easily generated by rival communities of believers was later adapted, in the countries with which we are dealing (details shortly), to similarly douse the flames of hatreds born of ideological differences. We use the word "neutrality" with some caution, recognizing that some governments of some neutrality societies have occasionally pushed the meaning of the word to the breaking point, but we are confident that our readers will know that there is a dividing line between this type of society and the type that is formally committed to a religion, such as the rival Christian societies of early modern Europe or ancient or modern Islamic societies, or to an ideology, such as communist or fascist societies found in different parts of Europe in the twentieth century. Some readers may think that "secular" would be a better word for what we have in mind, but as secularity has too often itself become an ideology, even, perhaps, a religion, we prefer "neutrality."

Modern neutrality society delivers to massive numbers of people relatively large amounts of freedom and safety. We define relative freedom and safety in the simplest of terms, to do with the capacity of individuals to pursue their own goals with statistically little chance, compared to other eras or other parts of the world, of them being physically harmed by other individuals as they do so. While other types of society, either in other parts of the world now, or in any part of the world in the past, may deliver, or may have delivered, higher levels of freedom and safety to *a small number of* people, no type of society, at any time or in any place, delivers or has delivered what modern neutrality society delivers to such massive numbers of people.

Modern neutrality society is not, by our argument, the natural consequence of some innate human tendency toward higher reason and higher morality, as if humans have a natural drive toward perfectibility. Rather, it is an historical artefact. It emerged in early modern Europe as a consequence (partly intended, partly unintended) of the security produced by the development of an equilibrium between politics and law. This equilibrium soon included the modern state as a force in its own right, as a product of the tense politics–law relation and its notion of sovereignty. To be more exact, modern neutrality society emerged in England, France, Germany, and the Netherlands, though of course it has since spread to other parts of Europe, to the United States, to Canada, to Australia and New Zealand, and, at least in part, to some countries in Asia, and Africa.

If this politico-legal understanding were the only available understanding of this type of society, our task would be relatively straightforward. If we could assume that all our readers accept as obvious the basic story of society, state, and security contained in the above paragraphs, then we might, for example, have to deal only with issues of periodization and geographical spread, defending our definition of "early modern" as roughly 1450–1700 and defending the aforementioned idea that the origins of modern neutrality society lie in just four countries. But this is not how the land lies for any who dare to enter into the debate about the nature and role of modern neutrality society. The terrain is much harsher, littered with intellectual landmines. Indeed, where casual attire is all that is required to discuss the timing and the location of modern neutrality society, full intellectual battle dress must be donned as soon as one moves beyond these polite issues (which we do right here) and confronts the fact that the politico-legal understanding is not the dominant understanding in most university disciplines that seek to study this type of society.

The dominant understanding is one we call the abundant-reason/abundant-morality understanding, or usually, to make it less cumbersome, just the reason-morality understanding. The "abundant" refers to the fact that it is actually the abundance of reason and the abundance of morality that is the main distinguishing feature between the politico-legal understanding and the reason-morality understanding. The politico-legal understanding does include a consideration of the importance to society of *some* reason and *some* morality, but nothing like as much as feature in the reason-morality understanding. The advocates of the reason-morality understanding are very confident of their dominance, so much so that they see their champion not as *an* understanding of *modern neutrality* society but as *the understanding of society per se*. For these advocates, their understanding expresses exactly the form of society given to humans by nature (or, in some older versions, by God).

The rivalry between the reason-morality and politico-legal understandings is one of the two main themes of our chapter. We emphasize before going any further that we are using "understandings" here in the manner of Max Weber's ideal types. As Stephen Turner argues, Weber's "self-proclaimed technique is to intentionally emphasize certain facts in a 'one sided way' as a method of analysis, but his point very often is also to conceptually define a domain or conceptual space in which even the most extreme actual cases have elements of the 'opposite' conceptual category" (Turner 2002:1).

In focusing on these two rival understandings, our chapter is not concerned directly with the most basic sense of society, as an agglomeration of interacting human beings.

In this basic sense, the term is applicable to all agglomerations of human beings (and even to some agglomerations of animals).[2] It can be used to cover very small and particular agglomerations (for example, the school debating society) and very large agglomerations (for example, European society in the Middle Ages or American society today). It is used in everyday speech and in specialist intellectual fields. Examples of such specialist fields include qualitative sociology, which focuses on the details of the microoperation of societies (see, for example, Silverman 1998; Silverman 2007) and long-sweep historical studies of societies or types of societies. For the latter case, consider the following instance from J.H. Burns's introduction to *The Cambridge History of Political Thought 1450–1700*: "A watershed between 'medieval' and 'modern' European history has conventionally been located in the late fifteenth and the beginning of the sixteenth [century] . . . Yet the society of the three centuries following that period has increasingly been represented as a 'world we have lost'" (Burns 1991:1). The only other point we wish to make about this basic sense of society here is to emphasize that of the two rival understandings with which we are dealing, only the politico-legal understanding respects the basic sense as an important separate understanding. The reason-morality understanding does not do so because it considers itself to be the basic sense. In its terms, there is nothing more basic than the abundance of reason and morality that humans have within them as a gift of nature (or God). Many humans may well not make the most of these two gifts but in the minds of reason-morality thinkers that does nothing to diminish the bedrock status of both "gifts." For reason-morality thinkers, this is to say, all interactions between humans—and hence all societies—feature reason and morality, albeit sometimes more potentially than actually, as we will discuss in more detail shortly.

In the first section of the chapter, we will elaborate upon these sketches of the two rival understandings of modern neutrality society in setting out our argument in favor of the politico-legal understanding. We will keep this section as short as possible, drawing on some other pieces of writing one of us has done elsewhere (Wickham 2006a,b, 2007, 2008a,b,c; Wickham and Freemantle 2008), thereby making as much room as we can for the chapter's second main section. In line with a key theme of the book, this will be an exploration of the role of the formation of particular types of subjects (or persons) in the emergence of, and the maintenance of, modern neutrality society. In short, in promoting the politico-legal understanding of society, we want to explore at least some of the factors involved in a remarkable change that took place during the early modern era in the handful of European countries listed above. This was the shift from, on the one hand, the predominance of subjects loyal to their religion or to some millenarian sect ahead of any allegiance to a separate politico-legal ruler or ruling body to, on the other hand, the predominance of subjects who had surrendered to the new sovereign rulers and states—those rulers and states who and which came into existence in the period and places on which we are focusing—the task of deciding upon the goals of their agglomeration, which included them agreeing not to make the pursuit of salvation a public goal of government. These were (and remain) subjects capable of enjoying the newfound security gained by this surrender. Even more remarkably, some of them were (and remain) capable of separating their private personae, including their personae as "believers," in favor of their neutral public personae as officials and representatives of the sovereign rulers and states. In this second section, we will show how the reason-morality understanding features a very different account of subject formation and a very different account of what is to be counted as the ideal subject of modern neutrality society.

The Rivalry between the Reason-Morality Understanding and the Politico-Legal Understanding of Modern Neutrality Society

The Reason-Morality Understanding

The reason-morality understanding has its roots in Plato's and Aristotle's understandings of sociality, particularly through the Platonic premise of *homo-duplex*, whereby humans are seen to have two natures; a lower nature by which they experience the world and a higher nature by which they can rise above their base experience and realize their abundant capacity to reason. This understanding picked up a few Christian edges in its journey from the ancient to the modern world, through the likes of Augustine, Thomas Aquinas, Luther, and Calvin, but gained most of its current strength through Kant and his various heirs (see esp. Colas 1997).

For this understanding, society is an outcome of our abundant reason-driven quest for the moral perfection, which nature sets for us as our goal. For this understanding, society, alongside culture and community, is an ally of our abundant reason and our natural morality as they struggle to reduce the influence of and/or to control each of politics, law, and the state. In other words, for reason-morality thinkers, society, alongside culture and community, is concerned with the formation of fully reasoning, morally aware individuals and groups, the true building blocks of modern life. On the other hand, for this understanding, politics, law, and the state have no fundamental relation to reason and morality; politics, law, and the state can and do still have worth, but only if they serve reason and morality, which is what Kant tried to make them do and what those working in his wake still try to make them do (we will return to Kant later). For this understanding, this is to say, politics, law, and the state can be useful forces in the promotion of reason and morality, but only if they are strictly servants. They definitely have no place in the coalition of forces that is meant to rule human interactions—reason and morality, as expressed through culture and community.

It needs to be always remembered that for the reason-morality understanding, society is the supposedly natural extension of the aforementioned rule by reason and morality through culture and community. Those who are guided by this understanding therefore cannot possibly accept that politics, law, and the state have produced society. In their eyes, society is the stage on which the dramas of politics, law, and the state are played out. This is why such reason-morality thinkers focus so much of their intellectual energies on criticising modern neutrality governments. These thinkers do not want modern neutrality society governed in line with the demands of politics, law, and the state. They believe that modern neutrality society should instead be governed in line with the perfectibility thesis suggested in the introduction: that because of their innate drive toward higher reason and higher morality, humans have a natural drive toward perfectibility. Modern neutrality governments, it follows, are to be incessantly criticized because, instead of seeking perfection, they seek to do the best they can with the resources they have to hand, the resources of politics, law, and the state. The reason-morality thinkers are thereby forever using "the politically unattainable best" as "a stick with which to beat the attainable good" (Turner 1995:397).

The Politico-Legal Understanding

For its part, the politico-legal understanding has its roots in the much harsher "humans are dangerous animals in need of great discipline" Epicurean and Stoic understandings of sociality/sociability (see esp. Hunter 1992-2). Human beings, by this picture, have some reason—enough to allow them to see that they need strong rule, that they cannot trust themselves to rule by reason alone—but their will far outweighs their reasoning capacity. The politico-legal understanding, on its journey to the modern world, picked up a few Christian edges of its own, as well as a few Judaic, neo-Epicurean, and neo-Stoic edges, but gained most of its direction through the work of thinkers faced with the mayhem of religion-inspired civil wars, like Thomas Hobbes in England, dealing with the English Civil War, and Samuel Pufendorf and Christian Thomasius in Germany, dealing with the Thirty Years War, as well as earlier thinkers like Niccolo Machiavelli in Italy, Jean Bodin in France, and Hugo Grotius and Justus Lipsius in the Netherlands (Bodin 1962 [1576]; Grotius 1925 [1625]; Hobbes 1994 [1651]; Hunter 2001, 2002, 2003, 2204b, 2005, 2007; Lipsius 2005 [1584]; Machiavelli 1961; Pufendorf 2003; Saunders 1997, 2002; Thomasius et al. 2007).

For this understanding, as we said at the outset, modern neutrality society is an achievement of the equilibrium that developed between politics and law, producing the state via the notion of sovereignty. It is an achievement that relies upon a very basic element, which Hobbes describes in *Leviathan* in the following terms: "Fear of oppression, disposeth a man to anticipate, or to seek aid by society; for there is no other way by which a man can secure his life and liberty" (Hobbes 1994 [1651]:59 [Part I, Ch. XI: Para. 9]). Crucially for our argument, Hobbes insists that society is not natural, arguing that Aristotle was wrong to compare the natural societies of bees and ants with human society (Hobbes 1994 [1651]:108-109 [Part I, Ch. XVII: Paras 6–12]). The main blow he strikes on behalf of the politico-legal understanding is offered as part of his famous claim that in the state of nature "the life of man" would be "solitary, poor, nasty, brutish, and short": "In such condition, there is no . . . industry; . . . no knowledge of the face of the earth; . . . no arts; no letters; no society" (Hobbes 1994 [1651]:76 [Part I, Ch. XIII: Para. 9]). In other words, society is something which we cannot take for granted, something which requires enormous political and legal effort, something which both marks peace and helps achieve peace, and, in this sense, something which can be lost, if we are not careful.

To be more exact, for the politico-legal understanding, modern neutrality society did not emerge until the aforementioned equilibrium was able to contain the power of morality, culture, community, and religion. For this understanding, morality is not natural at all but is made up of a series of historical conventions, only some of which are conducive to the peaceful rule of individuals and groups. For this understanding, morality must be contained by bringing culture—the formation of strongly willful and only partially-reasoning individuals and groups—under control, such that new, more restrained persons are formed as new moral personae, in the manner suggested above and to be discussed in more detail in the second section. For this understanding, community is the agglomeration of the individuals and groups around different moral goals (and therefore always potentially dangerous to those who would seek to rule them). For this understanding, religion, if it is not contained as a private form of spirituality, is a special, particularly powerful form of morality, culture, and community, and so considered especially dangerous. And of course, for this understanding, as we have been at pains to make clear throughout, society itself is a domain of relatively peaceful, relatively safe interaction between individuals and groups, a fragile domain achieved only by the aforementioned equilibrium. Where all else had failed, this is to stress, especially, all theological avenues, the equilibrium of politics, law, and state succeeded.

The mechanisms behind the emergence of the equilibrium, and hence of modern neutrality society, included the development of the absolutist state, especially in France, the separation of a private religious conscience from a public legal conscience, especially in England, the development of forms of public law, especially in Germany and England, and the increasing deployment of neo-Stoic and neo-Epicurean techniques for making new types of subject, like constancy and decorum, especially in the Netherlands, England, and Germany. We do not have room to deal with all these mechanisms here (for more discussion, see Wickham 2006a,b, 2007, 2008a,b,c; Wickham and Freemantle 2008). In this chapter we will deal only with the techniques for making new types of subject (in the next section) and with public law (shortly). Before we reach the public law example, however, we need to briefly explain what we mean by each of politics, law, the state, and sovereignty, which will involve us further explaining the operation of the equilibrium and modern neutrality society's relation to it.

The Equilibrium of Politics, Law, and State and Modern Neutrality Society

For the politico-legal understanding, politics, at its core, is that set of relations which Carl Schmitt described in his famous essay, *The Concept of the Political* (1996 [1932]): friend–enemy relations, with no universal or timeless basis for determining either friend or enemy, but instead with constant shifting between the two and with an imperative that friends try to kill off enemies and vice-versa, an imperative that is more often than not displaced, into discussion, diplomacy, treaties, etc., but always potentially active. Around this "displacing" of violence, it is worth noting, some writers draw a distinction between "the political" (Schmitt's formulation at is most powerful) and "politics" (the activities around the task of managing a human agglomeration, particularly a city or state). We are not unsympathetic to this distinction, particularly as it is drawn by Martin Loughlin (2003:32–52), but we do not always feel the need to employ it, happy instead to use formulations like, on the one hand, "the Schmittian sense of politics" or "raw politics." and, on the other, "sovereignty politics." The Schmittian sense of politics is politics at its most raw and, in many senses, its most powerful. While sovereignty politics, with its panoply of offices and duties and its massive machinery, can be thought of as much more sophisticated than raw politics, it cannot be said to be more powerful. For raw politics is politics driven by the will, and without the will, all the offices, duties, and machinery in the world are useless.

For the politico-legal understanding, law is defined as both a servant of politics—it helps politics to rule—and as a check upon the excesses of its rule. This is the very basis of the equilibrium: neither politics nor law trusts the other yet both gain strength from the other, with the proviso that, as Schmitt rightly insists, in exceptional circumstances politics always trumps law. Of course, while politics is always playing with an upper hand, its hand can never be so "upper" as to drive law out of the relation altogether—something that could define a slide into fascism (of which Schmitt has been often charged, not without justification; Loughlin 2003:69; see also Pels 1998; Weiler 1994)—but it is "upper" nonetheless. As Loughlin puts the matter:

> [W]e should not forget that law's function—the duty of all officers of the law—is to maintain and bolster the sovereignty of the state. The constitution, as Justice Robert Jackman once explained, is not a suicide pact . . . Law plays a critical role in explicating

in the form of rules, regulations, rights, and responsibilities the character of sovereign authority. But if public law is to be taken seriously, we need to recognize that, not withstanding certain rhetorical flourishes about the appeal to "higher", "fundamental" or even "natural" law, the determination of the limits to sovereign authority, even when articulated by courts, must be political. (Loughlin 2003:91–2)

The equilibrium can operate under monarchs, military figures, etc., but it gained and maintains its importance as the source of the modern neutrality state. For the politico-legal understanding, this type of state is defined both by its potential to achieve goals like individual liberty and security and by the underlying fact that it gave the power of politics under sovereignty a massive boost over raw politics, allowing it to reach further than raw politics ever had, both in its capacity to control its target population—that within the territory it rules—and in its capacity to use that control for external purposes—whereby sovereign forces, whether states or nonstates, turn their political energies outward, toward the populations of other territories, thereby allowing more space for the rule of internal populations by ever more peaceful means, including discussion, civil law, etc.

In this way, for this understanding, as was mentioned earlier, the state quickly became a force in the crucial equilibrium in its own right. This is to say that the state was the product of the tense relation between politics and law, a product that was soon able to interact with both of them (politics and law) and even to seek to control them (as noted, in exceptional circumstances, states can claim to totally control law, but those same circumstances mean that even states themselves can always be trumped by politics). This did not, and still does not, we hasten to add, make governing through the modern neutrality state somehow angelic, somehow immune from the usual litany of political motivations, the grubby, power-hungry motivations no less than the noble ones. As Michael Oakeshott puts it, this style of governing has entirely contingent origins, being born as nothing more than "'the activity of attending to the general arrangements of a set of people whom chance or choice . . . brought together'" (in dreadful circumstances) (Oakeshott, quoted in Loughlin 2003:79) Our support for the idea of governing through the modern neutrality state, this is to say, endures in spite of its all-too-human failings. It endures because this style of governing and the equilibrium of which it is part actually managed to create civil peace in the most trying of conditions, when no other style of governing could, least of all those driven by reason and morality. Despite many dreadful lapses, it is still the best bet, as we keep saying, for delivering relative freedom and safety to the greatest number of people.

As for modern neutrality society itself, once the equilibrium was achieved, in the manner described above, this type of society was slowly able to come into its own, to effectively become a fourth force in the equilibrium, albeit a weaker fourth force. This can be most easily seen in the emergence, in the nineteenth and twentieth centuries, of pointedly "social" mechanisms of government, like social insurance and social security (see esp. Ewald 1987).

Public Law as an Important Mechanism behind the Emergence of Modern Neutrality Society

Public law is best thought of as a form of law developed to assist the task of government, by restraining and attempting to direct politics. In this way it is concerned only with the government of this world, in direct opposition to the idea that law should serve mainly to assist in governing toward the salvation of souls. In describing some aspects of public law, we turn to Loughlin's extremely useful guide *The Idea of Public Law* (2003). For Loughlin, "the basic tasks of public law . . . can briefly be defined as those concerning the constitution, maintenance and regulation of governmental authority" (Loughlin 2003:1). Focusing mainly on Britain, he argues, consistent with our position here, that governments of modern neutrality societies are concerned primarily with the provision of "security, liberty, and prosperity." In this context, he notes that, "The scale of modern power has . . . grown in tandem with the development of techniques that have strengthened the capacity of governments to appropriate and deploy available resources in furtherance of these basic tasks." Worthy of particular attention, he adds, are the administrative capacities: "With the transmutation of the king's servants into officers of the state, a decisive step was taken in establishing an impersonal, specialized administrative apparatus that could exploit developments in printing, record-keeping, indexing, and such like" (Loughlin 2003: 8; see also Brewer 1989).

Loughlin argues that sovereignty is essential for public law. He defines sovereignty as "an institutional framework established for the purpose of maintaining and promoting peace, security, and welfare of citizens" (Loughlin 2003:92). He regards Hobbes's interventions on representation as an especially important step on the road to the cultivation of this type of sovereignty, the type of sovereignty that lies at the heart of modern neutrality government. To help understand what Loughlin has in mind here, in highlighting representation, it is worth including a few points from Hobbes himself, taken from his *English Works* (Hobbes 1845, hereafter Hobbes *EW*). Principally, Loughlin is stressing Hobbes's point that a sovereign, whether an individual sovereign or a sovereign assembly, can only be truly sovereign—a public common power who or which stops "private men" doing to one another "a great deal of grief" by keeping "them all in awe" (Hobbes *EW*, Vol. III: 112–113)—if the individual or assembly concerned is *publicly* made sovereign by the covenants of the subjects (Hobbes *EW*, Vol. III: 161; Vol. II: 101). This is why it does not much matter to Hobbes which man, woman, assembly, or part of an assembly is made sovereign, for in every case the individual or assembly immediately becomes a (singular) public "person," the "representative of all and every one of the multitude," the "person" who or which always carries the force of the multitude (Hobbes *EW*, Vol. III: 171; Vol. II: 140, 158). Three other points help to clarify the importance of representation to Hobbes: (1) the sovereign "represents" the multitude in the sense that when "the major part hath by consenting voices declared a sovereign; he that dissented must now consent with the rest" (Hobbes *EW*, Vol. III: 162; Vol. II: 73–74); (2) sovereign power is only as strong as the multitude can imagine it to be (Hobbes *EW*, Vol. III: 195, 346; Vol. II: 88); and (3) everything a sovereign does must be understood by the multitude to be for the ultimate public good—"the common peace and security" (Hobbes *EW*, Vol. III: 235).

In line with this, Loughlin contends, Hobbes thinks of the representatives to a ruling assembly not as "natural persons" but "artificial persons" (Loughlin 2003:56). "For Hobbes," Loughlin continues, "the public capacity of representatives . . . must be differentiated from the private life of the individual" (Loughlin 2003:57). He makes this point even clearer when he quotes Hobbes's formulation concerning the times at which those who serve the sovereign are actually "public": they are only "'Publique Ministers,'" Hobbes says, "'in the Administration of the Publique businesse'" (Hobbes, quoted in Loughlin

2003:57). Representation, then, provides "the structural unity of public law," it helps to ensure that "certain standards are attached to, and certain limits imposed on, the office of the representative," and it "emphasizes the fact that public law deals mainly with duties that attach to such offices" (Loughlin 2003:57). Whether the sovereign is an obviously artificial person (an assembly such as a parliament) or a person with private as well as public attributes (such as a king, queen, or prince), sovereignty must be understood to have an "intrinsically public nature" constructed for the purposes of government: "the sovereign holds an office impressed with public responsibilities and for the realization of which he is vested with absolute sovereign authority" (Loughlin 2003:59). We will return to Hobbes's account of person formation in our second section.

To summarize, politics, law (especially public law), sovereignty, the modern neutrality state, and modern neutrality society emerged as parts of the same package of developments, the package which helped to overcome the crippling effects of ongoing religious civil war and helped to create a peace that allowed much greater freedom and safety to individuals living in those countries where the developments occurred. As our final point in this section, we stress that when we speak of modern neutrality society as a relatively free and safe domain, we mean the phrase "relatively free and safe" in a thoroughly historical sense. In other words, not only must the levels of freedom and safety be understood against what has come before in these countries (as well as against what exists in other parts of the world), the notions of freedom and safety themselves must be thoroughly historicized, in order to understand the complexities of terms like "liberty," "freedom," "safety," and "security." In this way, consideration should be given, for instance, to the careful way in which Pufendorf refused the idea that freedom is a natural right accompanying humans' reason and instead allowed it to have an empirical status only as a product of subjects' (or citizens') recognition of a superior, a superior charged with creating and enforcing social peace (see esp. Hunter 2003). Consideration might also be given to the work done by Pocock on the way a republican understanding of freedom, to do with the freedom to participate in the affairs of the state, was slowly transformed as it made the journey from late-medieval Florence to early modern and modern England and America, morphing into different types of liberty along the way (see esp. Pocock 1975, 1987; see also Skinner 1998).

The Formation of Particular Types of Subjects in the Emergence of, and the Maintenance of, Modern Neutrality Society

A Tradition of Work on Subject Formation

In turning to the formation of subjects, we are drawing on a developing tradition of historical and sociological investigation, what we call studies of personae. Studies of personae broadly encompass histories of philosophy, of person formation, and of political thought. The tradition is more a collection of family resemblances than a homogeneous corpus of ideas or perspectives. Examples of works that feature in the tradition include: Norbert Elias' historical sociology, in particular his trilogy on forms of life-conduct (Elias 1983; Elias 1994 [1939]; Elias 1996); Weber's work on forms of life-conduct (Weber 1989 [1930]; Weber and Mills.:. 1991; Weber and Spiers. 1994) and histories of ethics such as Peter Brown's work on early Christian forms of person (1988a,b), the second and third volumes of Michel Foucault's *History of Sexuality* (1986a,b), Pierre Hadot's study on the transformative aspects of philosophical exercises (1995), James Davidson's consideration of manners in ancient Athens (1999), and the recent collection *The Philosopher in Early Modern Europe* (Condren et al. 2006). One thing these works all share is the idea that no piece of political, social, or philosophical thought is without its own history. Evidence is gathered in pursuit of one or any number of such histories and/or against any attempt to grant to some piece of thought or other the status of a timeless universal truth, that is, to grant it immunity from its own particular circumstances. Rather than espousing yet another "theoretical framework," these works "open the door to a fundamentally non-Kantian approach to the self, treating this not in terms of a subjectivity transcendentally presupposed by experience, but in terms of one historically cultivated to meet the purposes of a particular way of life" (Hunter 2001:23).

Two Extreme Examples of Subjects before the Emergence of Modern Neutrality Society

We begin our account of the formation of the particular types of subject so important to the emergence of modern neutrality society with a glimpse at two types of subjects in Europe from a period well before this, 1096 to 1146. These two types were formed by religious/cultural identities slightly different from one another and against a backdrop of economic circumstances extremely different from one another. One type was the pious knight, regarded by Pope Urban II as the ideal Crusader, the other type was the poor Crusader who went along on foot, driven by religious passions not necessarily consistent with the church's official doctrines but no less powerful because of it. We acknowledge that these are extreme examples, chosen to make a stark contrast with the types of subjects that had to be formed as part of modern neutrality society's emergence. The details are drawn from Norman Cohn's *The Pursuit of the Millennium* (1970 [1957]).

Cohn describes the economic conditions for each of the strata from which these types were drawn (Cohn 1970 [1957]:53–60). The knights were from land-owning families. This meant that they were vastly richer than the other type, the members of the "poor army," but their wealth was far from secure, especially for the younger sons, who were unlikely to inherent a large parcel of land, new land in Europe being very difficult to come by in that era. In this way, the knights might be said to have had an economic motivation to join the Crusade, although their religious motivation—Cohn talks about the extent to which they were physically moved by the prospect of serving God as Crusaders—was paramount. The economic conditions of the poor were, except in rare periods when high agricultural yields coincided with a shortage of labor, vastly inferior to those of the knights. Cohn describes grinding poverty and hunger and a desperation to seek deliverance to a better existence via an apocalyptic transformation. In this way, the poor were far more receptive to the charisma of itinerant figures claiming to be the resurrected Christ, or Charlemagne, or Frederick, or some other such leader. More than this, or rather as an extension of it, the poor were extremely bloodthirsty. Cohn's picture of the actual conduct of the two types as they journeyed across Europe toward the Holy Land (1970 [1957]:61–88) suggests that the level of restraint that is so vital to the operation of modern neutrality society was present in the knights in only an embryonic form and not present in the poor army at all. The knights responded to the commands of their leaders after a fashion—mainly when their economic incentives combined with their religious convictions and with their family training to convince them that behaving in a more orderly way was worth their while—whereas the poor army were like a giant mob, following various charismatic leaders and, especially, their lust for blood (the charismatic leaders usually leading the way in this, too, which was part and parcel of their charisma). Especially pertinent in this regard is Cohn's account of the conviction by members of the poor army that they would not be as ready as God wished them to be to slaughter Muslims in the Holy Land if they did not kill as many Jews as possible as they trekked across Europe; as such, they actively sought out and destroyed the Jewish population of each town they passed (1970 [1957]:74–80).

The Reason-Morality Understanding's Account of Subject Formation

As Kant provides far and away the dominant reason-morality means of thinking about subject formation, as part of his dominant philosophical framework for tying reason and morality together—the formidable basis for the reason-morality understanding of modern neutrality society—we will concentrate here upon his influence.

For Ian Hunter, "the modern humanities academy is . . . saturated by Kantian styles of thought" (Hunter 2001:274) in the form of philosophically informed critical techniques, which,

> have given rise to an expansive and vehement apologetics in which a whole series of mutually hostile dyads—the formal and the material, the semiotic and the economic, the sociological and the psychoanalytic, the logic of *différence* and the logic of society—do battle for the privilege of foundational status or else seek peace in an endless series of dialectical reconciliations. (Hunter 2006:79)

Rather than appreciating these techniques as historical artefacts, each with its own historical trajectory, in the reason-morality tradition they are put forward as harmonizing techniques for establishing universal truths. As David Saunders puts it, "Kant's commitment to the one all-transcending end—humanity's advance to the pure rationality of moral reflection"—means that all empirical modes of life become merely "provisional modes of being, pending our ascent to morality" (Saunders 1997:100), "all spheres of positive conduct—courtly, legal, administrative, military, commercial—become no more than "semblances of morality" (Saunders 1997:67).

In line with these points, Hunter argues that the fundamental aim of Kantian moral philosophy is to impose the foundational principle of a metaphysics of morals. For Kant, Hunter goes on, the metaphysics of morals must be addressed a priori, that is, without empirical knowledge of human beings and their behavior. For Kant, "it is of the utmost necessity to work out . . . a pure moral philosophy . . . completely cleansed of everything that may be only empirical and that belongs to anthropology." In Kant's own words:

> For, that there must be such a philosophy is clear of itself from the common idea of duty and of moral laws. Everyone must grant that a law, if it is to hold morally, that is, as a ground of an obligation, must carry with it absolute necessity; that, for example, the command "thou shalt not lie" does not hold only for human beings [*Menschen*], as if other rational beings [*vernünftige Wesen*] did not have to heed it, and similarly

with all other genuine moral laws; that, therefore, the ground of obligation must not be sought in the nature of the human being or in the circumstances of the world in which he is placed, but solely a priori in concepts of pure reason. (Kant, quoted in Hunter 2002:911)

For Kant, then, and for the reason-morality understanding itself, the ultimate principle of morality must come from a metaphysics of morals, the moral law, which is conceived so abstractly that it is capable of guiding us to the right action in application to every possible set of circumstances. In Kantian terms, this law must have the formal property of universality, by virtue of which it can be applied at all times to every moral agent (Audi 1999:940). The subjects of modern neutrality society, by the reason-morality way of thinking, have to be formed as potentially fully reasoning, fully moral individuals, whether they realize that potential or not, simply because *all* human subjects are formed in this way.

The Politico-Legal Account of Subject Formation

An important feature of the politico-legal account of subject formation, as we have hinted on several occasions, is the idea that techniques and practices of the self are not bound to a necessary moral ideal at all. In place of the centrality of the necessary moral ideal, this account of subject formation focuses upon "definite means for 'conducting' a life, or part of a life—'an ensemble of techniques and practices' for making oneself act in one set of ways rather than another" (Hunter 1992:348; see also Hunter 2008). We turn now to some aspects of the contribution made to this means of describing subject formation by each of four key early modern figures, all of whom were mentioned earlier: Lipsius (writing in the late sixteenth century), Hobbes (writing from the 1630s until his death in 1679), Pufendorf (a keen follower of Hobbes, writing from the 1660s to the 1690s), and Thomasius (Pufendorf's pupil, writing at the end of the seventeenth and into the eighteenth century).

Justus Lipsius

Where later writers, like Hobbes, Pufendorf, and Thomasius, were concerned with the formation of the types of persons needed to run the institutions that made up the emerging state—officials and representatives capable of thinking and acting beyond their confessional allegiances and in the interests of what we would now regard as "good administration"—Lipsius, the main neo-Stoic writer of the period, sought to confront a crucial preliminary step—teaching the subjects concerned to remain firm and patient in the face of deadly violence.

Having witnessed the carnage of religious conflict, in the form of the Dutch revolt against Spain, Lipsius had, by the middle of the sixteenth century, became frustrated with Greek philosophy. It was, he felt, totally impractical. In its place, he took up the Roman Stoicism of Seneca and Epictetus and used it to build a secular political ethics for his country's civil servants, merchants, and military officers (Oestreich 1982:5–9, 14–15, 31). In this way, Lipsius sought to unite the conflicting confessions by the use an active yet undogmatic faith suited to Catholicism *and* to the Protestant confessions, a type of rational impartiality, combining humanistic piety and the reason of Roman Stoicism, thus giving birth to early modern neo-Stoicism (Oestreich 1975:182).

Of particular importance are Lipsius' three main "steering" doctrines, as Gerhard Oestreich calls them:

> In the triad *constantia, patientia, firmitas* (steadfastness, patience, firmness) Lipsius gave to his age, an age of bloody religious strife, the watchword for resistance against the external ills of the world. His . . . philosophy acquired a leading position in European thought . . . The Neostoic philosophy which it inaugurated became common property. (Oestreich 1982:13–14)

Lipsius' most influential work was *De Constantia*, first published in 1584 (Lipsius 2005 [1584]). This book takes "the form of a conversation between the author," fleeing the religious violence destroying his home town of Louvain, "and an older friend committed to the Stoic doctrines," especially the three referred to above. "The aim of constancy was to achieve a 'right and immoueable strength of the minde,'" while the aim of patience was "to resist the importunities of passion, and . . . to avoid one's reason being overtaken by *opinio*, that is, by 'vain imagining'" (Saunders 1997:86, quoting Lipsius and Oestreich). The firmness adds the steel, to make up the ideal individual, one "who acts according to reason, is answerable to himself, controls his emotions, and is ready to fight." In this way, Lipsius' "neo-Stoic man of constancy was a secular alternative to the contemporary enthusiasm for Christian models," and it was the centerpiece of his "contribution to the Dutch achievement of producing personnel for military, juridical and administrative offices, men equipped to set aside their religious beliefs in order to perform official functions for the State" (Saunders 1997:87). When combined with humanist piety, Stoicism gave Lipsius the perfect philosophy for separating inner values from the external world, which, in practice, provided a method for producing the type of person who could lead an active religious life without engaging in dogmatic confessional conflict (Oestreich 1982:33).

Thomas Hobbes

Where we earlier discussed Hobbes as part of our account of the basis of the politico-legal understanding of modern neutrality society, here we draw on a theme in his work that is perhaps less prominent than his directly political thinking. It was touched upon when we discussed Loughlin's account of sovereignty, in which, it will be recalled, Loughlin makes good use of Hobbes' distinction between natural persons and artificial persons. Loughlin is aware, where perhaps many thinkers are not, that behind Hobbes' political philosophy lies a commitment to the idea of the formation of types of subjects capable of both contributing to higher levels of safety and enjoying greater freedoms. It is worth bearing in mind that Blandine Kriegel calls Hobbes "the true founder of the modern doctrine of subjective rights," or "human rights" as they have come to be called, arguing that "at the heart of . . . security," as Hobbes advocated it, stands the "preservation of individual life" (Kriegel 1995:38–9), while Gershon Weiler insists that Hobbes was "at pains to make the idea [of the state] human i.e. rationally both illuminating and persuasive" (Weiler 1994:37–8).

It is in this context that we turn to an essay by David Burchell that highlights Hobbes's understanding of the project of subject formation and discusses Hobbes's debt to Lipsius.

Burchell is interested in Hobbes's "civic thought not as a contribution to modern conceptions of the social contract, but as a political picture of the formation of civic attributes and civic personality." In this way, Burchell seeks to place Hobbes's account "in the context of a much wider conception of the citizen—a conception . . . characteristic of much of the thinking aligned with the emergence of the early modern administrative states" (Burchell 1999:507). Burchell carefully draws out Hobbes's portrait of "the modern individual as a citizen created by discipline," a portrait put together as "a direct riposte to the classical Aristotelian assumption that the human capacity for civic sociability was natural and innate" (Burchell 1999:507–9).

In bringing the opening phase of his discussion to a close, Burchell makes much of the meaning of the word *disciplina* in the following Latin sentence from Hobbes's *De cive*: "*'Ad societatem ergo homo aptus, non natura sed disciplina factus est'*" (Hobbes, quoted in Burchell 1999:507). The contemporary English translator—unauthorized and hence anonymous—rendered *disciplina* as 'education' in translating the sentence thus: "'Man is made fit for society not by nature, but by education'" (Hobbes, quoted in Burchell 1999:509). Burchell argues that by Hobbes's time *disciplina* already "had a decidedly wider meaning than the English equivalent provided by his unauthorized translator. It covered the full range of instruction, tuition and teaching, yet was also used in classical Latin to denote all those subjects capable of instruction (science, art, morals, politics)." Furthermore, in "medieval clerical life," it "additionally denoted those techniques and rules which served to create an image of pious comportment" and "connoted most of the range of meanings attached to discipline in the modern English sense of the word, and some others besides: military discipline, the discipline of the household, as well as the science of government and statesmanship." Burchell summarizes his argument about this crucial (mis)translation in the following terms: "In short, it seems likely that Hobbes meant here not merely the effects of formal pedagogical instruction as such, but also the much wider range of 'disciplines' by which human beings are 'made fit' for the various social roles which they inhabit as responsible citizens" (Burchell 1999:510). We might, in the wake of Burchell's points and in the wake of our argument that Hobbes is a founding figure of the politico-legal understanding of society, usefully retranslate the Latin sentence as follows: "Man is fitted for society not by nature but by accomplished discipline" (our translation).

In the remainder of his piece, Burchell goes on to trace Hobbes's debt to "the later Renaissance humanists" in general and to Lipsius in particular (Burchell 1999:511–23). As we have already outlined Lipsius's contribution, we do not need to follow every contour of Burchell's argument, but it is well worth our while to summarize his conclusion, for here he makes clear, in terms perfect for our chapter, exactly why Hobbes was borrowing so heavily from Lipsius and other humanists—precisely in order to propose just the type of citizen required for politico-legal society, the type that is still very much required for the successful operation of modern neutrality society:

> Just as the "passive" model of citizenship . . . [of] the subject territories of the Roman empire "was relatively easy to extend to a large and heterogenous "population", the new subject-citizens of the Continental territorial states became a heterogenous "population" capable of being inducted into a common culture of citizenship defined by the virtues of self-discipline and the external disciplines imposed by the

framework of police... [T]he emergence of this conception of the subject-as-citizen, of the citizen whose primary tasks, in Pufendorf's words, were to show "respect, loyalty and obedience to the governors of his state" and to live in "peace and friendship" with "his fellow-citizens" . . . constituted the emergence of a distinctively modern conception of the mass of a relatively undifferentiated population as the potential citizens of a territorial administrative state. And this . . . is the same fundamental conception which, with a number of important modifications, has animated the citizenship of the modern . . . states. (Burchell 1999:524–5, quoting Walzer and Pufendorf)

Samuel Pufendorf

Pufendorf saw with his own eyes the devastating effects of the Thirty Years War, where large-scale killing stemmed from the fact that each of the rival Christian confessions claimed a monopoly on ticket distribution for the journey to heaven. As Saunders puts it, the war "had been pursued for a divine end: to gain one's citizenship in heaven by eradicating others' heresy on earth" (Saunders 2002:2174). Pufendorf sought to secure a new type of society "within the orbit of this life." The ideal subject of this new politico-legal society would lead a life "'in society with others' . . . for an end that was merely civil and nothing higher" (Saunders 2002:2174). In order to arrive at his position, Pufendorf cut "the knot of metaphysical anthropology" (the same knot Kant later spent so much energy re-tying). He knew full well that "this is where the threads joining civil authority and transcendent truth are tied the tightest" (Hunter 2001:152). He used this insight in formulating a new type of natural law, in which the separation of government and religion would result in the formation of a new type of society and, within it, new types of civil rulers and citizens.

According to Saunders, Pufendorf's intention was "to abolish in natural law all theological controversies" and all traces of metaphysical conceptions of morality (Saunders 2002:2180–1). Pufendorf wanted a natural law that would provide "rules only for civil peace and public security, not a stairway to salvation" (Saunders 2002:2179). He effectively substituted an ethics of civil conduct for a metaphysics of morality. In the terms of Pufendorf's position, each individual can occupy several "statuses" at any one time, thereby operating as different personae. Thus one "can simultaneously be the head of his family, a senator in parliament, a lawyer in a court of justice." Moreover, he proposed that "the obligations attached to any one state [status] may in their parts be derived from different principles," insisting that "no status is morally so fundamental that its rights transcend the rights attaching to other statuses." Crucially, especially for the politico-legal understanding, it follows that clerical duties do not entail "exemption from duties imposed by civil government." For Pufendorf's way of thinking, state and church have different aspirations and so different personae (Saunders 2002:2183). In this way, political jurists, like Pufendorf himself, "might be profoundly religious *as men*; however, in their office *as political jurists* . . . they could acquire the difficult capacity for religious neutrality" (Saunders 2002:2179). Saunders summarizes this achievement in the following terms: "Pufendorf's construction of natural law as conventional and imposed invites us to consider law and the civil institutions of the state in their historical positivity, that is, in their own terms, not in terms of nature, theology or morality" (Saunders 2002:2185).

Christian Thomasius

Thomasius, like Lipsius, tackled the matter of civil conduct within a deconfessionalized state by using a triad of "conceptual categories." Thomasius's categories were not the same as those used by Lipsius—where Lipsius had used *constantia, patentia,* and *firmitas,* Thomasius used *honestum, decorum,* and *justum*—but their intended effects were similar (Barnard 1971: 236–9). The main difference is that where Lipsius treated his ethic of *constantia,* or steadfastness, as a neo-Stoic type of inner-distance, Thomasius treated his ethic of *decorum,* at least in part, as a type of accountability, *Rechenschaft,* where the "*Rechen* part in *Rechenschaft,* like the account part in accountability, is not to be identified with cold rationality of the calculus"; it is, for Thomasius, neither "a strictly moral or legal category" but "a certain weighing of costs and benefits, and a 'reckoning' of consequences" (Barnard 1988: 590-591). As Saunders puts it, for Thomasius,

> The *honestum* is the sphere of moral conscience and governs our actions by inner piety and the spiritual pangs of conscience. The *justum* is the sphere of law and governs our actions by public legal sanctions. The *decorum* is the sphere of manners and politics, governed by social norms. The three spheres did not form a hierarchy in which *decorum* and *justum* were steps towards morality or *honestum.* On the contrary, Thomasius' aim was to insulate law and manners from the devastation that religious conscience and moral absolutes had wreaked when pursued into reality. (Saunders 1997:92)

It was *decorum* that came to play the most prominent role. "Decorum governed actions in accordance with norms of civility and peaceful sociability, a prudent middle way between religion and law". *Decorum* was, this is to say, "a definite new ordering of life," albeit one built from ancient models, particularly Stoic models (Saunders 1997:66).

Through his advocacy of *decorum,* Thomasius became one of Europe's most influential thinkers (see esp. Hunter 2007; Hunter et al. 2007; Thomasius 2007). He accepted that the best balance of forces for good government favored public authority over private freedom, but, anticipating one of the mainstays of modern neutrality society and subject formation, he insisted that the authority be used to protect and enhance private freedoms, not to deny or diminish them. He trusted that a combination of *honestum, decorum,* and *justum* could deliver the aforementioned balance (Barnard 1971:242). In other words, he thought that the imposition of legal duties by force alone could never be enough for successful rule, it must be accompanied by *honestum* and, especially, *decorum.*

In his role as an educational reformer—among other achievements, he set up the law faculty at the University of Halle—Thomasius made *decorum* an essential part of the curriculum. He argued that the theologians were mistaken when they refused to include a training in *decorum* alongside their substantive teaching: "the result will be graduates who are 'useful for nothing; who are a burden on themselves and others . . . who trample all reason under foot and with an irrational so-called conscience torment themselves and others'" (Thomasius, quoted in Saunders 1997:96).

The failure of systems of knowledge to recognize an ethic of *decorum* was, for Thomasius, symptomatic of the general failure of philosophy to conceptualize the extralegal and extramoral characteristics of the civil sphere, or politico-legal society. He addressed this failure by proposing "two ethics of mutuality": an ethic of "intrinsic" values and an ethic of "instrumentality" (Barnard 1988:582). According to F.M. Barnard, these two ethics distinguish "the ordering principle of political life from that of religious life," or, as Hunter puts it, they develop a "dual strategy . . . of spiritualising religion by secularising the visible church, and desacralising the state by establishing its religious neutrality" (Hunter 2001:258).

Conclusion

Our chapter has presented a very particular account of the emergence and continued operation of modern neutrality society. In doing this, it has stressed the role of the state—via politics, law, and sovereignty—and it has stressed the importance of security. In presenting our account, we have taken great pains to emphasize that it is an account designed not only to promote a particular understanding of modern neutrality society, what we have called the politico-legal understanding, but just as importantly it is an account designed to demote the understanding of this type of society that currently dominates the university study of it, what we have called the reason-morality understanding.

The chapter has also taken up the challenge of the final component of the book's title and sought to show how a set of early modern interventions—in particular those by Lipsius, by Hobbes, by Pufendorf, and by Thomasius—laid the ground for the formation of new types of subjects, subjects capable not just of operating the political and legal machinery behind modern neutrality society, but also capable of enjoying the freedom and safety it has produced, enjoying it in a way that does not threaten the crucial mechanisms themselves. In line with this, the chapter has also sought to show how Kantian reason-morality thinking works to undermine these achievements.

Notes

1. We would like to thank Ian Hunter, Gavin Kendall, Stephen Turner, the editors of the volume, and the participants in the workshop behind the volume for their helpful comments on various early drafts. We would also like to acknowledge the invaluable research assistance of Liam Stone.
2. We owe this point to Barry Hindess.

CHAPTER TEN

Anticolonial Nationalisms: the Case of India

Benjamin Zachariah

Introduction

Central to this collection is the question "how to secure the conditions for a civil and peaceful life together"? The state is the agency by which society is pacified is an assumption common to a number of the chapters in this collection. The early modern western state was prenationalist; accordingly, the terms of pacification did not have reckon with nationalism, whether it is identified with a community of faith or some other kind of shared values. In this chapter, I argue that once nationalism assumes an historical force, the state enters its embrace. Perforce, the assemblage that is the nation-state participates both in the instability of the connection between "state" and "nation," and must engage in some way with the discourse of "national values." Once this occurs, however civil and inclusive one version of national values may be, the discourse of national values as such readily invites sectarian versions of national values.

"National" is the surrogate term for state-led or state-endorsed, for the versions of nationalism that are validated in the public domain tend not to be able to exist without support from the state. At any rate, it is in the interest of the custodians of the state to conflate the state and the "nation." In this chapter, I treat them as fundamentally connected. "Civic," "ethnic," "developmentalist," "culturalist," or other variations on the "national" theme serve to map the pluralist versus particularist themes onto nationalisms and states.[1] The "national" invokes the legitimacy of popular sovereignty in the service of the state. Furthermore, we are dealing with the assumptions of a liberalism idealized by its supporters that sees the possibilities of pluralism as contained in its own ideologies as capable of being universalized.

The limitations and paradoxes of such approaches find their expression in the need to defend "national" values. Liberal sentiment is plagued by the conundrum of being forced to tolerate (others') intolerance in the name of liberalism, and surrender progressive principles in the name of diversity and culture. Particularist and communitarian values might make culturalist claims to being progressive and more inclusive than their competitors, thereby justifying (their own) intolerance in the name of liberalism. In some cases, then, the case for defending pluralism *becomes* a case for defending a community of faith or "values," whether this faith is called "tolerance" or "Western culture" or "liberalism."

Such observations have been made before, especially in the context of metropolitan nationalisms or states: for instance, the allegedly tolerant Dutch state is able to justify stigmatizing Muslims on the grounds of Islam's intolerance of homosexuality or its mistreatment of women. However, it might make sense to ground such observations in the periphery instead of at the centre. It has become commonplace to suggest that the universalist pretensions of metropolitan political thinking are in fact particularist *because* they are metropolitan.

The case of anticolonial nationalisms is instructive in this regard. These are projects that merge two categories, which would be analytically useful to separate: the anticolonial (amorphous, negatively defined) and the national (typologically predictable, and able to draw on a language of legitimacy in international, by which is meant interstate, politics). I suggest that anticolonial sentiment is disciplined to fit a necessarily elite-defined nationalist project that has implications for exclusions from the potential liberated state, which then reproduces the forms of oppression the nationalists claim to combat.

India in particular is widely regarded as a successful democratic and largely secular state. It is nonetheless possible to look at the metanarrative and the practices of Indian nationalism in terms of their implications for minorities' sense of security and belonging. Contestations related to defining Indian nationalism after formal independence took place against the backdrop of the formation of Pakistan, allowing Hindu nationalists to argue that the residual Indian state, now that Muslims had their own state, would be a Hindu state. Those on the left, backed by Jawaharlal Nehru, claimed that national belonging would not be defined by religion or ethnicity, but by virtue of common belonging to India. The resulting compromise formula, framed in secular and inclusive terms, was characterized by a refusal to define who exactly belonged to the nation. If nationalism must delineate the distinction between one nation and another, the official version of Indian nationalism, successfully backed by Jawaharlal Nehru, singularly fails to do so.

The central part of the formula that was Nehruvian nationalism relied on a socially progressive developmentalism that, in positioning the state as working for the collective good of the people in general, could claim to harness nationalism on its side *without actually needing to define that nationalism*. The people were the ultimate beneficiaries of development; the state was the agent of development; the nation and the state were, if not entirely identified with each other, at least in harmony. Unless challenged, therefore, the state was the nation. The "developmental" state sought to bypass the national question, while inevitably having to situate itself within a nationalist paradigm, which was the only available paradigm to legitimate a collective identity for the Indian state. Inasmuch as the state had to legitimate its borders, which were inherited from colonial rule, the "national" was a problem that could be deferred, but not suppressed. Furthermore, the "developmental" did not replace or precede the "cultural national" (the latter term being the polite way to refer to Hindu chauvinist version of nationalism in India that often verged on the fascist), and was never hegemonic, as admitted by its own protagonists. Developmentalism was a way for an elite who saw itself as progressive to keep its hold on the state.

This argument has problematic implications for formal democracy. The "Nehruvians," and Nehru in particular, were adept at maneuvering languages of legitimacy so that, in the context both of the Indian anticolonial struggle that had always claimed to be nonsectarian, and of the postwar period, where ethnocentric sectarianisms stood temporarily discredited in the public domain, a Hindu chauvinist nationalism had limited access to the language of public legitimation. Thus, the "cultural" in the "national" ("culture" of course being an euphemism for any number of things) was sought to be suppressed by a form of state-led developmentalism. But this was always very unstable. And the exclusions of the "developmental" state in India were different exclusions to those of Hindu nationalists, but were nonetheless exclusions. (Exclusions on a class basis, which of course the "national" idea attempts to gloss over, are one such set of exclusions.) What follows is a set of explorations of problems of exclusion in the course of trying to create an inclusive form of national belonging and citizenship in India.

The Elaboration of "Nehruvian" Nationalism

In this context, it might well be worth pointing out that *all* forms of argument that claimed "India" as a national unit relied on some form of invocation of an ancient past that was, by default at least, "Hindu." While "Hindu" and its relative expressions were never fully "national", because their multiple meanings spread well beyond the disciplining framework of the imagining of an Indian nation, or a future Indian state, the "national" in the Indian case was extremely reliant on one or another version of the "Hindu."[2] Nationalisms rely on the ancient-past-revived-in-the-present theme; and whether as geographical, cultural, or religious entity, the "Hindu" past was required for the present; and "developmental nationalists" too had no choice in this regard but to refer to it. "Tradition" and "indigeneity" tended also to be euphemisms that easily gravitated toward upper-caste "Hindu" practices; and whether it could or could not be proved that these were recently invented traditions, they were effective in creating solidarities around themselves. Debating the national, therefore, always relied on some debate around the category "Hindu".

But a *merely* Hindu identity was not desirable as the basis for a national identity to serve a new state. It had long been the contention of Nehru and the Congress Left that 'communal' identities were not true identities; they were made possible by the poverty of the people and their consequent search for resources of rather irrational hope and were manipulated by elites with a vested interest in sectarianism for their own narrow ends. The preferred way of overcoming this problem of false identities and consciousness was by economic means: greater prosperity for the masses would lead to greater awareness that the real issues were economic. This, with some justification, can be seen as developmentalism *in place of* sectarianism or "communalism," or indeed developmentalism in place of nationalism, for sectarianism or communalism can, I think, be seen as a nationalism that sets its boundaries in the wrong place. It depends of course on one's point of view what that wrong place is.

It is important, therefore, to look at Nehruvian nationalism in this context: an attempt to rely on solidarities based on elective affinity, not ethnicity, religion, or other forms of sectarianism. Nehru very seldom made specific pronouncements on the nature of Indian nationalism. His autobiography refers disparagingly to the early stages of mass nationalism as elite groups discover the peasants and poverty almost by accident (Nehru 1936). As Nehru was repeatedly to put it in public, nationalism alone was too narrow and parochial to solve any major problems. Thus, it was important to have an economic program for the raising of living standards and incomes (Nehru 1936:266, 587–90). But it was inevitable that a people not yet free would think in terms of nationalism. When they were free they would think in more broad terms, Nehru argued, because nationalism was a nineteenth century idea whose time had come and gone (Nehru 1946).[3] (He was to be less optimistic about this later in his life.) Socialism was the ideology of the future, because it sought to make real and significant changes in people's lives. This was not merely Nehru's personal fantasy; he was increasingly becoming the focal point of a group of political activists within the Congress who shared many of Nehru's assumptions and beliefs, and who were dissatisfied by Gandhi's leadership, his propensity for unilateralism and compromise, and his tendency to see businessmen as holding their wealth as "trustees" for the nation (Narayan 1936). Although the Congress Socialists believed Nehru to be one of them, he never formally joined the group. Nevertheless, socialist support went a long way toward creating the so-called Nehruvian consensus; it was in fact never a consensus across the Congress, and this was always acknowledged in internal discussions (*Congress Socialist* 1934–1938).

Here there is a similar argument to that of the communalism versus nationalism dichotomy, with which students of Indian nationalism are so familiar: communalism misled people into following false ideas that were not in their interest to follow. Even as the left wing of a nationalist movement put forward socialism as the true solution, nationalism was implicitly—in most people's thinking—better than communalism because it achieved the unity of all people against the British. This simply meant that a nationalism that was not broadly enough defined could be construed as communalism. Nehru however was not interested in nationalism as an ultimate solution. Development was potentially the solvent of sectarian identities. Socialism was in some earlier versions of this to be the achievable basis of development. It has been pointed out that somewhat later this changed to a state-led development where the state led by the Nehruvian elite would stand for the nation, use the rhetoric of collective belonging to the nation to direct developmental plans from above on behalf of the people (Chatterjee 1993:200–5). This is largely accurate; and this is therefore a version of a developmentalism that is a surrogate for nationalism, and can express itself in a language of nationalism. But is it really nationalism?

Nehru's statement on the nature of Indian nationalism appears quite late: in 1946. It was a time when Nehru, by his own admission, was not properly in touch with events in India and the world, having spent most of the period of the Second World War in prison; already by the early years of the war, he had begun to feel isolated.[4] Nehru set himself the task of trying to find a consensual statement of Indian nationalism that he, as a leading member of the Congress party, could use once he was back in the outside world. Having previously argued that nationalism was too narrow a creed whose time had come and gone, in *The Discovery of India*, published in 1946, Nehru stated, as he had done before, that an obsession with nationalism was a natural response to the lack of freedom: "for every subject country national freedom must be the first and dominant urge" (52). With the achievement of freedom the obsession would vanish; wider groupings of nations and states, and wider solidarities on the basis of internationalism would be possible. But the emotional pull of nationalism could not now be wished away. How could one find a common cultural and historical heritage for India that would serve to build a sense of the nation? There is a strong sense here that the need for such a statement appeared in the context of the growing strength of the Pakistan movement during the Second World War. The text itself thanks many of his compatriots in jail for discussing the nature of the national with him; and the text gives the sense of his having attempted a progressive synthesis of these statements (9).

"The roots of the present lay in the past," Nehru wrote. His concern was with trying to understand the history of India (25). This would be "a process similar to that of psychoanalysis, but applied to a race or to humanity itself instead of to an individual. The burden of the past, the burden of both good and ill, is over-powering, and sometimes suffocating, more especially for those of us who belong to very ancient civilisations like those of India and China" (36). So the anxieties generated by the past in relation to the present had to be confronted and resolved. As a matter of central importance, Nehru confronted the Hindu view of Indian-ness: "It is . . . incorrect and undesirable to use 'Hindu' or 'Hinduism' for Indian culture, even with reference to the distant past" (75). The term "Hindu" was used in a geographical sense to denote the Indian land mass by outsiders, derived from the river Sindhu or Indus. The "Hindu golden age" idea had been crucially shaped by the needs of Indian nationalism. This, he believed, was understandable. "It is not Indians only who are affected by nationalist urges and supposed national interest in the writing or consideration of history. Every nation and people seems to be affected by this desire to gild and better the past and distort it to their advantage" (104). But it was a version that was, he argued, historically false (he could not have missed the fact that he was himself attempting something not dissimilar; to narrate an acceptable past for the "nation," retrospectively to justify his own commitment to that "nation"). Although he acknowledged that some basic ideas and continuities had been preserved in popular and elite cultures, it was impossible to attribute this to one group of inhabitants of India. Historically, India was "like some ancient palimpsest on which layer upon layer of thought and reverie had been inscribed, and yet no succeeding layer had completely hidden or erased what had been written previously" (59). Each layer had enriched Indian culture, and had a place in a new national consciousness; the great rulers of India were the synthesizers who looked beyond sectional interests to bring together different layers. The alien nature of British rule centered on the British refusal to accept India geographically as a home, and its exploitation of India economically for the benefit of outside interests.

Nehru also warned against a view of India that overglorified the past—a danger, he noted, that was also present in China. He agreed that both civilizations had "shown an extraordinary staying power and adaptability" (144). But not all ancient things were worth preserving: caste discrimination, for instance, had to be struggled against—in its origins, he reminded his readers, in an etymological exegesis that not all scholars would agree with, the *varna* classification had been based on color. India was at present "an odd mixture of medievalism, appalling poverty and misery and a somewhat superficial modernism of the middle classes" (56). What was needed was to bring modernism to the masses, by the middle classes understanding and promoting the needs of the masses. He stressed his admiration for Russia and the Chinese communists in their attempts to end similar conditions.

Culture, of course, remained the sticky question if the purpose was to invent an inclusive nationalism. Nehru's solutions to the problem of Indian cultural unity were rather awkward. He himself claimed to have experienced this unity emotionally rather than intellectually, in his travels through India. On the intellectual side, however, he tended to fall back on stereotypes. Nehru's own language, then and later, tended to be imbued with some of the prevalent language of race and eugenics, as well as a patronizing and at times paternalistic attitude toward the masses: he spoke unselfconsciously of "sturdy peasants" and "finer physical types" (65, 68). "Good stock" was, for Nehru, the result not of ethnic or racial *separation* but on the creative intermingling of the races that made up India.) His accretion-and-synthesis view of Indian culture fitted in well with some cultural practices such as the worship at Sufi shrines of both Hindus and Muslims. In other cases, this view did not work quite so well: the peasants, he wrote, had in common oral versions of the great epics, the *Ramayana* and the *Mahabharata* (67). This might just have been true even of some Muslim and Christian "sturdy peasants," but was not true, for instance, of the northeastern "tribal" territories of India that were to be inherited by independent India because they had been within the borders of British India.

The difficulty of finding an inclusive culture that would encompass class, regional, and religious differences did not evaporate: in the 1940s, the communist-proferred model of an India of many nations and a projected multinational Indian state might have solved this problem better. Elaborated, this meant, according to the Communist Party of India's publications on the subject, that no nation would need a state in order to feel secure, and that every small national identity claiming a state would in fact produce the very insecurity it sought to combat (Adhikari 1943:5–9).

It is also worth noting that Nehru regarded his statement in *The Discovery of India* as an attempt to find a consensual description of what it meant to be an Indian, rather than merely as a statement of his own position. His acknowledgements in the book make it clear that he owed much of what he wrote to his conversations with fellow inmates in prison during the period of its writing (9); and he continuously distinguishes his personal views from those that he believes might have wider resonances. Moreover, he does not and cannot work his way round the problem of the slippage or identification of "Hindu" and "Indian." Instead, however, he tries to dilute the significance of the category "Hindu," disarming it of its communitarian and therefore sectarian implications. This is of course an impossible task.

Flashback: A Short History of the "National" Idea in India and the Problem of the "Masses"

Stepping back in time for a sense of context might be a way to proceed further with this chapter, if only to clarify what the long-standing questions being addressed by Nehruvian means were. In the latter part of the nineteenth century, nationalism was a possible way of legitimizing claims to collective existence and therefore collective rights. In learning to use the language of nationalism, elite groups in India were appealing to a powerful principle that was on the way to being a radical force in European history. And because a central part of the British claim to the right to rule India was either that India was not and never had been a "nation," or that British rule had the potential of making India, not yet a nation, into one, legitimate (Indian) collectivities under British rule had to take on a "national" form.

At the beginning of the twentieth century, a nationalist movement not particularly radical, nor particularly anti-imperialist or anti-British, could be said to have come into existence. In the main, it sought more representation for Indians in the government and administration of India. In its most vocal aspects, this was a movement led by an elite, largely secular, self-professedly modernizing and self-consciously modern group of professionals and businessmen, organized around a body that called itself the Indian National Congress (see McLane 1977; Seal 1968; Suntharalingam 1974; Sarkar 1983). Such men were well-versed in the histories of Britain, of British parliamentary practice, and of a liberal political vocabulary that could directly address the imperial center.

At the same time, by the turn of the century there were already persons and groups referred to as "Hindu revivalists" who believed that a revival and revitalization of an allegedly ancient tradition in the present would lift India to its proper place among nations. Despite the insistence of many of its ideologues, the claim of this neo-Hinduism to indigenous roots were shaky: it owed much to British Orientalist scholar-administrators' discoveries of Hinduism in the eighteenth and early nineteenth centuries; the sacred texts that formed the basis of its appeal to tradition owed their standing in many cases to British attempts to find the core principles of the society that they sought to rule in their early years in India (Marshall 1970). Every nation must seek its own indigenous genius to rediscover, and India was no exception. The "indigenous" and the "foreign" remained in tension; in some cases, a useful formula was found in which the material and spiritual spheres were separated: in the material sphere, it was possible to acknowledge that India had much to learn from the "West"—for instance, in terms of science and technology—whereas in the spiritual sphere, the superiority of the "East" in general and of India in particular was asserted (see Raina and Habib 1993; Raina and Habib 1995).

We are speaking here of inclusivity and exclusivity in belonging to actual or potential states; this problem did not escape the ideologues of Indian nationalism. Yet it is difficult to find the voice of the ordinary (potential) citizen. Until the second decade of the twentieth century, there is little indication that this figure was of any particular relevance to the self-proclaimed leaders that wished to claim him (and it was usually him). Thereafter, the attempts were mired in suspicion, fear, and various semicolonial assumptions.

"Swadeshi"

Among nationalist leaders who sought to direct and control "a nation in the making" (Banerjea 1925), there was a growing tension between the borrowed but also internalized liberal idiom of legalistic, "moderate" Indian political agitators that had so horrified Kipling in Calcutta (Kipling 1891), and the more "extremist" ones, who in the early years of the new century found prominence in the movement against the partition of Bengal and the ensuing Swadeshi ("of our own country") Movement (1903–08), (Sarkar 1973). The latter had to find ways of reaching out to the "masses," and sought therefore to find a suitable populist idiom.

The Swadeshi Movement set a pattern that was to be repeated with some variations in the years to come. It was a response to the division of the province of Bengal, ostensibly an administrative measure, which was widely felt to be an attempt to reduce the importance of Calcutta as a political center, and to create a counterbalance to the organized power of the Calcutta *bhadralok*, the middle-class "respectable people." The government created a new administrative and political center in eastern Bengal in Dacca and encouraged the founding of a new political group, the Muslim League, to encourage Muslims to organize separately from the Hindu-dominated, and allegedly anti-Muslim, mainstream of a rising nationalist movement. The resultant antipartition agitation was led by Calcutta-based, mostly upper-caste, Hindu agitators who stressed the brotherhood of Hindus and Muslims, and accused the government of deliberately pursuing a policy of divide and rule. *Swadeshi* also promoted indigenous manufactures, and self-strengthening education, particularly in scientific and technological subjects—incorporating earlier nationalist debates about the need for national self-sufficiency and the nature of valid borrowings from the "West." Boycotts and *swadeshi* demonstrations were organized across the country, in solidarity with Bengal, and giving rise to an extremist trend in the national movement.

But in the search for a popular idiom, the extremists drew strongly on Hindu—and often upper-caste—symbolism. This could obscure the genuine attempt on the part of the

Bengal *swadeshi* agitators to reach out across those limitations. Nevertheless, an undoubted legacy of the rise of extremist politics was a rise in Hindu rhetoric in nationalist politics: the attempt to glorify historical figures who had fought against Mughal rule, now cast as alien and foreign; the worship of Mother India as a Hindu goddess; and more explicitly a reference to a glorious and untarnished ancient Indian past, identified with Hinduism. The possibility of countermobilization on the basis of Islam had showed itself early on, especially as some of the more enthusiastic of the *swadeshi* volunteers used coercive measures to attempt to stop poor peasants in rural eastern Bengal (most of who were Muslims) from buying British-made goods. In the absence of cheap *swadeshi* alternatives, this was hardly practical—it could only be a sacrifice made by the more affluent. The result was sectarian tension and occasional violence as religious leaders, encouraged by government officials, told Muslims that their interests and those of the Hindu agitators were opposed.

Ostensibly successful (the partition was annulled in 1911), the movement nevertheless ran out of steam as a mass movement by about 1908, with its protagonists forced into a campaign of targeting individual British officials in acts of terrorism, inspired partly by Russian anarchism and partly by a Hindu revivalist insistence on the nation as a mother/goddess to be defended by valiant sons (see Heehs 1993, 1998). The "terrorist" tradition, as it came to be called, had a long afterlife; in Bengal in the 1920s and 1930s, there was a steady stream of casualties among British Indian administrators, and British civil servants were particularly afraid of postings in eastern Bengal (Carritt 1986).[5]

Gandhians

The Swadeshi Movement foreshadowed—the teleology is clearly laid out—the great Gandhian movements: Non-Cooperation (1920–22), Civil Disobedience (1930–31) and Quit India (1942–3), though it is doubtful that Gandhi had any control over the last of these.[6] The first of these was merged with the Khilafat Movement. Among Indian Muslims, the danger to the *khalifa* remained an emotive issue with immense mobilizational potential especially after the defeat of Turkey in the war and the harsh terms of the Treaty of Sevres, signed on May 14, 1920. Gandhi's proposed alliance with the Khilafat Movement, in June 1920, was on condition that it accepted nonviolence as its guiding principle. Many Noncooperators who thought of themselves as secular intellectuals, whether they backed Gandhi or not, appeared to accept the principle that the "masses" wanted religion and would not be moved by anything else. (The secular intellectual's misgivings were not Gandhi's misgivings: he said repeatedly that he thought a politics separated from religion would be devoid of morality and would be alien to Indian tradition.) Thus it was that nonbelievers were responsible for promoting a quasimystical religious style of politics. In this second-guessing of the "masses," claims had to be made in their name, but it was Gandhi who retained the right to interpret what correct behavior was, and it was he and his deputies who castigated the "masses" for not living up to the standards set for them.

The importance of "mass support" in a colony is of course not directly in democratic or electoral terms, given the lack of the requisite institutional structures in any but the most caricatured forms. The colonial government, when it wished to appear to negotiate, found persons to represent various predefined "interest groups" or "communities," predefined entities often imagined into being, and given their apparent rigidity, by the processes of imperial administration. With time, elections to local bodies, and still later, to legislatures elected on the basis of narrow property franchises and electorates divided into "communities," with severely constrained powers of legislation, came into being. This was a caricature of parliamentary democracy; it was nevertheless the highest form of institutional politics in colonial India: even in the last stages of so-called "training for self-government," at the end of the 1930s, a legislature's decisions could be overridden by the Governor of a Province or the Viceroy of India.[7]

In this context, making up numbers from among the masses was political theater staged before the colonizer. In order to force colonial rulers to recognize them, and therefore to negotiate with them rather than with the ruler's own loyalist notables, anticolonial nationalists had to demonstrate mass support—this was a prerequisite for effective bargaining with the government. By demonstrating mass support, a group could demand recognition by the rulers, posing as interpreter of the popular will, as intermediary between the "masses" and the government, and in effect offer to act as a buffer zone between potential popular unrest and the colonial rulers. Once a group was so recognized, it also gained a relative monopoly over voicing the demands of the masses it *claimed* to represent. Whether it actually did so or not is a different matter.

The Left

This instrumentalization of the masses was precisely what a more left-wing movement than Gandhi's could be expected to avoid. And the Indian nationalist movement's rhetoric, under the leadership of the Congress, had at least from the late 1920s given much space to the importance of the masses. The differences between left and right wings of the Congress were based on how far these masses were to be at the center of their politics. Gandhi's ability to control the masses—or at least the rural masses who were vulnerable to his ascetic holy man image—was useful to the right, who therefore chose to identify themselves as Gandhians. But the left, from the mid-1930s organized around the Congress Socialist Party (CSP), correctly pointed out that this version of looking after the masses was a form of control—of denying ordinary people a say in important matters concerning their well-being, their earnings, and their survival.

Therefore, the left's challenge to the right was in terms of organizing and representing ordinary people: the *kisan sabhas* (peasant associations), the mass contact program, and the trade union movement broadly under the patronage and with the support of the (Congress) left, were the organizational forms that were to achieve this. With the growing importance of the communists inside the Congress at the time of the Popular Front from 1935 onwards,[8] the reach of the Congress toward ordinary people could be said to have increased. This caused some anxiety on the right, but on the whole the numbers game of both electoral and agitational politics meant that they would tolerate this as long as they could protect their interests. But because even the left agreed that the Congress was going to be allowed to identify itself with the movement for Indian national liberation (Dev 1934), this meant that "class struggle" might be interpreted narrowly to mean struggles on behalf of the lower classes carried out within the Congress by its— often self-proclaimed—representatives.

However, and this was where coalitional politics led to its own problems: businessmen's demands against colonial domination became *national* demands against *imperialist exploitation*. The cause of fighting *imperialists* because they were stifling legitimate

Indian aspirations to *development* could disarm left wing critiques of *Indian capitalists* who were at least in certain contexts on the nationalist side. In some contexts, for instance when the Congress formed provincial governments under the 1935 Government of India Act from 1937 to 1939, this became a particularly difficult problem: the right wing of the Congress dominated the governments, and worked closely with British imperial officials to suppress workers and peasants. Meanwhile the left wing of the Congress became the opposition (Markovits 1985:128–78).

Insofar as the records allow us to make this judgment we can, however, say that this was still proxy class war, with factions of middle-class political activists dividing in terms of their loyalties to their class or to others' class. They cannot speak for themselves, they must be spoken for, was the left's implicit line, especially as communal conflict and caste discrimination provided evidence of the masses' irrational behavior. This was a central aspect of organizational politics. Although there was the possibility of an emergent leadership that was more "organic" (Gramsci 1971:1–48) than that of the Congress members who were concerned with the masses, because they did not fully participate in Congress politics their credentials were not recognised.[9] Moreover, even if the Congress left tried to get them involved, the Congress right would have none of it. The CSP in Bengal complained, for instance, that the *praja samities* and *krishak samities*, peasant organizations that might have allied with a Congress left, gravitated toward the Krishak Praja Party, a predominantly Muslim-led party of mostly Muslim peasants, which was eventually swallowed up by the Muslim League, and the indigestible bits of it were later spat out.

The Right

There was a relative absence of explicitly procapitalist or proimperialist right wing positions in colonial Indian politics; industrialists and proindustrialists could hide behind a Gandhian rhetoric. Industrialists themselves claimed to be imperfect Gandhians in a less-than-perfect world: they held their wealth in trust for society, according to Gandhi,[10] and were therefore legitimized by him, but had no intention of giving up their machines as Gandhi claimed was desirable. Proper Gandhians of an ascetic persuasion remained antimachinery; they are sometimes identified as anarchists of sorts, but it is far from clear that this is an accurate description, given the authoritarian and controlling tendencies of Gandhi and his followers.

There was of course a radical right: some of them former extremists and terrorists, who had served time in (among other places) the dreaded Andaman Cellular Jail, where prisoners' deaths were routine but which was the zone of contemplation from which many terrorists emerged with new ideologies; some, indeed, became communists through their period of study (Laushey 1975). From the 1920s, there was in India a wide interest in fascism, not necessarily fully understood; but there were sections of opinion that did more than vaguely admire Mussolini or Hitler, or the successes in national discipline, economic mobilization, and collective action that seemed apparently the central characteristics of fascism. A determined group of ideologues of a Hindu race-nation-state set about producing an "indigenous" form of fascism in earnest. Mobilization through paramilitary groups modeled on the Black Shirts and Brown Shirts, providing schooling and indoctrination, martial arts, and quasimilitary training, became central to this project. Defining the nation in *völkisch* terms, men like V.D. Savarkar, M.S. Golwalkar, K.B. Hegdewar, and B.S. Moonje argued that the *pitribhumi* (fatherland) must also be the *punyabhumi* (sacred land), and since Muslims' sacred lands were outside India they could not be Indians unless they changed (see Savarkar 1928; Golwalkar 1938).

"Collaborators," Outcast(e)s, and Other Marginal Figures

There is a definite difficulty as far as all of this is concerned; the audible voices are not only of elite groups, which is a historian's inevitable problem of sources, but also of those with a recognized place in the mainstream of a "national liberation movement." It might also have been noted that the colonizer often appears as a sort of reified and undifferentiated figure in the colonized's views of him. This is a problem I have addressed at some length in another context: the colonized, as much as the colonizer, operates by conventionalized and stereotypical constructions of the operative Other in any given argument (see Zachariah 2005:25–79); the result is a conventionalized and unreal argument with a straw man (usually a man)—which is not of course to suggest an equivalence of power relations in the two sets of stereotypes (cf. Said 1978). Difficulties arise when the oppressor and oppressed refuse to be readily identifiable polarities; or where a collective coalition of the oppressed did not line up unproblematically under the banner of the national movement.

In India, with the exigencies of the anti-imperialist struggle placing even the communist left, potentially at least skeptical about the consequences of nationalism, in alliance and eventual entanglement with nationalism, the worst and most unforgivable of politics consisted in refusing the coalition of the national movement. Women, in this scheme of things, were expected by the national leaders to preserve the virtue of the nation as mothers and wives, embody national virtue, occasionally even emerge from respectability in exceptional circumstances in support of the national movement, only to be ordered back home upon the completion of a campaign of civil disobedience, noncooperation or *satyagraha*, strikes, or mass mobilization campaigns. Many campaigns in support of issues considered to concern women—the age of consent for women being a strong case in point—provoked "traditional" (and often male) outrage at the possible use of colonial legislative authority in a matter so indigenous as sexual intercourse, especially within a (child's) marriage.[11]

To the Gandhians, women's proverbial frailty was the downfall, potentially, of the virtuous movement as their love of luxury and ornament undermined attempts to wear khadi, coarse handmade fabric that was heavier than the finer foreign-machine-made goods (they were often silent on the wearing of the domestic-machine-made goods). Frail and ornamented women might also tempt the virtuous away from their duties to the nation and their vows of *brahmachari* (a word that means something in between celibate and student), or cause the male to fail in his duty to preserve his sperm and thereby his masculinity (Alter 1996). And yet when they were not frail and ornamental, women also transgressed. Gandhi publicly denounced "terrorist women" whose participation in armed struggle against the British was to him not only not nonviolent but contrary to their "nurturing" nature. During the Quit India Movement of 1942–43, Gandhi was particularly keen to persuade women guerrillas to give up violence and to give themselves up to the British.[12]

These unnatural women were paradoxically often part of a terrorist movement that provided Gandhi the dialectic of his success; for if not for the presence of potential violence, why was it important for the British to negotiate with Gandhi? As he came in later campaigns to be seen by the British (encouraged by his businessmen allies) as a "moderate" (Birla 1949), the continued importance of terrorist and communist alternatives—movements in which women had some prominence and some, albeit still limited, agency—gave Gandhi his bargaining power with the British as the lesser evil or the lesser danger. It has been well recorded that British civil servants were very afraid to enter into a rural posting in Bengal; almost inevitably, they would get shot (Carritt 1986). When the Hindustan Socialist Republican Army was beginning to organize itself, it sought advice and assistance from Bengal terrorist groups (see Habib 2007).

Women saw for themselves an important role in radical movements to the left of the nationalist mainstream. They were able to overcome the constrained and constraining roles imposed upon them by a convention-ridden society extremely touchy about social change that appeared as if it might be the impact of the colonizer.[13] In practice, the (male) guardians of "tradition" could present themselves thereby as cultural nationalists, protecting an inner and pure domain of the nation from the depredations of the colonizer. But the radical left movements, both in theory and in practice, challenged this. Or did they? Women in the communist movement, typically eschewing marriage or at least the visible accoutrements of traditional marriage that they saw as symbolizing domestic subjugation, could be seen as breaking the bounds of respectability that was allegedly central to their ability to reach out to workers and peasants; they had to visually retraditionalize themselves. (In a similar vein, Muslim men were sent to propagandize Muslims, thereby reifying the "traditional" in the categories "women" and "Muslim").[14] As for the potential of these movements to liberate people at least intellectually from bondage to old values: it is significant that the journal of the United Front, the *Congress Socialist*, suppressed discussions on sexual freedom versus bourgeois marriage at about the same time as they suppressed the Trotskyist heresy.[15]

The problematic example of caste uplift movements under colonial rule is best illustrated by the career of Dr B.R. Ambedkar, of the Mahar caste, whose education (he had a PhD from Columbia University, New York) he owed to his patron, the ruler of the princely state of Baroda (Omvedt 2004). Ambedkar's championing of the cause of lower castes, his refusal to have his movement coopted into the upper-caste dominated generic category of Hinduism and his willingness to use British legislative and legal protection to further his cause has led to an embarrassment among historians as to how to place him in the metanarrative of Indian nationalist heroes. Was his response to the British Empire that of a collaborator? What does it mean to strategically use British—or other—legislative authority, or more generally to use governmental capacity in the absence of one's own ability to wield it? Was his an instrumental use?

If one is permitted to read Ambedkar's academic writing on public finance, one finds this to be very much in the economic nationalist tradition (Ambedkar 1925). But he seems to have been unafraid to put himself at odds with the nationalist movement. It is arguable that Ambedkar was used as a counterweight to the Congress by the British government in a protracted series of negotiations leading up to the Government of India Act of 1935, in which the British attempted to refute the Congress's claim to speak for all of India by finding as many voices as possible that claimed not to be represented by the Congress. At the same time, Ambedkar's attempts to protect his perceived constituency through leaning on British power and legislative authority were crucial in enabling some sort of representation in public arenas for untouchables and low castes[16] excluded both from the nationalism of the Congress's variety (which is now commonly seen as majoritarian if not sectarian) and of the more frankly Hindu upper-caste dominated *völkisch* tendencies of the Hindu Mahasabha, the form taken by the Savarkar brand of nationalism, even though both of these habitually expressed publicly the desire to eliminate the practice of untouchability and the social disabilities that went with it. By demanding separate electoral representation for Backward Castes, Ambedkar appeared to be diluting the national movement and undermining the Congress's universalizing claim.

Indeed, it is the Ambedkar maneuver that raises an important question about majoritarianism, sectarianism, and colonial Indian politics. If untouchables, backward castes, tribals, and other liminal peoples in India were not considered by default "Hindu," then Hindus could not be considered the majority in India at all. (Tribals, in particular, had been the subject of great contestation between Christian missionaries on the one hand and upper-caste Hindu reformers on the other, both groups attempting to coopt them and to reinvent them in their own image.)[17] Given the fact that Hindu is to a large extent a residual category, taking positive shape and new forms under and in response to British rule, and continuing to be reshaped well into the twentieth century, a separate organization of untouchables outside the category Hinduism was a blow to both the majoritarian politics of the Congress and the attempted (instrumental) inclusions of nonupper-castes into the category Hindu that was necessitated by the deliberately fragmented and sectarianized electoral politics of colonial India. In the end, at least on this point, Ambedkar was outmaneuvered by Gandhi, who went on a "fast unto death" until Ambedkar withdrew his demand. Gandhi insisted that Untouchables were Hindus, and should not be separately represented; they could have seats in the legislature reserved for them as a proportion of the general (Hindu) seats. Ambedkar (1946:40–102) later described this blackmail bitterly and succinctly:

> I had to make a choice between two different alternatives. There was before me the duty, which I owed as a part of common humanity, to save Gandhi from sure death. There was before me the problem of saving for the Untouchables the political rights which the [British] Prime Minister had given them. I responded to the call of humanity and saved the life of Mr. Gandhi by agreeing to alter the Communal Award in a manner satisfactory to Mr. Gandhi.

Ambedkar (1946:38–9) maintained, however, that "[t]o tell the Untouchables that they must not act against the Hindus, because they will be acting against their kith and kin, may be understood. But to assume that the Hindus regard the Untouchables as their kith and kin is to set up an illusion." The two men made what is called the Poona Pact in 1932, with tremendous consequences for the colonial numbers game. Hindus were now, by definition, a majority in India.

Muslim Politics

It might have been noticed that Indian Muslims do not appear in central positions in this narrative so far. We have largely been following the mainstream narrative; and Muslims only appear in that narrative as anomalous or as stubbornly recalcitrant, refusing to accept the imperatives of a mainstream Indian nationalism.[18] There is a separate narrative and genealogy of Muslim separatists or separatism: a genealogy of the development of Muslim political consciousness that in many narratives is a tale of the tragic and misguided "two-nation theory" that led eventually to the formation of Pakistan. The narrative suggests that Muslims were backward in Western education and late to realize the benefits of national consciousness; when they did, they organized late and separately. Marxist and quasi-Marxist versions of this narrative rely on the separate development of a Muslim bourgeoisie as the explanation of a separate Muslim nationalism; but the case for a coherent and separate Muslim nationalism in India is as difficult to make as one for a coherent Indian nationalism. Institutional histories of the Mohammadan Anglo-Oriental College, or biographies of the educationist and social reformer Sir Syed Ahmad Khan, at first allegedly an Indian nationalist and then the father of the two-nation theory set up this narrative in its nineteenth century version (Lelyveld 1978). The imperfections and incoherences of (separatist) Muslim nationalism in India (usually, among Indian writers, not dignified with the normative term "nationalism") have come in for more close criticism than the allegedly more "complete" Indian nationalism.

The separatism of Muslims is often attributed to British divide-and-rule tactics, dating back to the creation of the Muslim League at the time of the Swadeshi movement. This is not inaccurate; for instance, it is undeniable that the successful separation by the British of Muslims from the terrorist movement in Bengal in the 1920s and 1930s relied on such tactics.[19] This is an incomplete story. Though some anarchists (as they often called themselves) later became communists, or participated in the *praja* movement, which comprised mainly Muslim peasants, outside certain minor successes of nonsectarian or cross-sectarian collective politics, a certain mistrust existed for a variety of reasons (see Roy 1999). The fear of being swallowed up in a majoritarian mainstream that did not represent their interests is a theme that can be followed closely in Muslim responses to empire as much as in backward caste ones.

The relative absence of Muslims from the Congress-led Indian national movement was a matter of their learning the art of watching and waiting—sections of Muslim intellectuals, at least, watched with interest the way the Indian National Congress turned in the 1930s: if it moved strongly to the left, Muslims would seek to join. If not, the Congress could not, as a Hindu sectarian party despite its public utterances, hold Muslims and represent them. Histories of Muslims, as a potentially insecure minority or a disempowered and impoverished slight majority (in Bengal) need to be written without recourse to a narrative structure that is centrally concerned with their failure to be true nationalists. There are other questions: fractures of class, political affiliation, and social position cannot be answered in generic and nonindividuated terms. Conservative Muslims interested in their faith, or in social control (for instance of women in public places), progressives with a liberal view of Islam, as well as many who were nominally Muslim but had no particular connection with Islam other than being identified by non-Muslims as Muslims, all ended up to a greater or lesser extent, and sometimes by default, supporting the "Pakistan movement." This is too complicated a tale to tell as a teleology of separatism or Muslim nationalism (in India).

Numbers, Negotiations, and the Mistrust of the Masses

A purist answer to the question of whether the disempowered leave coherent voices for the historian's retrospective access discourages us from looking in the gaps left for us by the above narratives, as also from looking at what these or alternative narratives cannot tell us. Perhaps, though, we can look at the last days of the British Empire in India's explicit presence (discounting the long afterglow of unfinished business, financial and economic linkages, cold war, and Commonwealth deals) in terms of the relative agency and renewed disciplining of the masses (see Singh 1993; Moore 1987; Charrier 1995).

To step back a bit by way of providing context: from the 1920s, British constitutional maneuvers for India warmed up, with slightly higher stakes after the 1935 Government of India Act. Indians could easily find themselves imprisoned in the colonial numbers game, debating whether a reserved seat here or there could be conceded, whether a proportion of the population was to be defined as Hindu, Backward Caste, or Muslim. Two processes were discernible: one was that of formal politics set up and manipulated by British governments in India and in Britain. The other sought to organize popular movements and speak for underprivileged groups in Indian society—with varying degrees of success.

In the course of the Second World War, and certainly after the Quit India Movement, it became clear that Britain did not have the will or the military resources to hold India by force after the war. The Viceroy, Lord Wavell, a military man, now saw the virtues of an orderly transfer of power to a government that Britain would be able to deal with after the war. Much rather this than popular initiatives that led in unknown directions, the line of reasoning went from at least late 1944, if not earlier. The problem now, as the British saw it, would be to create enough agreement among the two main players in the negotiations, the Congress and the Muslim League, to effect such an orderly transfer. In large measure, it had been due to *British* recognition of the Muslim League as representing Muslims that the League could, post-ex facto, gather the support of Muslim groups behind itself, and thereby also inherit the supporters of these other Muslim groups during the war (see Moon 1973).[20]

Yet it was after the Second World War that the politics of the masses had its moment, in part threatening to break away from the control of its self-appointed leaders, in particular in 1945 and 1946, the time of the trials of the Indian National Army (INA) who had fought the British Indian army alongside the Japanese, the Royal Indian Navy (RIN) mutiny, the Great Calcutta killings, and their aftermath, and the *Tebhaga* movement of sharecroppers, led by the Communist Party of India among Muslim peasants who were often at the same time supporters of the Pakistan movement (Cooper 1988; Sen 1972; and on the INA and the RIN revolt and its aftermath Roy 1999:163–218). It is difficult to disaggregate the various motivations for popular unrest. The postwar situation had led to massive cuts in employment levels as soldiers and auxiliary staff were demobilized across the country. The anger and bitterness of the Quit India and famine years had not receded. To this were added further causes for concern by the day.

Where, however, popular politics at times seemed to be in a position to set the agenda, in the end *elite interpretations* of the "people's will" won the day. What political leaders saw was unrest, strikes, violence of various kinds, and almost millenarian expectations of momentous change. The timetable for British departure was hastily adjusted forwards. The colonial power and their two interlocutors, the Congress and the Muslim League, were in effect negotiating details while claiming to represent people on the basis of their interpretations of events that were impossible to clearly interpret. All three sets of negotiators feared that the masses and their activities might take over control of events. And all of them agreed implicitly, if not explicitly, that this had to be avoided: outcomes would then be too messy, too unpredictable, too disorderly and above all too radical for all parties concerned. This had major consequences for the period of freedom after 1947.

Inclusions and Exclusions after Independence

To return now to such statements of national identity and inclusivity as laid out by Nehru in 1946, their most obvious limitation was that they were not grounded in practice. The left's ultimate optimism that economic man would inevitably replace sectarian man, as ordinary people began to recognize their real interests, was an untested assertion. Meanwhile, with the events surrounding the Partition of India and the creation of Pakistan becoming central, ideologues such as Nehru had no answer to questions of identity as expressed in the Partition massacres and the postindependence tendency of organized mobs of Hindus or Sikhs to turn on Muslims. Right through this period of violence, Nehru and his government or his socialist colleagues could do no more than make statements on the irrationality of events and muse on the atavistic tendencies of mobs.[21] If they had wanted to see these events in terms of types of nationalism, they found such readings exceedingly difficult. Nonetheless, the transfer of power was made according to a simplified understanding of events that regarded widespread and unprecedented violence as indication that Hindus and Muslims now could not live together in peace. Those who knew or suspected that things were not quite as uncomplicated as that were not those who drew the lines on maps or made the government operate.

Questions of national identity were entangled in the internal politics of the Indian National Congress as the successor to the British. Before independence, the Congress had claimed to be the representative body capable of speaking for the nation as a whole. But the inclusive claims made by the Congress in public, as its internal correspondence makes amply clear, were supported only by its left wing. The Congress as a whole had no coherent vision of India, and within it, there were many who wished to exclude Muslims in particular and nonupper-caste Hindus in general from political power and social status. Behind the scenes, they argued that after the partition of India, that the matter had been decided: Pakistan was a Muslim state; the residual India would therefore be a Hindu state. Nehru disagreed strongly, refusing to reduce Muslims and other non-Hindus in India to the implicit status of foreigners. He intervened frequently in the affairs of the Home Ministry, which he believed was unnecessarily harassing Muslims in claiming to maintain law and order. And largely on the strength of claims that the Congress had repeatedly made in public, he was often able to force the issue towards a nonsectarian definition of being Indian, in the Constituent Assembly, where it was written into the new Republic's Constitution, and elsewhere. But there were moments where the allegedly nonsectarian Indian state betrayed the implicit communitarian logic of its actions, as in the question of the repatriation of abducted women to Pakistan and India in the years after Partition. Repatriation was often in disregard of the wishes of the women themselves, and with the working assumption that "originally" Hindu women who lived with Muslims in Pakistan belonged back in India, and so on (Menon and Kamla 1998).

Nehru himself admitted that he was out of joint with public opinion, and with opinion inside the Congress, at the time of independence. "I find myself in total disagreement with this revivalist feeling," Nehru wrote to the Gandhian Rajendra Prasad, in response to Prasad's request that Nehru ban cow slaughter on the day of independence,

15 August, "and in view of this difference of opinion I am a poor representative of many of our people today."[22] Rajendra Prasad had demanded that Nehru announce a ban on cow-slaughter as part of the independence celebrations; Nehru had refused to envisage a measure "purely on grounds of Hindu sentiment."[23] He believed such opinion to be anti-Muslim and pro-Hindu upper caste, and he believed that at the time of independence, the current of public opinion would have been on the side of the Congress right, which despite the formal separation of the Hindu Mahasabha as a Hindu communal party from the Congress in 1938, could not as yet be sufficiently distinguished.[24] His strengths were his international connections and his acceptability across the political spectrum: as Gandhi's anointed successor, as the Harrow- and Trinity-educated intellectual who could parlay with the British on equal terms, and as the acceptable face of the Indian left. His language could become the language of legitimacy of the new Indian state. But to what extent was this language merely one in which *public* arguments had to be made? Those whose sentiments or goals were not very different from the Hindu Mahasabha's, for instance, could still hide in the Congress. And by pushing the tendency into an enforced silence, problems had been made more difficult to identify.

What, then, was the developmental alternative to a culturally defined, and therefore pro-Hindu, nationalism? The goal of national self-sufficiency as an escape from what Nehru described as "the whirlpool of economic imperialism" (Nehru 1946:398), and industrialization as a central plank of that self-sufficiency as India attempted to "catch up" with the advanced countries, drew on an older tradition of nineteenth century economic nationalism that demanded protection for "infant industries" so that they could, with time, compete with foreign industries. In effect, then, the postindependence political economy was set up as a protected national economy, run on capitalist lines with a strong state sector. And with socialists committed to a "transition period," it could be all but admitted that the shared goal was one of achieving a relatively successful capitalism rather than anything that could be recognized as "socialism"[25]—but the obligatory language of political legitimacy dictated that this was a step too far. The state's strong directorial role was not to everyone's liking, with old Gandhians like J.B. Kripalani, warning inter alia of the dangers of "investing the State with the monopoly of political and economic exploitation, which is what happens in the centralised economy of a communist or a fascist state" (Kripalani's speech on 15 November 1947 in Poplai 1959). The Gandhians' insistence that as an alternative to centralized state control, the economy could prosper on a decentralized system of rural self-sufficiency did not win much support.

Economics versus sectarianism: this was the formula on the basis of which many public battles were fought. And yet the dichotomy was an imperfect one. One of the earliest such battles was the one in 1947 over the first budget of the Interim Government, led by Nehru; the Finance Minister was Liaquat Ali Khan, Muslim League member and later to be Prime Minister of Pakistan. The central feature of Liaquat Ali Khan's budget was its taxation of the profits made by Indian businessmen through the war period. Liaquat drew the justification for this, he said, from many of the wartime speeches of Nehru himself and of other Congress leaders who deplored the tendency of Indian business to make large profits in collaboration with the government while Indian resources were exploited for the war effort without the consent of any representative body of Indians. Nehru, moreover, had approved the budget before Liaquat presented it to the Assembly. Now, the Congress right, led by Vallabhbhai Patel, vociferously attacked its own government's budget. Allegedly, Liaquat was leading a communal plot against the Hindus: since he knew that most businessmen were Hindus, he was, as a Muslim, being vindictive (Chattopadhyay 1986). The budget was forced to be modified; Nehru failed in public to back Liaquat on a point of principle. The economics versus sectarianism formula, it was clear, could also be manipulated by the right wing; it was a matter of using the conventions of argument well enough.

The central part of the formula had relied on a socially progressive developmentalism that, in positioning the state as working for the collective good of the people in general, could claim to harness nationalism on its side *without actually needing to define that nationalism.* The people were the ultimate beneficiaries of development; the state was the agent of development; the nation and the state were, if not entirely identified with each other, at least in harmony. Unless challenged, therefore, the state was the nation.

But the language of developmentalism was open to use also by a capitalist class that was, because it was relatively small, able to act relatively coherently. If a capitalist class could present its own role as that of furthering the progress of the nation as a whole, there was no reason that it could not utilize the same language of developmentalism that was being used to legitimize the state that a leftist group clustered around Nehru were using. This was clearly recognized: the authors of the Bombay Plan of 1944 (Thakurdas 1944), that much-publicized document in which Indian businessmen allegedly signed up to the postindependence socialist, or socially progressive agenda, were clear about what their task had to be:

> [t]he inevitability of a change in the direction of a socialist economy even in a country like India must now be recognised and leaders of industry would be well advised to take this into account and be prepared to make such adjustments as may meet all reasonable demands before the socialist movement assumes the form of a full fledged revolution. The most effective way in which extremer demands in future may be obviated is for industrialists to take thought while there is yet time as to the best means of incorporating whatever is sound and feasible in the socialist movement. One of the principal tasks of the Committee will therefore be to examine how far socialist demands can be accommodated without capitalism surrendering any of its essential features.[26]

Moreover, if an abstract ideal of "development" was something that was greatly desired in nationalist circles, for its own sake, for the uplift of the masses, and in some versions, to wean the masses off the false consciousness of communal concerns, it was perfectly possible for the terminology around development to become the legitimating window-dressing for several arguments that led away from these allegedly central developmental concerns. In particular, the masses began to be conceptualized in a rather abstract way. There was thus a definite tension between imagining an independent India that was to be for the benefit of the masses (the nation, represented by the nationalists-who-were-the-Congress, who would run the state) and imagining development in and for India, in which the masses (who would allegedly *ultimately* be the beneficiaries) were instrumentally cast as material to be molded to a project that was greater than they. This was enabled by the construction of a language of legitimacy that simultaneously centered on and marginalized the "masses" by subordinating them to a larger, allegedly national, project.

This is evident early on in the public statements around the economy emanating from the new state. The centrality of the anti-imperialist struggle had often led to a deferral of questions of labor rights, wages, and welfare, in which the left had been complicit and even proactive, on the grounds that the first enemy to be defeated was the imperialist one; this deferral, contrary to the claims made by the left, continued after independence. This happened simultaneously with attempts of sections of the nationalist movement, then organized on a coalitional basis, to mobilize labor behind the national movement, and thereafter behind the nationalist state. The nationalist leadership and the state it controlled thereafter claimed to represent labor and at the same time demanded discipline from the labor force for "national" goals.

The central myth that made this possible was that the postindependence Indian state was, or would be, a benign one, or at least a lesser evil. The masses were instrumentalized by the custodians of the national state, and the custodians of that state presented themselves as intermediaries between the exploiters (capitalists, landlords) and the exploited (workers, peasants). The instrumentalization of labor, allegedly for its own future good, was institutionalized in the split in the trade union movement, the older, All-India Trade Union Congress (AITUC), remaining with the Communist Party of India, which had become dominant in the AITUC by the end of the Second World War, and the newer Indian National Trade Union Congress (INTUC), dominated by the Congress party. The INTUC accepted the myth of the benign state: the state, being a national one, was now an impartial intermediary between business and labor, representing the interests of the nation as a whole.

Nehru himself made several statements on the need for collective national action, and of deferring conflict between classes for that greater cause. In a speech in which he referred to himself as the "First Servant of the Indian People" (invoking in his rhetoric the Soviet People's Commissars of the early days of the Russian Revolution), on August 15, 1947, he reiterated that the predominant problems faced by India were economic: the country was faced with inflation, the people with lack of food and clothing and adequate shelter. "Production today is the first priority," he explained; but on its own it would not be enough—the key social question would be one of distribution (Press statement in Nehru, 1963:27). An Industries Conference on December 18, 1947 agreed to maintain "industrial peace, and to avoid lock-outs, strikes, and slowing down of production for the next three years"; Nehru's address again stressed the primacy of production, lest there otherwise be nothing left to distribute.[27] Nehru maintained that the government could not afford to leave industrial disputes to be fought out in terms of strikes, "especially when there is something like a crisis in production."[28]

The rhetoric of the period after 1947 strongly stressed the need for collective and disciplined national progress, for production before distribution could be achieved, and consequently for harmonious industrial relations. Change would come, but it would be relatively gradual, consensual, and rely on the education of the masses and the initiatives of the state. Vested interests would be chipped away by the authority of the state, represented by the national government, which in effect was the Congress. But the masses were to be increasingly disarmed of their own right to decide on what their interests really were.

In its operation, therefore, the developmental imagination excluded the representatives of nonelite groups from making decisions pertaining to the nation. *Exclusion* based on a common commitment to a developmental project claiming to be for their benefit, in a paternalistic appropriation on the part of an allegedly benign state and its government, was, in being developmental, also largely noncultural; to what extent such exclusions, based on class, were less exclusionary than those potentially based on culture remains open to question.

Meanwhile, the everyday details of finding the identity of the new Indian state continued to run into difficulties. Opinion in the Constituent Assembly, the body assigned the task of writing a new Constitution, was, according to many, not exactly progressive or developmentalist. The Constituent Assembly was elected on a property franchise in 1946, in response to which many socialists boycotted it, refusing to accept that such an unrepresentative body could draw up a constitution that would command legitimacy in the years to come; its membership was also curtailed by the secession of Pakistan during its discussions. Minoo Masani, former Congress Socialist and soon to be the main spokesman of Indian capitalist interests, classified opinions in the Assembly along two axes: "modernists" and "traditionalists," "socialists," and nonsocialists (Masani 1982). Both modernist and traditionalist opinion divided along socialist and capitalist lines. Many followers of Gandhi claimed, as Gandhi himself occasionally did, though not consistently, to be socialists themselves. Gandhians and other defenders of tradition managed to assert themselves at times, making the constitutional document an ambiguous compromise of divergent tendencies that remained, and remain, in tension. Gandhi's own views on the necessarily spiritual basis for a morally upright and culturally rooted "authentic" Indian politics, which was underpinned by his own idiosyncratic Hindu views, sat uneasily with the need for a nonsectarian and nonreligious basis for Indian national belonging. Gandhi, of course, was not directly a party to debates in the Constituent Assembly and elsewhere; his major contribution to the silencing of Hindu sectarian and fundamentalist opinion was in being shot by a Hindu. Thereafter, Nehru and the Congress left were able to mobilize public opinion behind themselves and to discredit, in public debate, Hindu sectarian positions that had so recently claimed the life of the Mahatma.[29]

The "cultural" in the "developmental" needs to be highlighted. A developmental project required some sense of social reform, in the older sense known in India of reforming socioreligious institutions, as well as in the socioeconomic sense, for instance, of land reforms.[30] The boundary between social reform and religious reformation in many of these debates was made difficult by the fact that British Indian political discourse had positioned India as a fundamentally religious society (Inden 2000 [1990]). Social reform of various kinds was central to the claimed developmental agenda of the state: "backward" institutions should be swept away, caste distinctions abolished, and a form of citizenship that rendered questions of sectarian identity irrelevant had to be found. At the same time, all social reform also ran into questions of how far the state could interfere with tradition. There was the added danger that the adjudicators of tradition were conservative male leaders of sects or religious organizations. And if continuing special representation for the Backward Castes or Scheduled Castes ran into the question of whether this in fact militated against the avowed aim of destroying these distinctions altogether, the question of preserving or reforming Hindu or Muslim laws also raised the question of whether these should also be abolished.

The Nehruvian state worked largely on the basis that minorities should not be made to feel insecure in the new state by having their institutions subject to attack from the state. Treading softly on matters relating to minorities, the state therefore started on the reform of Hindu law, with the intention, allegedly, to tackle Muslim law at a later date, and with the avowed ultimate aim of a uniform and secular civil code. But the Hindu Code Bill ran into many difficulties as the self-proclaimed defenders of the community sought to defend "tradition." The president of the new Republic, Rajendra Prasad, opposed the Bill in a move that clearly had him overstep his constitutional position. Dr B.R. Ambedkar, the Law Member in Nehru's Cabinet, resigned in disgust in September 1951, and the Hindu Code Bill struggled on as four separate pieces of legislation, marriage, divorce, succession, and adoption. This eventually satisfied the demand for the state to take a proactive role in social reform as part of a developmentalist agenda, if more in symbol than in substance (Som 1994), but it also tended paradoxically towards *establishing the "normal" citizen as a Hindu.* As late as 1959, Nehru refused to open discussions on Muslim personal law, and would not even place monogamy on the agenda, at par with the Hindu Marriage Act, which was passed in 1955—there should be no impression that a Hindu majority was enforcing anything on a Muslim minority (Gopal 1972). The details are less important for the purposes of this essay than the question of how the debates operated: communities had laws and rights to themselves; custodians of the rights of a community were its leaders, usually self-appointed, and male; Muslims, by being left out of questions of social reformist legislation, were exceptional citizens.

The Erosion of the Nehruvian Vision

The erosion of this version of the Nehruvian vision can be attributed to the problems of the North East Frontier Agency and the Chinese borders. These were connected: just as the borders with China were ambiguous, the peripheral areas of India were only a part of the Indian Union through accidents of colonial history and its arbitrary borders. The tribal areas of North-East India, under colonial administration, were separated from the rest of India by an "inner line"; the "outer line" then divided it from the outside world— an "outer line" whose precise position was not clearly known. This division was inherited by independent India. Potential secessionist tendencies had been identified in the Naga areas of the northeast early on by Nehru, at the time of the Interim Government. But the retention of these areas in India was impossible to justify by virtue of national models. At the time of the separation of Burma from India in 1935, British administrators had toyed with the idea of attaching these areas to Burma rather than India. There was no particular reason why they should have shared an Indian nationalist sentiment, as Nehru himself acknowledged: "Our freedom movement reached these people only in the shape of occasional rumors. Sometimes they reacted rightly and sometimes wrongly" (June 1952, quoted in Singh 1989:2). (By this, apparently, Nehru applied to the behavior of the "tribals" a yardstick of legitimacy that was based on a "right" attitude to Indian nationalism.)

After independence, Nehru believed, the Naga areas ought to be a part of India and of Assam. He offered concessions: "It is our policy that tribal areas should have as much freedom and autonomy as possible so that they can live their own lives according to their own customs and desires." They could expect protection from being "swamped by people from other parts of the country" and consequently from being exploited.[31] He seemed quite unconscious of the patronizing language and the colonial rhetoric of his pronouncements. In April 1953, Nehru, now accompanied by the Burmese prime minister U Nu, attempted to address a gathering of Nagas; they turned their backs on the two prime ministers and walked out of the meeting (Gopal 1979:208). Indian attempts at nation-building by force of arms, with the Indian defense forces in culturally alien territory indulging in large-scale killing and rape were hardly the best ways of demonstrating to the North-East of India the warm and enveloping joys of belonging represented by Indian nationhood. But Nehru's centralized state could not afford to have fuzzy edges. It was in the North-East of India that the Nehruvian vision took on its most brutal and violent forms.

Connections to the eventual border conflict with China are obvious: the question of inheritance of colonial borders and the question of who belongs within them. The developmental and the cultural found themselves in direct confrontation here: Nehru initially argued that it was not worth fighting over wasteland that no one inhabited. Various other Indian groups, including socialists, refused to cede any ground to the *mlecchas* who were defiling the sacred soil of India. Nehru was gradually pushed into more and more assertive positions (Maxwell 1970). Meanwhile, developmentalists who were looking closely at Chinese experiments with cooperative farming were forced away from these efforts as everything Chinese became anathema (Frankel 1978: 167–8). Then, when the border dispute flared up into direct warfare in late 1962, citizenship rights were withdrawn from Indians of Chinese origin.[32]

Since the problem of Indian citizenship and belonging usually takes the form of looking at Muslims, this often goes unnoticed. But this particular pairing of examples exposes the problems of a nationalism that attempts to refuse to define itself except as a common project of citizenship intended toward collective development or progress. "We" all belong within our borders, within which we conduct development; that assumes a stability of borders and also an *enforcement* of belonging within those borders. In addition, moments of crisis and uncertainty expose certain groups to the possibility that they will suddenly find themselves excluded. This is not *within* the logic of a developmental nationalism, but it seems that the implicit cultural assumptions behind belonging to the nation (state) can emerge at such moments. The developmental nationalism is thus always also, at least potentially, a cultural nationalism whose chauvinist assumptions are held in reserve.

Inconclusions

This analysis cannot wind down without questioning the possibility of *any* national identity or state-led ideology being nonexclusionary and progressive, or indeed, anything other than a form of sectarianism. Which leads us to the problem that any state-led ideology, whether it is explicitly nationalist or not, whether it avoids definitions or descriptions of national values or the nature of belonging or not, is potentially a form of sectarianism. Or is it possible for state-led ideologies to avoid appealing to particular values?

Historians are notorious for refusing to offer a resolution to tricky problems of politics. Is it possible to avoid having an implicit conception of the "normal" citizen? To what extent do(es) a state('s custodians) make this implicit conception explicit in moments of perceived crisis? And why is it necessary to look to the state to create the conditions for "a civil and peaceful life together"? Is the state not equally often the obstacle to such a life?

What sort of state? Whose state? Is it possible to have recourse to ideas of citizenship without recourse to ideas of national belonging?

Notes

1. For the purposes of this paper, I do not require clarity on the question of what the nation is or how it is imagined; I would place myself on the side of those taking a "constructionist" position, and examine how contemporaries attempted to conceptualize national belonging.
2. This argument is further developed in chapter 4 of Zachariah (forthcoming). See van der Veer (1994) for a strong version of this argument.
3. Unless otherwise indicated, in the remainder of this section references to Nehru (1946) are in page numbers only.
4. Jawaharlal Nehru, article for *Daily Herald*, London, typescript dated 9/12/41, Jawaharlal Nehru Papers, Nehru Memorial Library, New Delhi, Part III Sl No 85.
5. Carritt was an exceptional figure: he was a member of the Communist Party and worked in the Indian Civil Service as well as with the Communist Party of India.
6. On the Gandhian movements, see (Minault 1982; Sarkar 1976; Pandey 1988; Damodaran 1992).
7. Section 93 of the Government of India Act, 1935.
8. The so-called Dimitrov Line of the Comintern proclaimed a popular front of all democratic forces against fascism. But in the Communist Party of India's interpretation, fascism was capitalism in crisis at home, and imperialism was the overseas manifestation of capitalism, so the popular front in India was one against imperialism.
9. The Kisan Sabhas, for their part, did not fully merge with the Congress organization, merely loosely affiliating themselves to the CSP, for fear of losing their autonomy and agenda (Ranga 1937).
10. On Gandhi's "trusteeship" theory, sympathetically interpreted, see Dasgupta 1996: 118–131.
11 This was of course one strand of the debate. The debates on the Sarda Act to raise the age of consent for women from 12 to 14 years (in 1929) came close on the heels of the responses to the American Katherine Mayo's book (1927) that provoked nationalist outrage by highlighting gender relations as an aspect of the inferior nature of India's civilization. As a result, criticism of "indigenous" social norms such as child marriage was placed in a context where nationalist solidarity against 'outside' criticism had to be maintained, thereby strengthening the "traditionalists." Katherine Mayo herself followed this up with her own second contribution, provocatively entitled Volume Two (1931). See also Sinha 2006: 192–6.
12. Gandhi's letters to Aruna Asaf Ali, copies in the Nehru papers.
13. On this dynamic in another context, see Fanon (1965).
14. Yusuf Meherally, Muslim Mass Contact, *Congress Socialist*, June 26, 1937, No. 25, pp. 12–13.
15. See Kamaladevi Chattopadhyay's writing on Alexandra Kollontai in the *Congress Socialist* (1935).
16. "The reader will find that I have used quite promiscuously in the course of this book a variety of nomenclature such as Depressed Classes, Scheduled Castes,

Harijans and Servile Classes to designate the Untouchables. I am aware that this is likely to cause confusion especially for those who are not familiar with conditions in India. Nothing could have pleased me better than to have used one uniform nomenclature. The fault is not altogether mine. All these names have been used officially and unofficially at one time or other for the Untouchables. The term under the Government of India Act is 'Scheduled Castes.' But that came into use after 1935. Before that they were called 'Harijans' by Mr. Gandhi and 'Depressed Classes' by Government," (Ambedkar 1946:i–vi).

17. Elwin (1964) describes these manoeuvres from the point of view of a maverick ex-missionary turned anthropologist who by some accounts "married his own fieldwork." On Elwin, see Guha (1999).

18. Those who did were referred to, paradoxically, as "nationalist Muslims" (see Hasan 1997).

19. The classic case of this was the 1931 Chittagong, instigated by British and Muslim police officers in the colonial police force after the killing of a Muslim police officer by a terrorist: Muslims were encouraged to attack "Hindu" terrorists intent on setting up a "Hindu raj" (see Das 1991:133–41).

20. This is also a central argument in Jalal (1985).

21. See for instance, Nehru's speech at Khusrupore, November 4, 1946, in Gopal (1984, vol. 1:55); his letter to Vallabhbhai Patel, November 5, 1946, in Gopal (1984, vol. 1:62–5).

22. Jawaharlal Nehru to Rajendra Prasad, August 7, 1947, in Gopal (1984, vol. 3:191).

23. Jawaharlal Nehru to Rajendra Prasad, August 7, 1947, in Gopal (1984, vol. 3:191).

24. Z.A. Ahmad's notes from his talk with Jawaharlal Nehru, June 1945, "not to be shown to anyone else without PC Joshi's [General Secretary, Communist Party of India] permission," 1945/9, PC Joshi Archive, Jawaharlal Nehru University, New Delhi.

25. This has been pointed out by retrospective scholarship: see for instance, Byres (1994).

26. P. Thakurdas papers, Nehru Memorial Library, File 291 Part II: Post-War Economic Development Committee, ff. 265–6.

27. Gopal (1984, vol. 4:570–9).

28. December 15, 1947, Gopal (1984, vol. 4:564). There were strikes in Bombay and Kanpur in December and January, as well as a food crisis; a December 29 strike of 60 labor unions in Bombay (with dockyard and port trust workers demanding higher wages) had been called on December 14, before the "truce" call of December 18.

29. "The light has gone out of our lives," All India Radio broadcast by Nehru, January 30, 1948 in Gopal (1984 vol. 5); resolutions on Gandhi's death, February 2, 1948, in Gopal (1984, vol. 5:37–8).

30. On land reform debates, see Sen (1998).

31. Letter to Naga National Council, published in the *National Herald* of 2/10/46, reprinted in Gopal (1984, vol. 2:604).

32. Roy (2007:186, n.116), mentions the "ethnicisation of the nation" in connection with the China War and cites the relevant legislation.

CHAPTER ELEVEN

The Sense of Existing and Its Political Implications (on François Flahault's "General Anthropology")

Jeffrey Minson

Introduction

"What is government itself but the greatest of general reflections on human nature? If men were angels, no government would be necessary" (Hamilton et al. 1961:319). Are not Madison's reflections on man's imperfection as the basis for modeling government a hallmark of conservatism? The citation also conflicts with powerful metaphysical images of the autonomous person. This chapter introduces François Flahault's un-angelic "general anthropology," which offers images of humankind counter to those envisioned in a metaphysics of autonomy, yet which is distinct from conservatism.

My aim is more expository than critical. I outline Flahault's central concepts, methods, and especially his treatment of *malice*: its psychological sources and unsettling relations to morality and politics. And I indicate how his anthropology yields a variant on social-solidaristic views about social deprivation, which Flahault links to a *psychical* insecurity that cannot be addressed by redistributive measures alone.

I also locate his anthropology in relation to various issues and traditions. In particular, I pick out affinities with the anthropology informing an early-modern "civil prudence"-based ethic of state. Though Flahault does not work on "the state," his anthropology lends itself to constructing an ethically inflected "political realist" account of state-and-citizen.

Agency and Ethics of State: Background Issues

In setting out my agenda I have implied that Flahault's anthropology speaks to several contemporary issues. One pertains to the conservative connotations of "human nature"; another, to connections between ethics and "political-realist" accounts of state sovereignty; a third is about how to conceive the limits of the redistributive focus in social policy. Cutting across these is debate about the form and limits of human freedom.

> One could test all theories of state according to their anthropology and thereby classify these as to whether they consciously or unconsciously presuppose man to be by nature . . . a dangerous being or not. (Schmitt 1996 [1932]:58)

Doesn't Carl Schmitt's sense of the dangerousness of "man" and its authoritarian implications for political rule epitomize the conservative mind? References to humanity's darker propensities—often allied to an Augustinian view of original sin—have long been used to brace conservative-communitarian arguments for tough-minded "alterations" (Honderlich 2005) designed to restore the moral authority and social discipline vested in the national community's core institutional pillars of family, church, state.

The other side of this conservative coin is mistrust of social change framed by emancipatory moral principles (Quinton 1973; Oakshott et al. in Muller 1997). Conversely, influential theoretical advocates for radical change repudiate the very notion of human nature as a constraint upon social-transformational possibilities. To be human is to be capable of transcendence of any givens or constructs that would close off possible futures for what we might be. It is to be capable of unconditionally "beginning something anew" (Arendt 1971:9). Though counterexamples can be mustered, it is hard to shake the assumption that conservatives hold the franchise over views that government and its limits should be indexed to human dangerousness.

Let us turn to the *second* issue, around ethicizations of "political realism." Broadly speaking, political realists' starting point is the disconnect between the actual *capacities* of states and the first principles of justice, liberty, equality, and democratic self-government to which states are obligated in "idealist" normative conceptions of political field (e.g. Khilnani 1991:196–204). The issue at hand is whether, as is widely believed, political realism requires construing the sovereign state—insofar as it is not subject to the authority of moral principles—as an amoral *Machtstaat*. Two political-realist approaches to registering the ethical edges of states can be distinguished.

The most common approach frames itself as a *dialectics* of idealism and realism. E.H. Carr made a classical realist case for the need to bridge the divide between "utopian" standards of value, purportedly constructed independently of politics, and the realists' conservative acquiescence in the world of amoral political fact (Carr 1939; Niebuhr 1960). This dichotomy trades on a questionable equivalence between the ethical realm and transcendent ideals. Conversely, it presumes that the state as such is merely a power entity, which can only acquire "provisional" ethical legitimacy (Ellis 2005) to the extent that it approximates those ideals. So defined the amoral realist and impractical idealist self-evidently need each other. Yet the persistent ingenuousness, or disingenuousness, of dialectical bridge-building only underlines the realist-idealist divide. There is the wishfulness of legitimations of the state based on (inevitably "tacit" or "hypothetical") popular *consent* (Geuss 2001:64–8). There is the habit of talking about the State by means of *euphemisms* with demo(cra)tic connotations, like "nation," "society," "community." In a formulation like: "[T]he strength of a nation lies ultimately not in arms but in its ability to provide decently for its people" (Hulsman and Lieven 2006:26), it is as if the sovereign entity *were* the people over whom protection and power is exercised. A third, again American, instance is the history of deploying democratic sovereignty and rights discourses as a means to constrain the states and "stimulate the growth of federal power" (Schudson 1999:261; see also Morgan 1988).

A less frequently taken ethical-realist stance asks: What if the State's ethical mission were shaped not by reference to transcendent ideals (or amoral self-interest) but by a worldly ethic of its own? A prototype of this way of normatively modelling state authority is the seventeenth century natural law jurisprudence of Samuel Pufendorf (1991). At a minimum, a sovereign political entity must be capable of protecting its citizens and its own capacities from external and internal harms, not least from its own derelict officials, *and* is under an *ethical obligation* to do so. It must refrain from foisting sectarian beliefs on a culturally heterogeneous population. For Pufendorf, natural law was grounded not in independent (divine) reason, but in the existence of a civil state power plus reasons for supporting it, *which presuppose its hegemony*. In the Pufendorfian tradition of statist ethics, political science and jurisprudence known as *prudential civilis* (Oestreich 1982: 90, 155–65); or as it was also known, "civil philosophy" (Hunter 2001:63–94), the state, a moral entity distinct from both government of the day *and* the governed, is conceived as a complex of partly independent, partly interconnected *offices*. Office-holders are bound by standards, purposes and *modi operandi* of good government that are built into the functioning of their distinct yet interdependent offices.

Unambivalent modern equivalents of this *civil-prudence*-based ethic of state are rare, though Raymond Geuss (2001) comes tantalizingly close. He starts from the position that the modern state as such is irreducible to states' capitalist, liberal, human rights based, and democratic features. Adapting Max Weber, Geuss argues that the (early-) modern sovereign state was constructed, independently of, or in opposition to these features, as a complex—multiple office based—form of *involuntary political association* (Geuss 2001:28–30, 49–51). He approves this form of state supremacy. But because it cannot be justified by a putatively "independent" moral theory he would not grant it "full" *ethical* status (Geuss 2001:42). This is but one example of how difficult it is to find an unambivalent realist ethic of state.

A third issue to which Flahault's work speaks arises out of the frequently voiced objection to government programs, which ignore aspects of social existence unamenable to utilitarian, capitalist, and/or economic calculations of losses and remittances. The question is: how should the shortcomings of such programs be conceived? A common line of critique conceives the nonutilitarian/economic/capitalist phenomena occluded in these programs as a *beyond*. One such critique exhorts social policy to address yearnings for redemptive "meaning," or "our deeper needs . . . for love, cooperation, nurturance, community, friendship and dedication to higher purposes" (Wachtel 1998:198). Now a policy, for instance, of educational tax credits to lower-income families would be unlikely to solicit reference to a politics of love, or prefigure the end of capitalism. Hence not only "neoliberalism," but also redistributive schemes to counter adverse impacts of market forces are exposed to this critique. The question is whether there exist other ways of thinking about nonfungible foci of social policies. Are human needs for "cooperation, nurturance, community, friendship" unintelligible outside the "deeper" registers of love and uppermost ideals?

The metaphysics of autonomy touches all of the above issues, but I will concentrate here on its implications for the human-nature/state nexus. In Kant's version, humans are members of a community of thinking-willing *spirits*. While tied by its sensuous nature to the causal-phenomenal world, humankind transcends it *via* an unlimited *contracausal* capacity for acting on the basis of *self-imposed* maxims. We *allow* ourselves to be swayed by malicious desires, and social or characterological pressures. Consequently, to attribute a *nature* to humans implies we are but a locus of natural forces: actions would not be "morally imputable" (Kant 1960:20).

Correlatively, a natural human incapacity for collective self-governance cannot be invoked as justifying a state's right to impose constraints on citizens. Through the metaphysical optic of radical autonomy, government is legitimate only insofar as morally self-governing citizens author or consent to the laws governing them. In the concise formulation of a latter-day neo-Kantian champion of radical democracy—reminding us that, before Marx, Kant envisioned the withering away of the state—true citizenship "would no longer be identical with subjection for anyone" (Balibar 1994:12).

So, the issue of metaphysical autonomy presents us with a choice. On the antiautono-mist model of civil prudence, however constrained in its ruling capacities a sovereign state may be by its democratic (and other "liberal") features, it remains a locus of supreme decision, imposing a quantum of political subjection. In the antithetical view, governed by the ideal of the self-governing community of citizens, Geuss' affirmation that a state is an "involuntary political association" is nothing but a charter for *servility*.

To be sure, there is a middle ground. But is it ever free of the sorts of fudging illustrated in my examples of realist-idealist dialectics? In my "ethical realist" book, an honest package of standards for registering shortcomings and permissible or worthwhile objectives in a civil state must accept that citizen status includes limited *political subjection* or *dependence*. But there is no gainsaying the prestige and appeal of images of the transcendently free person. To counter that imputation of servility attaching to political self-dependency, there's a need for *detranscendentalized anthropological counterimages*, which do not imply a generalized disapprobation of dependency.

Flahault: Dependencies and the Illimitation of Personal Existence

François Flahault's work is a rich source of such counterimages. In a recent polemic on the injunction to "be yourself" he calls his field of study "general anthropology" (Flahault 2006:243). This he envisages as a nascent cross-cutting intellectual field, which can be an object of contemporary social-scientific, psychological, anthropological, literary and (chastened) philosophical investigations, while also furnishing directional indicators for reformist social government. In extensive literary research, Flahault (2001) uncovered a cross-cultural strain of antiperfectionist reflection on the human condition implicit in folk tales. His published work includes studies of domestic discord, the constitution of senses of self in children, a history of faces, and the limits of capitalism (Flahault 1987; Flahault 1989; Flahault 2005). Best known to Anglophone readers is his (2003) study of malevolence. At the center of my exposition of his thought is a treatise (and a translated paper) on what Flahault dubs "the sentiment of existing," loss of which, he argues, is a fundamental source of malevolent dispositions (Flahault 1993, 2002).

What lends consistency to these wide-ranging studies is their mode of attention to intersections of human nature and the social. Flahault distances himself from specula-tive, aprioristic, and deterministic conceptualizations, which yield simplistic one-line predictive generalizations about man as a self-interested or benevolent individual. Such generalizations only reinforce social and political scientists' tendency to regard human nature as either *ultra vires*, philosophers' business, or to be avoided on principle. Flahault targets aspects of the human condition which, though replete with philosophical implications, are more commonly registered in dramatic or fictional forms, or in every-day commonplaces than in philosophy itself.

His picture of human nature is premised on antipathy to philosophical constructions of autonomous selfhood, which is driven by a "persistent desire for a redemption through thought, through a truth that would raise us above our ordinary human existence." Flahault's *"cure de désidéalization"* aims "as far as possible to add nothing to life such as we live it. No message. No meaning. Nothing elevating or exalting" (Flahault 2002:32–3). As we will see, that disclaimer does not preclude his anthropology's occupying a certain moral low ground.

In Western thought, the wish to add an ultramundane dimension to human life derives from Judeo-Christian conceptions of man's duplex—divine-but-fallen—nature, especially as modulated by (neo-) Platonic philosophies. Historiographical challenges to the presumption of a unitary "Enlightenment project" (e.g. Pocock 1999:5–9; Schutz 2005; Hunter 2001:1, 4–5, 14–5) have yielded increased appreciation that modern autonomist images of the person have differently enlightened competitors and are a reprise rather than repudiation of the religious *homo duplex* figure. Flahault adds to that challenge, focusing on the modern metaphysics of autonomy's *Promethean* twist to this religious figure. In Marx, Bataille, Sartre, and Heidegger, Flahault (2002:311–3; 2006: 109–14) finds a self-transcending image of the human as *plasticator*: "a creator who can model himself" free of constraints deriving from pre-given natural attributes.

Or herself. See how Flahault's "cure" for Promethean self-idealization operates in his bifocal response to a classic twentieth century feminist philosophical argument. That role-comportments associated with women are socially constructed is a constant theme in polemics against conservative representations of natural womanhood. Flahault concurs. He is not about defending invocations of human nature as a means to reinforce the social disadvantage of particular human groups, or to occlude the morally corrosive effects of bad social conditions. However, *pace* Simone de Beauvoir, from the fact that the *housewife role* is a cultural construction, it does not follow that one is not born a *woman* but made one. For the ethical force of her aphorism derives from the more questionable existentialist-Promethean image of the self as *plasticator*—an image which is hardly congruent with other feminist accounts of human beings' social interdependencies (Flahault 2002:303–5; compare Baier 1994:51–75).

Proponents of the self's metaphysical autonomy, continues Flahault (1993:249), conceptualize humans' inner being as suspending the principle of causality. This core of human being owes nothing to its social surrounds, which can only serve to enable or stultify its self-realization. Such assumptions run back to theometaphysical constructions of human souls as owing nothing to their parents. To the contrary, argues Flahault (2002:64–5), the psychical-social "tissue" of child–parent interactions comprise a non-voluntary constituent of ourselves.

Idealization of a socially transcendent selfhood is common ground in the standoff between pessimistic conservative-Augustinian moral anthropologies and optimistic secular-progressivists. The Augustinian view is that the causes of human wickedness lie in the perversity of the will (or "heart") as a consequence of the Fall. Postlapsarian man's incapacity to master the temptations of the body and the social, and their tumultuous consequences, is part of Christian *raisons d'être* for political authority to maintain social order. Notwithstanding Augustine's hereticizing polemics against philosophical overestimations of man's capacity for self-mastery, he remains an ur-metaphysician of autonomy in his insistence on the soul's independent capacity for willing good or evil.

How Flahault sloughs off what he dubs the *piano nobile* (Flahault 2002:58) of the neo-Augustinian autonomous self is nicely exemplified in his engagement with the great seventeenth century French Jansenist Pierre Nicole's essay "On the weakness of man."

Here is a seemingly orthodox sermonic contrast between the properly autarkical relation of the Christian souls to their alluring worldly surrounds when the heart is opened to God, and their too-common tendency to act as though their sustenance and consistency depends on social nexuses and worldly goods. However, argues Flahault, something misfires rhetorically. But let us first see a sample of Nicole's essay, in John Locke's translation:

> . . . [T]is the common lot of man . . . to be tumbled into a quiet and easy posture, but this state of tranquillity is so weak . . . that the least matter is enough to disturb it. The reason whereof is, that man supports himself not by fixing on some solid Truth . . . but rests himself upon a variety of slender props, and is, as it were, held up by an infinite number of small and fine threads (*fils faibles et delié*), fastened to as many empty bubbles, that depend not upon him; so that, some of them always failing he receives a jolt. We bear ourselves up upon the little circle of friends and admirers . . . our employments, that take up our thoughts, the hopes we entertain, the . . . businesses we undertake, make part of our supports; and a garden, a country house, or a closet of curiosities, are places of repose. (Nicole 1828:79–81; partly cited and discussed in Flahault 2002:29–33)·

Corresponding to these worldly domestic and workaday dependencies, Nicole observes, is the "feeling of infinite emptiness" (*vide infini*) that can afflict the dying, as their condition deprives them of the worldly relations, enjoyable activities and things that seemed to give life its *élan* (Flahault 2002:29–31).

What has gone awry? Nicole's inscribed orthodox Christian reader is supposed to experience this tableau of the soul's dependencies as a reminder of its deficiency and need for redemption. The trouble is that Nicole's matter-of-fact and touching representations of our dependencies are apt to induce effects of both recognition and acceptance: *c'est la vie*. In which case the several slender threads on which our sense of self may depend, like satisfying employment, children, a home or garden, good friends, health, are more humanly significant than empty bubbles. They do not portend a degrading situation requiring spiritual reversal. Rather, the soul is not *made* to be self-sustainable, but must find support from outside itself. Nicole's re-descriptions of human social dependencies undermine his redemptive interpretive framing of them.

Moreover, these dependencies can be *severed* from that frame. On one hand, Flahault's broader gambit is to retain something like an Augustinian sense of the soul's lack of self-sufficiency—and malignant capacities. On the other, he rejects *both* representations of its social dependencies as a moral and spiritual lack; *and* the correlative image of the fallen soul as possessed of a scintilla of contracausal autonomy from the social that enables it (aided by grace) to strive for self- redemption. Flahault challenges these ultramundane idealizations of the person by constructing nonderogatory counterimages of socially dependent selfhood, such that the social now appears as (to an extent) a positive means of sustaining selfhood. This two-step allows him to place himself at a symmetrical distance from *both* sides of the stand-off regarding human nature.

See how he treats the optimistic-progressivist *anti*-Augustinian supposition that the causes of human wickedness do not originate in the perverse soul of fallen man, but are always social products, which are in principle sociopolitically transformable. This shibboleth emerged out of influential eighteenth century Enlightened attacks (most famously by

Rousseau) on the Augustinian doctrine of original sin. The attacks, Flahault acutely observes, rarely extended to questioning the Augustinian axiom that prelapsarian man was possessed of godlike innocence. Rather this was reaffirmed. No account was taken of the internal relations between the "fallen man" story's three internally related "moments": primal innocence, sin, and redemption. Small wonder then that so much enlightened progressive thought generated secular equivalents of the Fall narrative. As in Rousseau, instead of the devil in serpentine disguise the demonic precipitator of man's fall from grace becomes "society." Explanations of human misdeeds in terms of social oppressive structures or forces too often imply, unnecessarily, that human beings, as such, like the prelapsarian Adam, have no inherent malevolent propensities. Taking the place of redemption are aspirations of social justice, predicated on radical social transformation (Flahault 2003:3–4, 12–14, 26–7, 90). Illustration of this conceptual reoccupation and its implications for the politics of benevolence is best reserved for our discussion of malice.

Furthering this work of detaching human dependency and dangerousness from Judaeo-Christian salvation doctrines—and again cross-cutting the secular-religious divide over human nature—is Flahault's critical discussion of the *monotheistic* footings of redemptive anthropologies and his contrasting evocation of the neglected conceptual resources of "pagan" cosmologies. In orthodox Christian theology life is a creation *ex nihilo*, and a reflection of God's infinite perfection. Chaos, symbolized by Satan, is evil *tout court*. Whereas, in pagan cosmologies, the beginning is a limitless, barely differentiated, abyssal Chaos, a primordial infinite and ill-defined mass sometimes embodied in creation myths as monsters (Behemoth, etc). Pagan creation consists in giving this mass form, a work of differentiating, containing, distancing, delimiting. In pagan creation stories, Chaos figures not simply as evil, but as a source of "limitless energy, which so long as it can be contained by forms, can nourish the dynamism of life" (Flahault 2003:26). In this perspective, infinite chaos—e.g. as reflected in folktales representing the jungle in relation to the order of a village—represents both a threat *and* a promise, good *and* evil.

Following anthropologist Marc Augé (1982), Flahault reads these Christian and pagan cosmologies as feeding into rival—but at times interwoven—moral anthropologies. Judeo-Christian monotheisms are an important source of universalist Western idealizations of freedom, justice, equality, democracy. Normative political philosophy supplies an array of justifications and edifying images of these ideals. But Flahault argues that to understand some less edifying reasons "why we are so fond of them" it is necessary to take account of this blending of rival moral anthropologies and cosmologies (Flahault 2003:140). Affective investments in Western ideals, he suggests, may have to with how they tap into the infinite or limitless dimension of existence, or "illimitation" as Flahault calls it. Protestant and secular-promethean intensifications of individual autonomy equally rest upon taking human beings' interiority as a mark of ultramundane transcendence (Flahault 2003:141). "The price of monotheism" has been the loss of pagan cosmologies' sense of the above-noted ambivalence of this infinite dimension. Monotheism identifies the infinite with moral and spiritual perfection. This equation blinds it to the maleficent edges of limitlessness—the "bad infinite" (Flahault 2003:16–33).

The human self is not just a limited dependent social creature but also in some sense has to be seen as embodying this "fount of limitlessness." The attractiveness of Milton's Satan is not only due to his embodying a spirit of revolt. Rather, like us, Satan is "racked by infinitude." Unlike most of us, he refuses to live a limited life of interdependent coexistence with others. He abandons himself to the urge to omnipotence, to the pleasures of creating mayhem (Flahault 2003:121–5). But we (Milton's readers) can vicariously partake in these pleasures.

Two aspects of Flahault's "cure" for idealizations of the autonomous self have been introduced: his detachment of the self's dependencies on social supports from the Christian metaphysical bifocal image of fallen-yet-redeemable man; and the critical distance he creates from monotheistically derived conceptions of the infinite/transcendent aspects of human subjectivity. Together these moves prepare the ground for the crux of his conception of human nature: "the sense of existing."

A Difficulty: To Exist

The sentiment of not existing, states the opening line of his sprawling magnum opus, *Le Sentiment d'Exister*, is both a commonly reported experience (*constat de plus banals*) and a breach in the self-evidence of the Cartesian *cogito*. No more than having a headache, consciousness thinking (or objective indicators of mental activity) gives no unconditional guarantee of a sense of existing or "*feeling* of being alive" (Flahault 2002:1).

He illustrates how feelings of not existing find expression in various literary testimonies (e.g. William Styron discussed by Flahault 2002:36–7). But to flesh out its meaning, let us begin with Flahault's account of a less sophisticated testimony to a feeling of nothingness reported in a popular magazine article featuring a bored provincial teenager who had been charged with committing "pointless" acts of vandalism. These acts, he says, makes him and his friends feel that they exist. Flahault compares these comments with scenarios of nothingness in the spiritual exercises and cultural circles of Heideggerian philosophy. In this milieu reflection on human finitude is supposed to induce an intensely anxious experience of nothingness in the face of superinstrumentalized modern life. The experience of not-being is treated as a means of elevating oneself above quotidian life and thereby opening oneself up to a glimpse of that Being about which modernity has forgotten. In contrast, these teenage delinquents testify to suffering from an inability to live an animated urban existence (Flahault 2002: 22–3, 32).

There is then nothing ethereal about the experience of (not) existing. It is the kind of consciousness you have when, for example, in circumstances of chronic unemployment (with its exclusionary effects), the days blur into one another, presenting no reason to get up in the morning. It may consist in a milder feeling of deadness or colorlessness with respect to one's immediate surrounds and life activities. It may involve feelings, often transient, of not really being there in one's place or body, of not counting for something (say, at a dinner party dominated by shop-talk in which one has no part). Or, contrary to the desire for self-affirmation, someone else is in your place, spoiling your enjoyment of life. Poverty, illness, hated neighbors, abject relations to intimates or to anyone, including "equals," with the power to block your wishes, can induce a feeling of "less-being." Conversely, certain experiences (an electrifying cabaret performance, a political demonstration, may induce sentiments of "more-being." One is infused with happiness, energy, vitality (Flahault 1993:252–3).

How does the sense of existing furnish an alternative to metaphysical images of autonomous agency? Because it draws further attention to the constitutive role of social others, to whom you can be useful; who have affection for you; or—if you are someone who loudly proclaims they do not care what anyone thinks of them—who will sustain your sense of existing by reflecting your non-conformist self image back to you. Quotidian cosmopolitan life no less than folk tales teach us that "to live we need to not be reduced to ourselves" (Flahault 2002:25; 2006:11–2).

So, our relations to other people, institutions, possessions may be a source of delight and psychical sustenance, or they may menace or irritate us (Flahault 2006:8). For the self-confirming effects of social relations are inseparable from their delimiting function with respect to the self qua repository of chaos, illimitation. Coexistence and cooperation, realizing our need for and attraction to others, are inconceivable apart from self-restraint, compromises, delimitations, etc. Even among the most altruistic, these sociable capacities must collide with the will to an infinite or undetermined freedom—to wish that the good shall triumph primarily, if not exclusively, through one's own efforts (Kierkegaard 1966:87–91).

In short, we are caught between "the impossibility of not depending on others and the impossibility of reaching self-completion through them" (Flahault 2003:112). Notice the absence here of morally asymmetrical weighting. If there is an endogenous impulsive cause of human dangerousness, it lies in this bedrock fact: "our being is formed both on the basis of a fount of limitlessness and on the basis of limitations that cut us off from it" (ibid., 30).

The sense of existing, Flahault (2002:1) suggests, here expressly invoking Hume, is more an impression than an idea. He characterizes its subjective register as "a subject of existence" as distinct from "a subject of knowledge." What he is mainly gunning for through this contrast is images of the self, which are projections of the self-image of the metaphysical thinker, and which downplay the all-the-way-down social dependencies of selfhood. Flahault profiles aspects of common personal existence, which rationalist metaphysics cannot readily recognize but which furnish background preconditions and hence *limits* for such thought.

For all its resistance to formal theoretical articulation, sentiments of existing, and of more- or less-being, are not inexpressible or recondite. The meaning and reference of the *sentiment d'exister* is closely bound up with Flahault's conception of the means of accessing it. A prominent surface of emergence of the "subject of existence" is fiction. Granted, fictional works may share similar pedagogical objectives with more formalizing philosophical discourses, e.g. to build a sense of injustice. Still, fictions usually cater to audiences that wish to be moved, excited, entertained. And it is in moments when social relations and individuals' mental universes are dramatized, when authors' and readers' moral guard is down, that human dispositions, which do not readily mesh with moral philosophical images of good or bad personhood hove into view. I will illustrate Flahault's use of literature in the course of sketching how, the sense of existing feeds into his account of malice.

Malice and Morality

Malice often involves calculation (how to maximize its object's suffering), but it is preeminently compulsive. This driven and extreme character of malicious attitudes and conduct is precisely what is lost in conventional moral philosophical conceptions of malevolence as a species of self-interest. Anglophone readers may be familiar with Albert Hirschman's (1977) and Stephen Holmes' (1995:42–68) demolition of this viewpoint via their recovery of seventeenth and eighteenth century "polite" philosophers' arguments for a partly self-interest-inflected-form of sociability. Among the antonyms of self-interest constructed in these philosophies of sociability we encounter the self-destructive, noncalculative, and even altruistic faces of malice. Acknowledging Hirschman, Flahault extends this decoupling of malice and self-interest by linking malice to an egoism of a very different order. Self-interest accounts for wishing to gain at another's expense, not for the desire to destroy them (Flahault 2003:6, citing Arendt).

Rather, the source of malice is argued to lie in human drives to illimitable self-assertion, insofar as this generates retributive aggression toward whatever is felt to diminish one's sense of existing (recall Flahault's claim that responsibility for a sense of "less-being" may be attributed to another.)

This emphasis on the urge to endlessly confirm the *sentiment d'exister* as a defining component of malice is reminiscent of psychoanalytical challenges to the image of the morally self-governing person and to that of morality as synonymous with order and restraint. Summarizing Freud's interest in morality's compulsive aspect, Jacques Lacan (1992:89) notes "a special quality of malice" coloring the superego's characteristically cruel and exorbitant demands. Irreducible to self-interest, aggressive malice, driven by an illimitable urge toward self-assertion, cannot be dissociated from altruism. Flahault also reprises Freud's (1985:284–5) comments on the difficulty of distinguishing between civilized challenges to institutional injustices and infantile, decivilizing assertions of egoistic freedom from moral constraints.

Flahault explores these unsettling contiguities of malice and struggles for justice in his discussion of the ambivalences of "the impulse to liberty" driving them. Libertarian sensibility embraces more than rationally warranted moral emotions, like resenting humiliations. "What a pleasure it is to hate when the hatred is fed by a legitimate accusation" (Flahault 2003:66). "Full enjoyment of legitimate hatred" can head justice-seekers into acting out a destructive rage for omnipotent self-completion. He backs up this contention with a reading of the eighteenth century progressive-enlightened philosopher William Godwin's novel, *Caleb Williams*. This was written to illustrate the progressive principles of social and political justice and associated picture of human innocence (absent an oppressive society) set out in his treatise, *Enquiries Concerning Political Justice*. But those principles are at odds with the infernal, accumulating rancor exhibited by his protagonist when he is subject to a series of injustices.

In a similar vein Flahault (2003:108–18) offers a jaundiced view of contemporary trust in "warm feelings" toward oppressed or otherwise suffering people in distant lands as the affective lynchpin of the contemporary social conscience. These feelings he sees as a further legacy of metaphysically enlightened-progressive reoccupations of the Christian fall narrative. The problem is not benevolence per se, but a "puritanism of good feeling," a widely cultivated experience of benevolence, which functions as self-protection against real differences and tensions and problems. This experience generates disingenuous images of the innocent and virtuous character of both the objects of oppression and the conscientious beholder, who is thereby licensed to regard morally ugly conduct of the oppressed as rendering them unworthy of assistance.

In sum, Flahault has painted a picture of human beings as by nature possessed of an ambivalent twofold predilection for limitless self-assertion and for self-restraining cooperation. For him, there is no ideal solution to the conflict between sociable and malicious propensities, no striving for dialectical balance. It can only be "managed" through mundane give-and-take, compromise, or a civilly circumscribed *agon*. Moral maturity is "mak[ing] the best of our incompleteness" (Flahault 2003:30, 57–8, 66, 108–18). In this account of personal-prudential settlements with oneself and others— "*bonnes ententes*"—we glimpse how, despite his insistence on not reaching for moral elevation, his general anthropology after all has an ethical edge. This is also discernable in Flahault's (2003:114) comment on "our worldly moral consciousness," which "corresponds to the feeling that must personally strive for the maintenance of everything that brings about a certain co-existence, a state from which one benefits, and to which, consequently one owes something."

Locating Flahault: Avatar of Civil Prudence?

Where to locate Flahault's work? Perhaps the salience of "the sense of existing" and his distinction between "subject of existence" and "subject of knowledge" make him an existentialist . . . yet of a peculiarly worldly kind. For in his accounts of Sartre and Heidegger the distance between his alternately stony and cheerful, but always unedifying authorial persona and the Promethean-redemptive cast of existentialist philosophy is clear. I also noted some affinities with psychoanalytical thought. Yet the Freudian unconscious is not a central category for Flahault. In Freudian terms, the sense of existing belongs in the *pre*conscious; for our need to exist is less repressed than prone to denial (Flahault 1993–6). His work has footings in psychoanalysis, but perhaps only to the extent—too tangled a matter to enter into here—that a more *naturalistic* Freud can be detached from lines of psychoanalytic thought and practice which are invested in an antinaturalistic (neo-Kantian) concept of human autonomy.

Other "locations" for the sentiment of existing might be investigated: "biopolitics" for example. For present purposes I propose to concentrate on some shared ground between Flahault and the civil prudence tradition as exemplified by Pufendorf. Flahault's affinity with its valorization of mundane forms of civility, sociality, and prudence is clear. I also suggested parallels with three other thinkers who are at least partly locatable in the civil prudence tradition: David Hume, Stephen Holmes, and Albert Hirschmann. But there is also a particularly telling homology between Pufendorf's and Flahault's anthropologies.

Such a comparison may seem unlikely. Pufendorf is a philosopher of state jurisprudence whereas the state as such does not figure in Flahault's work. Equally discouraging is Pufendorf's "demarcation argument." The ethical and political interests of the state in its citizenry should be limited to their public conducts and capacities, withdrawing from concerns with the state of his *soul* (Pufendorf 1991:6–13 and the editorial gloss, xxi–xxiv). That argument converges with Pufendorf's (1990) moral-anthropological backstory of human imperfection. Our intelligence, sociable dispositions, and organizational capacities do not suffice to protect us against malevolence and aggression, including our own. Civil peace cannot therefore be secured by depending on citizens schooled in a rational morally autonomous exercise of virtue. Rather, for political, legal and administrative purposes, the comportments of citizens and public officials must be constructed around impersonal "offices" (Hunter 2001, esp. pp. 154–68). Now why would an ethic of state so circumscribed have any interest in *psychological* sources of its citizens' or officials' misconduct?

These doubts are significant and I will return to them. But they hardly gainsay the parallel between the anthropologies bracing Flahault's "de-idealizing cure" and what Hunter (2001:169–80) terms Pufendorf's "de-transcendentalization" of political ethics. Pufendorf's anthropology reprises the Augustinian depiction of man's "furious pleasure in savaging his own kind" overshadowing our sociability and reason. But breaking with Augustine and the entire metaphysical-Christian natural law tradition, Pufendorf contends that natural law ethics should *not* presume any knowledge of man's Godlike "primeval integrity," to serve as "a model to which civil laws and customs must be conformed." Rather, "we will always presuppose a human nature tainted with depravity" (Pufendorf 1990:111–2).

Compare Flahault (2003:27): "It is possible to imagine the construction of the human psyche as being ambivalent *by nature, not because of a fall,* an evil by which it has become contaminated" (my emphasis). By different routes Pufendorf and Flahault both construct a desacralized image of the human which challenge rationalist images of the person as capable of autonomous self-government.

There is no doubting Pufendorf's disinterest in the psychological. But must this be off-limits to a contemporary rendition of a Pufendorfian ethic of state? Since Pufendorf's time, *psychological* interiority has become an object/effect of intense cultural and governmental investments. Can a plausible contemporary story about human nature ignore human beings' irreducible "psychological reality" (Wollheim 1999:3–6)? The proviso is—as Flahault's anthropology testifies—that to treat human beings and their interactions as a psychical space is not necessarily to attribute to the psychological a *transcendent(al)* (supracausal) dimension.

As well, a sense of the sources of human malignity might be relevant to addressing a stubborn problem for an ethics of office. Even in institutions consciously articulated around office-based tasks and turfs, cultural training is not exclusively office-based. At the level of operational units institutions such as armies incorporate a guild-like bonding ethos. A psychological supplement to a detranscendentalized anthropology might be thought to be less likely to forget that the human tendencies that necessitate civil government may induce pathologies of governing at the intersections of office- and guild-based sources of obligation and engagement. And in some contexts, it might be useful to draw on Flahault's view of humans' conflicted attitudes toward the social and the compromises needed to cope with these.

But what of the absence of the state in Flahault's anthropology? One consequence of this absence is that (unlike Pufendorf or Hume), Flahault does not supplement his view of social relations as constitutive supports of the self with a problematization of *social community,* in some forms and circumstances, as *itself* a source of civil discord. I am persuaded by his formulation that human beings are caught between the impossibility of not depending on others, and the impossibility of reaching self-completion through them. Yet human sociability may also express itself in the form of unremitting identification with an in-group imagined as a source, of self-completion rather than an obstacle to it. Hence not all forms and circumstances of social relations have a moderating effect on human self-assertion. From there, it is not a great step to the civil-prudential point that there may be nonsocial, *political,* conditions for social relations to sustain whilst moderating the self: viz.: vis, the setting up of some civil-sovereign entity) capable of limiting the sway of unsociable communities over other communities and over their own members. But this is not a step taken by Flahault.

Might a civil statist perspective be grafted onto his project? There are precedents in the civil prudence tradition, where it segues into the European "police" literature, to extend its purview from modeling the sovereign security-state into questions of administrative, constitutional, and social government that cannot be equitably addressed before the question of sovereignty is settled. Which brings us to our final expository topic, how Flahault's anthropology segues into a governmental philosophy, and how he offers to theorize the less quantifiable aspects of social deprivation.

Social Government as Reflection on Dependencies of Personal Existence

"Here we are, condemned to live in the world as it is." (Furet 1988:505).

Few late twentieth century texts have been as reviled by the French left as Francois Furet. The above citation comes from his historical diagnosis of the revolutionary hope, which came to be invested for so long by so many Western Europeans in the idea of communism and in its primary custodian, the Soviet Union, fuelled partly by a passionate hatred of "bourgeois" existence. Furet is invoked by Flahault (2002:57) as setting a nonutopian horizon for hopes of social betterment. Flahault's philosophy of social government seeks ways of kicking the political reformist's habit of retaining a political lexicon predicated on *société á la ideal* and "desire to be more than what one is" (2002:57, 46).

Former French socialist politician Michel Rocard is cited as a case in point (Flahault 2002:818), along with philosopher/economist Amartya Sen. Regarding the question of limits to capitalist, utilitarian, or economic calculation as the basis of social government, both recognize the import of noneconomic goods, but can only conceive them in terms of distributive justice. The noneconomic equates to values of individual self-realization and equality. Flahault's response is to pick out a connection between Sen's view of the social as distributable resources and his idealizing anthropological assumption of an autoeffective and omnipresent self, which can only be aided or impeded by society (Flahault 2002:809–12).

Flahault uses his counterimage of socially dependent, partly involuntary selfhood to present a more qualitative yet worldly reformist conception of noneconomic goods and bads. His reformist outlook is nicely epitomized in T.H. Marshall's notion of a *hyphenated* relation to capitalism rather than one based on the promise of transcending it. Except that Flahault insists that capitalism cannot be conceived as essentially an economic regime, along with its political and social supports. It can be "a source of vitality which is itself beneficent"—a force for social good and individual animation—*if* its tendency to crowd out or destroy other beneficial goods can be checked (Flahault 2002:805). One way of coming at the limits of capitalist/utilitarian calculation, he argues, is to attend to the worldly sociable meanings of sayings like "there's more to life than money." Many aspects of social existence escape quantitative and individualist-distributive logics insofar as they are only enjoyed in company (Flahault 2002:814–5). The social is not only a resource to be shared out for the benefit of an autoeffective and omnipresent self. We should also attend to "the means of achieving existence that social life offers" (Flahault 1993:249–50).

Conditions for sustaining a sense of existing, he argues, are implicit in empirical studies of what the "poverty of poverty" consists in, aside from lack of income, for social groups who are unemployed and concentrated into derelict housing projects (Flahault 2002:817–8). "[T]he problem raised by the aggravation of unemployment is, how to exist without working" (Flahault 1993:261). Contrary to the social-scientific tendency to equate talk of human nature with philosophy, he draws attention to a cluster of empirical factors surrounding poverty in which unsociable relations and natural psychological states are melded. These privations are at once social and spiritual, and involve relations to possessions as well as people. Recall Pierre Nicole on the "slender threads" – including our homes, more than solely an economic resource, or testimony to self-interested strivings— which sustain the sense of self (victims of the current subprime mortgage crisis might testify to that).

Such social-psychic privations render life psychologically insupportable. Some respond with malicious, nihilistic aggression, others give up on life. As to the latter, from the Hurricane Katrina disaster there emerged reports of able-bodied flood victims' passively waiting to be evacuated. This passivity provoked liberal-conservative ire based on imputing inherent human capacities for enterprise and self-responsibility. Anticonservative responses denied the imputation (blaming inadequate public transportation). Perhaps such "irresponsibility" should neither be denied nor elicit moralizing about "agency," if it reflects the corrosive effects of poverty and governmental neglect on the capacity to sustain a sense of self, a sentiment of existing.

Concluding Remarks

Earlier I cited François Furet's realist remark in *The Passing of an Illusion* about being "condemned to live in the world as it is" as emblematic of Flahault's attempt to de-idealize the social-solidaristic vocation of welfare. Yet in concluding, Furet reprises Western philosophers' habit of "investing society with unlimited hope." If the communist idea of revolutionary emancipation is dead, perhaps the messianic baton can be passed onto "democracy," which "by virtue of its existence creates the need for a world beyond the bourgeoisie in which a genuine human community can flourish" (Furet 1988:505). Furet's flip-flop into the romance of democratic community typifies the assumption *Le Sentiment d'Exister* sets out to challenge: that an amelioristic politics—including some vibe of hope—has to be staked on preserving revolutionizing ideals of self and society. And it highlights the rarity of Flahault's attempt to show that it is possible to think imaginatively and productively *inside* the frame of a welfare-capitalist policy philosophy.

The centerpiece of his challenge, and of this chapter, has been the "deidealized" depictions of the person in his "general" anthropology. In this picture, the dependencies of our sense of self on workaday, neighborhood, and domestic supports are not a problem from which we need deliverance, but facts of common life which sustain our very core of self. Where dependence on "society" collides with the self's ("illimitable") side, well, that urge for "completeness" too has pros and cons. It is to be coped with rather than idealized or demonized. The sense of existing is a challenge to images that "allow individuals to connect themselves through some [idealized] figure of completeness to an unconditional source of being" (Flahault 1993:267).

It is in connection with problems of political order posed by this runaway side of ourselves, and with problematizations of the political status quo, which are hitched to metaphysical ethoses of autonomy, that I saw parallels between Flahault's de-idealizing anthropology and the antiredemptive civil prudence tradition. Partly overlapping, partly colliding with other models of civil statehood assembled in this volume, civil prudence embodies a feeling for the difference a legal and administrative state makes—to citizens' security, coordination, social welfare, and personal or political freedoms, including the possibility of working for moral-political ends that civil prudence itself can only accommodate to a compromising degree. For it is an ethics and politics of imperfection. Civil states are a way to cope with an ethical *lack:* a limited capacity to put brakes on the will to self-assertion for purposes of collective and individual self-government.

Yet, for those committed to metaphysics of autonomy, such considerations of what a state is good for typically fail to outweigh its implication of political subjection. Despite his disinterest in the state Flahault' work may be pertinent to sustaining a civil-prudential model. It reprises the de-transcendentalizing gesture performed in Pufendorf's anthropology. It offers counterimages to celebrations of transcendent autonomy, accentuating the *dignitas* of social self-dependencies. And Flahault's philosophy of social government repudiates the assumption that supposing man to be dangerous by nature (Schmitt) is necessarily the hallmark of a conservative political stance.

Bibliography

Abram, J. 1996. *The Language of Winnicott: A Dictionary of Winnicott's Use of Words*. London: Karnac Books.

Acorn, A. 2004. *Compulsory Compassion: A Critique of Restorative Justice*. Vancouver: University of British Columbia Press.

Adhikari, G. 1943. "National Unity Now!" In *Pakistan and National Unity*, ed. G. Adhikari. Bombay: People's Publishing House, 5–9.

Agamben, G. 1993. *The Coming Community*. Minneapolis: University of Minnesota Press.

—1998. *Homo Sacer: Sovereign Power and Bare Life*. Stanford, CA: Stanford University Press.

—1999. *Potentialities: Collected Essays in Philosophy*. Stanford, CA: Stanford University Press.

—2003. *Stato di eccezione*. Torino: Bollati Borlinghieri.

—2005. *State of Exception*. Chicago, IL: University of Chicago Press.

Alter, J. 1996. "Gandhi's Body, Gandhi's Truth: Nonviolence and the Biomoral Imperative of Public Health." *Journal of Asian Studies* 55(2):301–22.

Ambedkar, B. R. 1925. *The Evolution of Public Finance in British India: A Study in the Provincial Decentralisation of Public Finance*. London: P.S. King.

—1946. *What Congress and Gandhi Have Done to the Untouchables*. Bombay: Thacker & Co.

Anderson, B. 1983. *Imagined Communities*. London: Verso.

Anderson, R. 1992. *Clinical Lecture on Klein and Bion*. London: Tavistock/Routledge.

Arendt, H. 1965. *On Revolution*. New York: Viking Press.

—1968. *Men in Dark Times*. New York: Harcourt Brace & Co.

—1998 [1958]. *The Human Condition*. Chicago, IL: University of Chicago Press.

Arjomand, S. A. and Tiryakian, E. A. eds. 2004. *Rethinking Civilizational Analysis*. London: Sage.

Audi, R. ed. 1999. *The Cambridge Dictionary of Philosophy*. 2nd ed. Cambridge: Cambridge University Press.

Augé, M. 1982. *Genie du Paganisme*. Paris: Gallimard.

Badiou, A. 2005a. *Being and Event*. London: Continuum.

—2005b. *Infinite Thought*. London: Continuum.

—2005c. *Metapolitics*. London: Verso.

—2006. *Polemics*. London: Verso.

Baier, A. 1994. "Hume, The Women's Moral Theorist?" In *Moral Prejudices: Essays on Ethics*, ed. A. Baier. Cambridge, MA: Harvard University Press, 51–75.

Balakrishnan, G. 2000. *The Enemy: An Intellectual Portrait of Carl Schmitt*. London: Verso.

Balibar, E. 1994. "Subjection and Subjectivation." In *Supposing the Subject*, ed. J. Copjec. London: Verso, 1–15.

Ball, K. 2000. "Trauma and its Institutional Destinies." *Cultural Critique* 46(Fall):1–44.

Banerjea, S. 1925. *A Nation in the Making*. London: Oxford University Press.

Barnard, F. M. 1988. "Fraternity and Citizenship: Two Ethics of Mutuality in Christian Thomasius." *The Review of Politics* 50:582–602.

Bateson, G. 1972. *Steps to an Ecology of Mind: Collected Essays in Anthropology, Psychiatry, Evolution, and Epistemology*. Chicago, IL: University of Chicago Press.

Bauman, Z. 1987. *Legislators and Interpreters*. Cambridge: Polity Press.

Beard, C. A. and Beard, M. R. 1962. *The American Spirit*. New York: Collier.

Beck, U. 2006. *Cosmopolitan Vision*. Cambridge, MA: Polity Press.

Bell, D. 1975. *The End of American Exceptionalism*. Cambridge, MA: Harvard University Press.

—2003. *Paranoia*. Cambridge: Icon Books.

Bendersky, J. W. 2004 [1934]. "Introduction: The Three Types of Juristic Thought in German Historical and Intellectual Context." In *On the Three Types of Juristic Thought*, ed. C. Schmitt. Westport, CT: Praeger, 1–42.

Benhabib, S. 2000. "Arendt's Eichmann in Jerusalem." In *The Cambridge Companion to Hannah Arendt*, ed. D. Villa. Cambridge: Cambridge University Press, 65–85.

Benjamin, J. 2004. "Beyond Doer and Done to: An Intersubjective View of Thirdness." *Psychoanalytic Quarterly* 73:5–46.

Benjamin, W. 2003. *Selected Writings, Vol. 4, 1938–1940*. Cambridge, MA: Harvard University Press.

Berg-Sørensen, A. 2004. *Paradiso-Diaspora. Reframing the Question of Religion in Politics*, Published PhD Thesis. Copenhagen: Department of Political Science, University of Copenhagen.

Berlin, I. 2002. "Two Concepts of Liberty." In *Liberty*, ed. H. Hardy. Oxford: Oxford University Press, 166–218.

Bhargava, R. 2000. "Restoring Decency to Barbaric Societies." In *Truth vs. Justice. The Morality of Truth Commissions*, eds. R. I. Rotberg and D. Thompson. Princeton, NJ: Princeton University Press, 45–67.

Bion, W. R. 1962. *Learning from Experience*. London: W. Heinemann Medical Books.

Birla, G. D. 1949. *The Path to Prosperity*. Bombay: Eastern Economist.

Blanchot, M. 1995. *The Writing of the Disaster*. Lincoln, NE: University of Nebraska Press.

Bodin, J. 1962 [1576]. *The Six Bookes of a Commonweale*. Cambridge, MA: Harvard University Press.

Bottici, C. and Challand, B. 2006. "Rethinking Political Myth: The Clash of Civilizations as a Self-Fulfilling Prophecy." *European Journal of Social Theory* 9(3):315–36.

Bowden, B. 2004a. "In the Name of Progress and Peace: The 'Standard of Civilization' and the Universalizing Project." *Alternatives* 29(1):43–68.

—2004b. "The Ideal of Civilisation: Its Origins and Socio-Political Character." *Critical Review of International Social & Political Philosophy* 7(1):25–50.

Breuer, S. 1991. "The Denouements of Civilization: Elias and Modernity." *International Social Science Journal* 128:401–16.

Brown, P. 1988a. *The Body and Society: Men, Women, and Sexual Renunciation in Early Christianity*. New York: Columbia University Press.

—1988b. *Power and Persuasion in Late Antiquity: Towards a Christian Empire*. Madison: The University of Wisconsin Press.

Brown, W. 2006. *Regulating Aversion*. Princeton, NJ: Princeton University Press.

Brudholm, T. 2008. *Resentment's Virtue. Jean Améry and the Refusal to Forgive*. Philadelphia, PA: Temple University Press.

Buchan, B. 2006. "Civilisation, Sovereignty and War: The Scottish Enlightenment and International Relations." *International Relations* 20(2):175–92.

Burchell, D. 1999. "The Disciplined Citizen: Thomas Hobbes, Neostoicism and the Critique of Classical Citizenship." *The Australian Journal of Politics and History* 45(4):506–24.

Burgess, G. 1999. *Absolute Monarchy and the Stuart Constitution*. New Haven, CT: Yale University Press.

Burkitt, I. 1996. "Civilization and Ambivalence." *British Journal of Sociology* 47(1):135–50.

Burns, J. H. ed. 1991. *The Cambridge History of Political Thought 1450–1700*. Cambridge: Cambridge University Press.

Butler, J. 1997. *Excitable Speech: Politics of the Performative*. New York: Routledge.

—2000. "Restaging the Universal: Hegemony and the Limits of Formalism." In *Contingency, Hegemony, Universality. Contemporary Dialogues on the Left*, eds. J. Butler, E. Laclau, and S. Žižek. London: Verso, 11–43.

Byres, T. J. 1994. "State, Class and Development Planning in India." In *The State and Development Planning in India*, ed. T. J. Byres. Delhi: Oxford University Press, 36–81.

Canovan, M. 2000. "Arendt's Theory of Totalitarianism: A Reassessment." In *The Cambridge Companion to Hannah Arendt*, ed. D. Villa. Cambridge: Cambridge University Press, 25–43.

Carr, E. 1939. *The Twenty Year's Crisis 1919–39*. London: Papermac.

Carritt, M. 1986. *A Mole in the Crown*. Calcutta: Rupa.

Caruth, C. 1995. "Introduction." In *Trauma. Explorations in Memory*, ed. Caruth, C. Baltimore: John Hopkins University Press, 3–12.

—1996. *Unclaimed Experience: Trauma, Narrative, and History*. Baltimore: Johns Hopkins University Press.

Charrier, P. J. 1995. *Britain, India and the Genesis of the Colombo Plan, 1945–1951*, Unpublished PhD Thesis. Cambridge: University of Cambridge.

Chartier, R. 1989. "The Practical Impact of Writing." In *A History of Private Life, Vol. 3: Passions of the Renaissance*, ed. R. Chartier. Cambridge, MA: Harvard University Press, 111–59.

Chatterjee, P. 1993. *The Nation and its Fragments*. Princeton, NJ: Princeton University Press.

Chattopadhyay, R. 1986. *Indian National Congress and the Indian Bourgeoisie: Liaquat Ali Khan's Budget of 1947–48*. Occasional Paper no. 85 of Centre for Studies in Social Sciences, Calcutta.

Christodoulidis, E. and Veitch, S. 2007. "Introduction." In *Law and the Politics of Reconciliation*, ed. S. Veitch. Aldershot: Ashgate, 1–8.

Clarke, S. and Hoggett, P. 2004. "The Empire of Fear: The American Political Psyche and the Culture of Paranoia." *Psychodynamic Practice* 10(1):89–106.

Cohen, J. 2006. "Sovereign Equality versus Imperial Right: The Battle over the New World Order." *Constellations* 13(4):485–506.

—2008. "Rethinking Human Rights, Democracy and Sovereignty in the Age of Globalization." *Political Theory* 36(4):578–607.

Cohn, N. 1970 [1957]. *The Pursuit of the Millennium*. Oxford: Oxford University Press.

Colas, D. 1997. *Civil Society and Fanaticism: Conjoined Histories*. Stanford, CA: Stanford University Press.

Coleridge, S. T. 1830. *On the Constitution of the Church and the State, According to the Idea of Each, with Aids Towards a Right Judgment on the Late Catholic Bill*. London: Hurst, Chance & Co.

Condren, C., Gaukroger, S. and Hunter, I. eds. 2006. *The Philosopher in Early Modern Europe: The Nature of a Contested Identity*. Cambridge: Cambridge University Press.

Cooper, A. 1988. *Sharecropping and Sharecroppers' Struggles in Bengal 1930–1950*. Calcutta: KP Bagchi.

Damodaran, V. 1992. "Azad Dastas and Dacoit Gangs: The Congress and Underground Activity in Bihar, 1942–44." *Modern Asian Studies* 26(3):417–50.

Das, S. 1991. *Communal Riots in Bengal 1905–1947*. Delhi: Oxford University Press.

Dasgupta, A. 1996. *Gandhi's Economic Thought*. London: Routledge.

Davidson, J. 1999. *Courtesans and Fishcakes: The Consuming Passions of Classical Athens*. New York: Harper Perennial.

Davis, M. 2001. "The Flames of New York." *New Left Review* 112:34–50.

de Swaan, A. 1995. "Widening Circles of Identification: Emotional Concerns in Sociogenetic Perspective." *Theory, Culture & Society* 12(2):25–39.

—1997. "Widening Circles of Disidentification: On the Psycho- and Sociogenesis of the Hatred of Distant Strangers-Reflections on Rwanda." *Theory, Culture & Society* 14(2):105–22.

—2001. "Dyscivilization, Mass Extermination and the State." *Theory, Culture & Society* 18(2–3):265–76.

Demertzis, N. 2006. "Emotions and Populism." In *Emotion, Politics and Society*, eds. S. Clarke, P. Hoggett and S. Thompson. Basingstoke: Palgrave Macmillan.

den Boer, P. 2001. "Vergelijkende begripsgechiedenis." In *Beschaving*, ed. P. den Boer. Amsterdam: Amsterdam University Press.

Denzer, H. 1972. *Moralphilosophie und Naturrecht bei Samuel Pufendorf. Eine geistes- und wissenschaftliche Untersuchung zur Geburt des Naturrechts aus der Praktischen Philosophie*. Munich: C. H. Beck.

Derrida, J. 1994. *Specters of Marx: The State of the Debt, the Work of Mourning, and the New International.* New York: Routledge.

Derrida, J. and Caputo, J. 1996. *Deconstruction in a Nutshell: A Conversation with Jacques Derrida.* New York: Fordham University Press.

Dev, A. N. 1934. "The Task before Us." At the Congress Socialist Party, 29 September 1934.

Donnelly, J. 1998. "Human Rights: A New Standard of Civilization?" *International Affairs* 74(1):1–24.

Dossa, S. 1989. *The Public Realm and the Public Self: The Political Theory of Hannah Arendt.* Waterloo: Wilfrid Laurier University Press.

Douzinas, C. 2007. *Human Rights and Empire.* Milton Park: Routledge-Cavendish.

Dreitzel, H. 2001. "Naturrecht als politische Philosophie." In *Die Philosophie des 17. Jahrhunderts, Band 4: Das heilige Römische Reich deutscher Nation, Nord- und Ostmitteleuropa,* eds. H. Holzhey and W. Schmidt-Biggemann. Basel: Schwabe.

Dryzek, J. S. 2005. "Deliberative Democracy in Divided Societies: Alternatives to Agonism and Analgesia." *Political Theory* 33(2):218–42.

du Toit, L. H. 2007. "Feminism and the Ethics of Reconciliation." In *Law and the Politics of Reconciliation,* ed. S. Veitch. Aldershot: Ashgate, 185–213.

Duerr, H. P. 1988. *Nacktheit und Scham.* Frankfurt a.M.: Suhrkamp.

—1990. *Intimität.* Frankfurt a.M.: Suhrkamp.

—1993 *Obszönität und Gewalt.* Frankfurt a.M.: Suhrkamp.

—1997. *Der erotische Leib.* Frankfurt a.M.: Suhrkamp.

—2002. *Die Tatsachen des Lebens.* Frankfurt a.M.: Suhrkamp.

Dyzenhaus, D. 2005. "The State of Emergency in Legal Theory." In *Global Anti-terrorism Law and Policy,* eds. V. V. Ramraj, M. Hor and K. Roach. Cambridge: Cambridge University Press, 65–89.

—2006. *The Constitution of Law. Legality in a Time of Emergency.* Cambridge: Cambridge University Press.

Elias, N. 1972. "Processes of State Formation and Nation Building." Conference Paper Presented at Transactions of the 7th World Congress of Sociology, September 1970, Varna, International Sociological Association.

—1983. *The Court Society.* Oxford: Blackwell.

—1986. "Soziale Prozesse." In *Grundbegriffe der Soziologie,* ed. B. Schäfers. Opladen: Leske en Budrich, 382–7.

—1988. "Violence and Civilization: The State Monopoly of Physical Violence and its Infringement." In *Civil Society and the State,* ed. J. Keane. London: Verso, 177–99.

—1991. *The Society of Individuals.* Oxford: Basil Blackwell.

—1996. *The Germans: Power Struggles and the Development of Habitus in the Nineteenth and Twentieth Centuries.* Cambridge: Polity Press.

—2000. *The Civilizing Process. Sociogenetic and Psychogenetic Investigations,* Revised Edition of 1994. Oxford: Blackwell.

Ellis, E. 2005. *Kant's Politics: Provisional Theory for an Uncertain World.* New Haven, CT: Yale University Press.

Elwin, V. 1964. *The Tribal World of Verrier Elwin: An Autobiography.* Bombay: Oxford University Press.

Engler, W. 1991. "Vom Deutschen: Reflexive contra selbsdestructive zivilisierung." *Sinn und Form* 43(2):268–83.

—1992. *Die zivilisatorische Lücke.* Frankfurt a.M.: Suhrkamp.

Erikson, K. 1995. "Notes on Trauma and Community." In *Trauma. Explorations in Memory,* ed. C. Caruth. Baltimore, MD: John Hopkins University Press, 183–99.

Ewald, F. 1987. "Risk, Insurance, Society." *History of the Present* 3:1–12.

Fanon, F. 1965. "Algeria unveiled." In *A Dying Colonialism,* F. Fanon. New York: Grove Press, 35–68.

Febvre, L. 1998 [1930]. "Civilisation: Evolution of a word and a group of ideas." In *Classical Readings in Culture and Civilization*, eds. J. Rundell and S. Mennell. London: Routledge, 160–90.

Felman, S. 2002. *The Juridical Unconscious. Trials and Traumas in the Twentieth Century*. Cambridge, MA: Harvard University Press.

Ferejohn, J. and Pasquino, P. 2005. "The Law of the Exception: A Typology of Emergency Powers." *International Journal of Constitutional Law* 2:210–39.

Fidler, D. P. 2001. "The Return of the Standard of Civilization." *Chicago Journal of International Law* 2:137–57.

Flahault, F. 1987. *La Scene de Ménage*. Paris: Denoel.

—1989. *Face a face: Essai sur la visage et le regard*. Paris: Plon.

—1993. "The sense of existing." *Salmagundi* 104–5:248–70.

—2001. *La Pensée des Contes*. Paris: Anthropos.

—2002. *Le Sentiment d'Exister: Ce Soi Qui Ne Va Pas De Soi*. Paris: Descartes et Cie.

—2003. *Malice*. London: Verso.

—2005. *Le Paradoxe de Robinson: Capitalisme et Société*. Paris: Milles et Une Nuits.

—2006. *Be Yourself!: Au Dela De La Conception Occidentale De L'individu*. Paris: Milles et Une Nuits.

Fletcher, J. 1997. *Violence and Civilization*. Cambridge: Polity.

Foucault, M. 1977. *Discipline and Punish*. London: Allen & Unwin.

—1986a. *The Care of the Self*. New York: Pantheon.

—1986b. *The Use of Pleasure*. New York: Pantheon.

Fousek, J. 2000. *To Lead the Free World: American Nationalism and the Ideological Origins of the Cold War*. Chapel Hill, NC: University of Carolina Press.

Franke, H. 1988. "Opvoeding als doelbewuste civilisering: Een penitentiar beschavingsoffensief in het interbellum." *Amsterdams Sociologisch Tijdschrift* 15(1):108–30.

Franke, W. 2007. "Preface. One the Apophasis as a Mode of Discourse." In *On What Cannot Be Said. Apophatic Discourses in Philosophy, Religion, Literature and the Arts*, ed. W. Franke. Notre Dame: University of Notre Dame, 1–7.

Frankel, F. 1978. *India's Political Economy, 1947–1977: The Gradual Revolution*. Princeton, PA: Princeton University Press.

Freud, S. 1917. *Mourning and Melancholia*. The Standard Edition of the Complete Psychological Works of Sigmund Freud, Vol. 14 (1914–1916), ed. J Strachey.

Friedeburg, R. v. 2003. "Natural Jurisprudence, Argument from History and Constitutional Struggle in the Early Enlightenment: The Case of Gottlieb Samuel Treuer's Polemic against Absolutism in 1719." In *Early Modern Natural Law Theories: Contexts and Strategies in the Early Enlightenment*, eds. T. J. Hochstrasser and P. Schröder. Dordrecht: Kluwer, 141–68.

Fukuyama, F. 1992. *The End of History and the Last Man*. London: Penguin.

Gauchet, M. 1994. "L'Etat au miroir de la raison d'Etat: la France et la Chrétieneté." In *Raison et déraison d'état: théoriciens et théories de la raison d'état aux XVIe et XVIIe siècles*, ed. J. C. Zarka. Paris: Presses Universitaires de la France, 198–205.

Geuss, R. 2001. *History and Illusion in Politics*. Cambridge: Cambridge University Press.

Glassner, B. 1999. *The Culture of Fear: Why Americans are Afraid of the Wrong Things*. New York: Basic Books.

Golwalkar, M. 1938. *We, or Our Nationhood Defined*. Nagpur: Bharat Publications.

Gong, G. W. 1984. *The Standard of "Civilization" in International Society*. Oxford: Clarendon Press.

Goody, J. 2002. "Elias and the Anthropological Tradition." *Anthropological Theory* 2(4):401–12.

—2003. "The 'Civilizing Process' in Ghana." *Archives Européennes de Sociologie* 44(1):61–73.

Gopal, S. 1979. *Jawaharlal Nehru: A Biography, Vol. 2: 1947–1956*. London: Cape.

Gopal, S. ed. 1984. *Selected Works of Jawaharlal Nehru*. New Delhi: Jawaharlal Nehru Memorial Fund.

—1972. *Selected Works of Jawaharlal Nehru*. New Delhi: Orient Longman.

Gouldner, A. W. 1981. "Doubts about the Uselessness of Men and the Meaning of the Civilizing Process." *Theory & Society* 10(3):413–8.

Gramsci, A. 1971. "The Intellectuals." In *Antonio Gramsci, Selections from the Prison Notebooks*, eds. Q. Hoare, and G. N. Smith. London: Lawrence and Wishart, 1–48.

Gross, O. 2003. "Chaos and Rules: Should Responses to Violent Crises Always be Constitutional?" *Yale Law Journal* 112(5):1011.

Grotius, H. 1925 [1625]. *The Law of War and Peace*. Oxford: Clarendon Press.

Guha, R. 1999. *Savaging the Civilised: Verrier Elwin, His Tribals, and India*. Chicago, IL: University of Chicago Press.

Habib, S. I. 2007. *To Make the Deaf Hear*. Delhi: Three Essays Press.

Hadot, P. 1995. *Philosophy as a Way of Life: Spiritual Exercises from Socrates to Foucault*. Oxford: Blackwell.

Haferkamp, H. 1987. "From the Intra-State to the Inter-State Civilizing Process?" *Theory, Culture & Society* 4(2–3):545–57.

Hamilton, A., Madison, J. and Jay, J. 1961. *The Federalist Papers*. New York: Signet.

Hammerstein, N. 1986. "Universitäten—Territorialstaaten—Gelehrte Räte." In *Die Rolle der Juristen bei der Enstehung des modernen Staates*, ed. R. Schnur. Berlin: Duncker & Humblot, 687–735.

Hasan, M. 1997. *Legacy of a Divided Nation: India's Muslims Since Independence*. London: Hurst.

Heehs, P. 1993. *The Bomb in Bengal: The Rise of Revolutionary Terrorism in India 1900–1910*. Delhi: Oxford University Press.

—1998. *Nationalism Terrorism, Communalism: Essays in Modern Indian History*. Delhi: Oxford University Press.

Heller, A. 2007. "The Shame of Trauma, the Trauma of Shame." In *Trauma, History, Philosophy*, ed. M. Sharpe. Newcastle, UK: Cambridge Scholars Press.

Hirschman, A. O. 1977. *The Passions and the Interests*. Princeton, NJ: Princeton University Press.

Hobbes, T. 1845. *The English Works of Thomas Hobbes of Malmesbury: Now First Collected and Edited by Sir William Molesworth, Vol. 2: Philosophical Rudiments Concerning Government and Society; Vol. 3: Leviathan: Or the Matter, Form, and Power of a Commonwealth, Ecclesiastical and Civil*. London: John Bohn.

—1994 [1651]. *Leviathan, with Selected Variants from the Latin Edition of 1668*. Indianapolis: Hackett.

—1996. *Leviathan*. Cambridge: Cambridge University Press.

Hoggett, P. 2005. "Blair's Mission Impossible." *British Journal of Politics and International Relations* 7(4):418–28.

Hoggett, P., Mayo, M. and Miller, C. 2007. "Individualization and Ethical Agency." In *Contested Individualization: Debates about Contemporary Personhood*, ed. C. Howard. New York: Palgrave Macmillan, 99–116.

Holmes, S. 1995. *Passions and Constraint*. Chicago, IL: University of Chicago Press.

Honderlich, T. 2005. *Conservatism: Burke, Nozick, Bush, Blair*. Pluto: London.

Hulsman, J. and Lieven, A. 2006. *Ethical Realism: A Vision for America's Role in the World*. New York: Pantheon.

Hunter, I. 1992. "Aesthetics and Cultural Studies." In *Cultural Studies*, eds. C. Nelson, P. Treichler and L. Grossberg. New York: Routledge, 347–67.

—2001. *Rival Enlightenments: Civil and Metaphysical Philosophy in Early Modern Germany*. Cambridge: Cambridge University Press.

—2002. "The Morals of Metaphysics: Kant's Groundwork as Intellectual Paideia." *Critical Inquiry* 28(4):908–22.

—2003. "The Love of a Sage or the Command of a Superior: The Natural Law Doctrines of Leibniz and Pufendorf." In *Early Modern Natural Law Theories: Strategies and Contexts in the Early Enlightenment*, eds. T. J. Hochstrasser and P. Schröder. Dordrecht: Kluwer, 169–94.

—2004a. "Conflicting Obligations: Pufendorf, Leibniz and Barbeyrac on Civil Authority." *History of Political Thought* 25(4):670–99.

—2004b. "Reading Thomasius on Heresy." *Eighteenth-Century Thought* 2:39–55.

—2005. "The Passions of the Prince: Moral Philosophy and Staatskirchenrecht in Thomasius's Conception of Sovereignty." *Cultural and Social History* 2:113–29.

—2006. "The History of Theory." *Critical Inquiry* 33(4):78–112.

—2007. *The Secularisation of the Confessional State: The Political Thought of Christian Thomasius.* Cambridge: Cambridge University Press.

—2008. "Critical Response II: Talking about My Generation." *Critical Inquiry* 34(2):583–600.

Huntington, S. P. 1993. "The Clash to Civilizations?" *Foreign Affairs* 72(3):22–49.

Inden, R. 2000 [1990]. *Imagining India.* London: Hurst.

Isaacs, S. 1989. "The Nature and Function of Phantasy." In *Developments in Psychoanalysis*, eds. M. Klein. et al. London: Karnac Books, 67–121.

Ivison, D. 2008. "Historical Injustice." In *The Oxford Handbook of Political Theory*, eds. J. S. Dryzek, B. Honig and A. Philips. Oxford: Oxford University Press, 507–24.

Jacobus, M. 1999. *Psychoanalysis and the Scene of Reading.* Oxford: Oxford University Press.

Jalal, A. 1985. *The Sole Spokesman: Jinnah, the Muslim League and the Demand for Pakistan.* Cambridge: Cambridge University Press.

James, E. 1972. *Pierre Nicole, Jansenist and Humanist.* The Hague: Nijhoff.

Jarausch, K. and Lindenberger, T. 2007. *Conflicted Memories. Europeanizing Contemporary Histories.* New York: Berghahn Books.

Kaldor, M. 1999. *New & Old Wars: Organized Violence in a Global Era.* Stanford, CA: Stanford University Press.

Kammen, M. 1993. "The Problem of American Exceptionalism: A Reconsideration." *American Quarterly* 45(1):1–43.

Kant, I. 1960. *Religion within the Limits of Reason Alone.* New York: Harper.

—1970. "Idea for a Universal History with a Cosmopolitan Purpose." In *Kant's Political Writings*, ed. H. Reiss. Cambridge: Cambridge University Press, 41–54.

—2000. *Critique of the Power of Judgment.* Cambridge: Cambridge University Press.

Khilnani, S. 1991. "Democracy and the Limits of Political Community." *Economy and Society* 20(2):196–204.

—1999. *The Idea of India.* New York: Farrar Straus Giroux.

Kierkegaard, S. 1966. *Purity of Heart is to Will One Thing.* New York: Fontana.

Kilby, J. 2002a. "Redeeming Memories. The Politics of Trauma and History." *Feminist Theory* 3(2):201–10.

—2002b. "The Writing of Trauma: Trauma Theory and the Liberty of Reading." *New Formations* 47:217–30.

Kipling, R. 1891. *City of Dreadful Night.* Allahabad: AH Wheeler.

Klein, M. 1935. "A Contribution to the Psycho-Genesis for Manic-Depressive States." Reprinted in 1975 in *The Writings of Melanie Klein Vol.1: Love, Guilt and Reparation*, M. Klein. London: Hogarth, 262–89.

—1946. "Notes on Some Schizoid Mechanisms." Reprinted in 1975 in *Writings of Melanie Klein Vol.3: Envy and Gratitude*, M. Klein. London: Hogarth, 1–24.

Klein, M. and Rivière, J. 1964. *Love, Hate and Reparation.* New York: W.W.Norton & Co.

Koskenniemi, M. 2001. *The Gentle Civilizer of Nations.* Cambridge: Cambridge University Press.

Kriegel, B. 1995. *The State and the Rule of Law.* Princeton, NJ: Princeton University Press.

—2002. "The Rule of the State and Natural Law." In *Natural Law and Civil Sovereignty: Moral Right and State Authority in Early Modern Political Thought*, eds. I. Hunter, and D. Saunders. Basingstoke and New York: Palgrave Macmillan, 13–26.

Kristeva, J. 1982. *Powers of Horror. An Essay on Abjection.* New York: Columbia University Press.

Kruithof, B. 1980. "De deugdzame natie: het burgerlijk beschavingsoffensief van het Maatschappij tot Not van 't Algemeen tussen 1784 en 1860." *Symposium* 2(1):22–37.

LaCapra, D. 2004. *History in Transit: Experience, Identity, Critical Theory.* Ithaca, NY: Cornell University Press.

Lasch, C. 1985. *The Minimal Self: Psychic Survival in Troubled Times*. New York: W. W. Norton.

Lasswell, H. D. 1934 [1930]. *Psychopathology and Politics*. Chicago, IL: University of Chicago Press.

—1965 [1935]. *World Politics and Personal Insecurity*. Glencoe, IL: Free Press.

Latour, B. 2005. *Reassembling the Social*. Oxford: Oxford University Press.

Laushey, D. M. 1975. *Bengal Terrorism and the Marxist Left: Aspects of Regional Nationalism in India, 1905-1942*. Calcutta: Firma KL Mukhapadhyay.

Lederach, J. P. 2005. *Moral Imagination: The Art and Soul of Building Peace*. Oxford: Oxford University Press.

Lefort, C. 1988. *Democracy and Political Theory*. Minnesota: University of Minnesota Press.

Leibniz, G. W. 1972. "On the Principles of Pufendorf." In *Political Writings*, ed. P. Riley. Cambridge: Cambridge University Press, 64-76.

Lelyveld, D. 1978. *Aligarh's First Generation: Muslim Solidarity in British India*. Princeton, PA: Princeton University Press.

Levi, P. 1988. *The Drowned and the Saved*. New York: Vintage International.

Leys, R. 2000. *Trauma: A Genealogy*. Chicago, IL: University of Chicago Press.

Linklater, A. 2004. "Norbert Elias, the 'Civilizing Process' and the Sociology of International Relations." *International Politics* 41(1):3-35.

Lipsius, J. 2005 [1584]. *De Constantia*. Bristol: Bristol Phoenix Press.

Locke, J. 1967. *Two Treatises of Government*. Cambridge: Cambridge University Press.

Loughlin, M. 2003. *The Idea of Public Law*. Oxford: Oxford University Press.

Machiavelli, N. 1961. *The Prince*. Harmondsworth: Penguin.

Malpas, J. 2006. *Heidegger's Topology: Being, Place, World*. Cambridge, MA: MIT Press.

Marchart, O. 2007. *Post-foundational Political Thought: Political Difference in Nancy, Lefort, Badiou and Laclau*. Edinburgh: Edinburgh University Press.

Markovits, C. 1985. *Indian Business and Nationalist Politics*. Cambridge: Cambridge University Press.

Marris, P. 1996. *The Politics of Uncertainty: Attachment in Public and Private Life*. London: Routledge.

Marshall, P. 1970. *The British Discovery of Hinduism in the Eighteenth Century*. London: Cambridge University Press.

Masani, M. 1982. *Against the Tide*. New Delhi: Vikas Publishing House.

Maxwell, N. 1970. *India's China War*. London: Jonathan Cape.

Mayo, K. 1927. *Mother India*. London: Jonathan Cape.

—1931. *Mother India. Volume Two*. London: Jonathan Cape.

Mazlish, B. 2004. *Civilization and its Contents*. Stanford, CA: Stanford University Press.

McCormick, J. P. 2004 [1958]. "Identifying or Exploiting the Paradoxes of Constitutional Democracy: An Introduction to Carl Schmitt's Legality and Legitimacy." In *Legality and Legitimacy*, C. Schmitt, ed. J. Seitzer. Durham: Duke University Press, xiii-xliii.

McCrisken, T. 2000. *American Exceptionalism and the Legacy of Vietnam: US Foreign Policy Since 1974*. Basingstoke: Macmillan.

—2001. "Exceptionalism." In *Encyclopedia of American Foreign Policy*, eds. A. DeConde, R. Burns and F. Longevall. New York: Charles Scribner, 63-80.

McGowan, I., Hamilton, S., Miller, P. and Kernohan, G. 2005. "Contrasting Terrorist-Related Deaths with Suicide Trends over 34 years." *Journal of Mental Health* 14(4):399-405.

McLane, J. 1977. *Indian Nationalism and the Early Congress*. Princeton, PA: Princeton University Press.

Melucci, A. 1988. "Social Movements and the Democratization of Everyday Life." In *Civil Society and the State*, ed. J. Keane. London: Verso, 245-61.

Mennell, S. 1990. "Decivilizing Processes: Theoretical Significance and Some Lines of Research." *International Sociology* 5(2):205-23.

Menon, R. and Kamla, B. 1998. *Borders and Boundaries: Women in India's Partition*. New Brunswick, NJ: Rutgers University Press.

Minault, G. 1982. *The Khilafat Movement: Religious Symbolism and Political Mobilization in India.* New York: Columbia University Press.

Minow, M. 1998. *Between Vengeance and Forgiveness. Facing History after Genocide and Mass Violence.* Boston, MA: Beacon Press.

—2000. "The Hope for Healing: What Can Truth Commissions Do?" In *Truth vs. Justice. The Morality of Truth Commissions,* eds. R. I. Rotberg and D. Thompson. Princeton, NJ: Princeton University Press, 235–60.

Mitzman, A. 1987. "The Civilizing Offensive: Mentalities, High Culture and Individual Psyches." *Journal of Social History* 20(4):663–87.

Monroe, K. R. 1996. *The Heart of Altruism.* Princeton, NJ: Princeton University Press.

Moon, P. ed. 1973. *Wavell: The Viceroy's Journal.* London: Oxford University Press.

Moore, R. J. 1987. *Making the New Commonwealth.* Oxford: Clarendon Press.

Morgan, E. 1988. *Inventing the People: The Rise of Popular Sovereignty in England and America.* New York: Norton.

Mouffe, C. 1999. "Carl Schmitt and the Paradox of Liberal Democracy." In *The Challenge of Carl Schmitt,* ed. C. Mouffe. London: Verso, 38–53.

—2000. *The Democratic Paradox.* London: Verso.

—2005. *On the Political.* Milton Park: Routledge.

Muller, J. ed. 1997. *Conservatism: An Anthology of Social and Political Thought From David Hume to the Present.* Princeton, PA: Princeton University Press.

Narayan, J. 1936. *Why Socialism?* Benares: All India Congress Socialist Party.

Nehru, J. 1936. *Autobiography.* London: The Bodley Head.

—1946. *Discovery of India.* London: Signet.

Nicole, P. 1828. *Discourses Translated from Nicole's Essays by John Locke, with Important Variations: On the Existence of a God, on the Weakness of Man, on the Way of Preserving Peace.* London: Harvey, Darnton & Co.

Niebuhr, R. 1952. "Culture and Civilization (a Summary)." *Confluence* 1(1):66–76.

—1960. *Moral Man and Immoral Society.* New York: Charles Scribner.

Nietzsche, F. 1982. *Daybreak: Thoughts on the Prejudices of Morality.* Cambridge: Cambridge University Press.

Oestreich, G. 1975. "Justus Lipsius als Universalgelehrter Zwischen Renaissance und Barock." In *Leiden University in the Seventeenth Century: And Exchange of Learning,* eds. T. H. Lunsingh Scheurleer and G. H. M. Meyjes. Leiden: Brill, 177–201.

—1982. *Neostoicism and the Early Modern State.* Cambridge: Cambridge University Press.

Olick, J. K. 2007. *The Politics of Regret. On Collective Memory and Historical Responsibility.* London: Routledge.

Olzak, S. 1992. *The Dynamics of Ethnic Competition and Conflict.* Stanford, CA: Stanford University Press.

Omvedt, G. 2004. *Ambedkar: Towards an Enlightened India.* New Delhi: Penguin.

Padoa-Schioppa, A. 1997. "Hierarchy and Jurisdiction: Models in Medieval Canon Law." In *Legislation and Justice,* ed. A. Padoa-Schioppa. Oxford: Oxford University Press, 1–15.

Pagden, A. 2000. "Stoicism, Cosmopolitanism, and the Legacy of European Imperialism." *Constellations* 7(1):3–22.

Pandey, G. ed. 1988. *The Indian Nation in 1942.* Calcutta: KP Bagchi.

Parker, N. ed. 2008. *The Geopolitics of Europe's Identity: Centers, Boundaries and Margins.* London: Palgrave Macmillan.

Pateman, C. 1979. *The Problem of Political Obligation: A Critical Analysis of Liberal Theory.* New York: John Wiley & Sons.

Pels, D. 1998. *Property and Power in Social Theory: A Study in Intellectual Rivalry.* London: Routledge.

Penglase, J. 2005. *Orphans of the Living: Growing up in "Care" in Twentieth-Century Australia.* Fremantle: Fremantle Arts Centre Press.

Pettit, P. 2002. "Keeping Republican Freedom Simple: On a Difference with Quentin Skinner." *Political Theory* 30(3):339–56.

Phillips, A. 2007. *Multiculturalism without Culture*. Princeton, NJ: Princeton University Press.

Pocock, J. G. A. 1975. *The Machiavellian Moment: Florentine Political Thought and the Atlantic Republican Tradition*. Princeton, PA: Princeton University Press.

—1987. "Between Gog and Magog: The Republican Thesis and the Ideologia Americana." *Journal of the History of Ideas* 48(2):325–46.

—1999. *Barbarism and Religion, Vol. 1: The Enlightenment of Edward Gibbon 1737–1764*. Cambridge: Cambridge University Press.

Poplai, S. L. ed. 1959. *India 1947–1950: Select Documents on Asian Affairs, Vol. 1*. London: Oxford University Press.

Preuss, U. K. 1999. "Political Order and Democracy: Carl Schmitt and His Influence." In *The Challenge of Carl Schmitt*, ed. C. Mouffe. London: Verso, 155–79.

Pufendorf, S. 1991. *On the Duty of Man and Citizen*. Cambridge: Cambridge University Press.

—2003. *The Whole Duty of Man According to the Law of Nature*. Indianapolis, IN: Liberty Fund.

Quinton, A. 1973. *The Politics of Imperfection: The Religious and Secular Traditions of Conservative Thought in England from Hooker to Oakeshott*. London: Faber and Faber.

Radin, B. 2006. *Challenging the Performance Movement: Accountability, Complexity and Democratic Values*. Washington, DC: Georgetown University Press.

Radstone, S. 2007a. "Trauma Theory: Context, Politics, Ethics." *Paragraph* 30(1):9–29.

—2007b. *The Sexual Politics of Time: Confession, Nostalgia, Memory*. London: Routledge.

Raina, D. and Habib, S. I. 1993. "The Unfolding of an Engagement: The Dawn on Science, Technical Education and Industrialisation." *Studies in History* 9(1):87–117.

—1995. "Bhadralok Perceptions of Science, Technology and Cultural Nationalism." *Indian Economic and Social History Review* 32(1):95–117.

Ranga, N. G. 1937. *Kisan Speaks*. Madras: Kisan Publications.

Rauch, L. and Sherman, D. 1999. *Hegel's Phenomenology of Self-Consciousness: Text and Commentary*. Albany, NY: Suny Press.

Riviere, J. 1936. "A Contribution to the Analysis of the Negative Therapeutic Reaction." *International Journal of Psycho-Analysis* 17:304–20.

Rosenfeld, H. 1971. "A Clinical Approach to the Psychoanalytic Theory of the Life and Death Instincts: An Investigation into the Aggressive Aspects of Narcissism." *International Journal of Psycho-Analysis* 52:169–78.

Rostbøll, C. F. 1998. *Human Rights, Popular Sovereignty and Freedom*. Copenhagen: Copenhagen Political Studies Press.

Rothfield, P. 2007. "Surviving Reconciliation, from the Social to the Singular." *Radical Psychology. A Journal of Psychology, Politics, and Radicalism*. Available from: RadPsyNet 6(1). [Accessed on October 13, 2007].

Roy, S. 1999. *Communal Conflict in Bengal*. Cambridge: University of Cambridge.

—2007. *Beyond Belief: India and the Politics of Postcolonial Nationalism*. Durham, NC: Duke University Press.

Ruane, J. and Todd, J. 1996. *The Dynamics of Conflict in Northern Ireland*. Cambridge: Cambridge University Press.

Rummell, R. J. 1997. *Statistics of Democide*. Münster: Lit Verlag.

Said, E. 1978. Orientalism. New York: Pantheon.

Saint-Bonnet, F. 2001. *L'état d'exception*. Paris: Presses Universitaires de France.

Sarkar, S. 1973. *The Swadeshi Movement in Bengal 1903–1908*. New Delhi: People's Publishing House.

—1976. "The Logic of Gandhian Nationalism: Civil Disobedience and the Gandhi-Irwin Pact (1930–31)." *Indian Historical Review* 3(1):114–46.

—1983. *Modern India 1885–1947*. London: Macmillan.

Saunders, D. 1997. *Anti-Lawyers: Religion and the Critics of Law and State*. London: Routledge.

—2002. "'Within the Orbit of This Life' – Samuel Pufendorf and the Autonomy of Law." *Cardozo Law Review* 23(6):2173–98.

Savarkar, V. 1928. *Hindutva: Who is a Hindu?* Nagpur: Bharat Publications.

Saward, M. 2008. "Democracy and Citizenship: Expanding Domains." In *The Oxford Handbook of Political Theory*, eds. J. S. Dryzek, B. Honig and A. Phillips. Oxford: Oxford University Press, 400–22.

Schaap, A. 2005. *Political Reconciliation.* New York: Routledge.

—2006. "Agonism in Divided Societies." *Philosophy and Social Criticism* 32(2):255–77.

—2007. "Political Theory and the Agony of Politics." *Political Studies Review* 5(1):56–74.

Schmitt, C. 1965 [1928]. *Verfassungslehre.* Berlin: Dunker & Humbolt.

—1985 [1923]. *The Crisis in Parliamentary Democracy.* Baskerville: MIT Press.

—1988. *Political Theology.* Cambridge, MA: MIT Press.

—1996 [1932]. *The Concept of the Political.* Chicago, IL: University of Chicago Press.

—1996 [1938]. *The Leviathan in the State Theory of Thomas Hobbes: Meaning and Failure of a Political Symbol.* Chicago, IL: University of Chicago Press.

—2003 [1974]. *The Nomos of the Earth: In the International Law of the Jus Publicum Europaeum.* New York: Telos Press.

—2004 [1958]. *Legality and Legitimacy*, ed. J. Seitzer. Durham, NC: Duke University Press.

—2004 [1934]. *On the Three Types of Juristic Thought.* Westport, CT: Praeger.

—2004 [1963]. *Theory of the Partisan.* New York: Telos Press.

—2005 [1934]. *Political Theology: Four Chapters on the Concept of Sovereignty.* Chicago, IL: University of Chicago Press.

Schneewind, J. B. 1996. "Barbeyrac and Leibniz on Pufendorf." In *Samuel Pufendorf und die europäische Frühaufklärung. Werk und Einfluß eines deutschen Bürgers der Gelehrtenrepublik nach 300 Jahren (1694–1994)*, eds. Palladini, F. and Hartung, G. Berlin: Akademie Verlag, 181–9.

Schneider, H. P. 1967. *Justitia Universalis. Quellenstudien zur Geschichte des "Christlichen Naturrechts" bei Gottfried Wilhelm Leibniz.* Frankfurt a. M.: Klostermann.

—2001. "Christliches Naturrecht." In *Die Philosophie des 17. Jahrhunderts, Band 4: Das heilige Römische Reich deutscher Nation, Nord- und Ostmitteleuropa*, eds. H. Holzhey and W. Schmidt-Biggemann. Basle: Schwabe.

Schudson, M. 1999. *The Good Citizen: A History of Civic Life.* New York: Free Press.

Schutz, A. 2005. "'Legal Critique': Elements for a Genealogy." *Law and Critique* 16:71–93.

Schwab, G. 1996 [1938]. "Introduction." In *The Leviathan in the State Theory of Thomas Hobbes: Meaning and Failure of a Political Symbol*, ed. C. Schmitt. Chicago, IL: University of Chicago Press, ix–xxxii.

Schwarzenberger, G. 1955. "The Standard of Civilization in International Law." In *Current Legal Problems 17*, eds. G. W. Keeton and G. Schwarzenberger. London: Stevens & Sons, 212–34.

Scott, J. W. 1992. "Experience" In *Feminists Theorize the Political*, eds. J. Butler and J. W. Scott. London: Routledge, 22–40.

Seal, A. 1968. *The Emergence of Indian Nationalism.* Cambridge: Cambridge University Press.

Segal, H. 1988. *Introduction to the work of Melanie Klein.* London: Karnac Books.

Seidler, M. J. 2002. "Pufendorf and the Politics of Recognition." In *Natural Law and Civil Sovereignty: Moral Right and State Authority in Early Modern Political Thought*, eds. I. Hunter and D. Saunders. Basingstoke: Palgrave, 235–51.

Sen, S. 1972. *Agrarian Struggle in Bengal.* Delhi: People's Publishing House.

—1998. *The Transitional State: Congress and Government in UP, c. 1946–1957*, Unpublished PhD Thesis. London: School of Oriental and African Studies, University of London.

Sennett, R. 1974. *The Fall of Public Man.* Cambridge: Cambridge University Press.

Shain, Y. 2002. "Jewish Kinship at the Crossroads: Lessons for Homelands and Diasporas." *Political Science Quarterly* 117(2):279–309.

Shapiro, E. 2003. "The Maturation of American Identity: A Study of the Elections of 1996 and 2000 and the War against Terrorism." *Organisational and Social Dynamics* 3(1):121–33.

Shapiro, T. 2001. *Great Divides: Readings in Social Inequality in the USA*. Mountain View: Mayfield Publishing Company.

Sheets-Johnstone, M. 1999. *The Primacy of Movement*. Philadelphia, PA: John Benjamins.

Silverman, D. 1998. *Harvey Sacks: Conversation Analysis and Social Science*. Cambridge: Polity.

—2007. *A Very Short, Fairly Interesting and Reasonably Cheap Book about Qualitative Research*. London: Sage.

Singh, A. I. 1993. *The Limits of British Influence: South Asia and the Anglo-American Relationship 1947–56*. London: Pinter.

Singh, K. S. ed. 1989. *Jawaharlal Nehru, Tribes and Tribal Policy*. Calcutta: Anthropological Survey of India.

Sinha, M. 2006. *Specters of Mother India*. Durham, NC: Duke University Press.

Skinner, Q. 1990. "Thomas Hobbes on the Proper Signification of Liberty." *Transactions of the Royal Society, Fifth Series* 40:121–51.

—1998. *Liberty before Liberalism*. Cambridge: Cambridge University Press.

Smith, A. 2006. *Chosen Peoples*. Oxford: Oxford University Press.

Som, R. 1994. "Jawaharlal Nehru and the Hindu Code Bill: A Victory of Symbol over Substance?" *Modern Asian Studies* 28(1):165–94.

Starobinski, J. 1993. *Blessings in Disguise, or: The Morality of Evil*. Cambridge: Harvard University Press.

Sullivan, V. 2004. *Machiavelli, Hobbes, and the Formation of a Liberal Republicanism in England*. Cambridge: Cambridge University Press.

Suntharalingam, R. 1974. *Politics and National Awakening in South India, 1852–1891*. Tucson: University of Arizona Press.

Symington, N. 2001. *The Spirit of Sanity*. London: Karnac.

Thakurdas, P. 1944. *A Plan of Economic Development for India*. Harmondsworth: Penguin.

Thomasius, C. 2007. *Essays on Church, State, and Politics*, I. Hunter, T. Ahnert, and F. Grunert, eds. Indianapolis: Liberty Fund, 49–127.

Thomassen, L. 2007. *Deconstructing Habermas*. London: Routledge.

Tomkins, A. 2005. *Our Republican Constitution*. Oxford: Hart Publishing.

Tuck, R. 1996. "Introduction." In *Leviathan, Hobbes*. Cambridge: Cambridge University Press, ix–xlvi.

Turner, S. 1995. "Obituary: Edward Shils (1 July 1910–23 January 1995)." *Social Studies of Science* 25:397–9.

—2002. "Weber, the Chinese Legal System, and Marsh's Critique." Comparative & Historical Sociology. *Newsletter of the ASA Comparative and Historical Sociology Section* 14(2):1–4.

Tutu, D. 2000. *No Future without Forgiveness*. London: Rider.

van der Veer, P. 1994. *Religious Nationalism: Hindus and Muslims in India*. Berkeley: University of California Press.

van Krieken, R. 1989. "Violence, Self-Discipline and Modernity: Beyond the 'Civilizing Process'." *Sociological Review* 37(2):193–218.

—1990a. "Social Discipline and State Formation: Weber and Oestreich on the Historical Sociology of Subjectivity." *Amsterdams Sociologisch Tijdschrift* 17(1):3–28.

—1990b. "The Organization of the Soul: Elias and Foucault on Discipline and the Self." *Archives Européennes de Sociologie* 31(2):353–71.

—1999. "The Barbarism of Civilization: Cultural Genocide and the 'Stolen Generations'." *British Journal of Sociology* 50(2):297–315.

—2002. "Reshaping Civilization: Liberalism between Assimilation and Cultural Genocide." *Amsterdams Sociologisch Tijdschrift* 29(2):1–38.

—2008. "Cultural Genocide." In *The Historiography of Genocide*, ed. D. Stone. London: Palgrave Macmillan.

van Velzen, H. U. E. T. 1984. "The Djuka Civilization." *Netherlands Journal of Sociology* 20(2):85–97.

Veitch, S. 1999. "Pro Patria Mori: Law, Reconciliation and the Nation." In *Courting Death: The Law of Mortality*, ed. D. Manderson. London: Pluto Press, 148–62.

Veitch, S. and Perrin, C. 1998. "The Promise of Reconciliation." *Law, Text, Culture* 4(1):225–32.

Verrips, K. 1987. "Noblemen, Farmers and Labourers: A Civilizing Offensive in a Dutch Village." *Netherlands Journal of Sociology* 23(1):3–16.

Volkan, V. 1997. *Bloodlines: From Ethnic Pride to Ethnic Terrorism.* Boulder, CO: Westview Press.

Von Tunzelman, A. 2007. *Indian Summer: The Secret History of the End of an Empire.* Toronto: McLelland & Stewart.

Wachtel, P. 1998. "Alternatives to the Consumer Society." In *Ethics of Consumption: The Good Life, Justice, and Global Stewardship*, eds. D. Crocker and T. Linden. Lanham, MD: Rowan and Butterfield, 198–217.

Warner, M. 2002. "Sorry: The Present State of Apology." Available from Open Democracy, 07 November 2002.

Watzlawick, P., Beavin, J. and Jackson, D. 1968. *The Pragmatics of Human Communication.* London: Faber.

Weber, M. 1948. "The Meaning of Discipline." In *The Meaning of Discipline*, eds. H. Gerth and C. W. Mills. London: Routledge & Kegan Paul, 253–64.

—1989 [1930]. *The Protestant Ethic and the Spirit of Capitalism.* London: Unwin Hyman.

—1991. *Essays in Sociology*, eds. C. W. Mills, H. Gerth. London: Routledge.

—1994. *Political Writings*, eds. R. Spiers and P. Lassman. Cambridge: Cambridge University Press.

Weiler, G. 1994. *From Absolutism to Totalitarianism: Carl Schmitt on Thomas Hobbes.* Durango, CO: Hollowbrook.

Whitebrook, M. 2002. "Compassion as Political Virtue." *Political Studies* 50:529–44.

Wickham, G. 2006a. "Foucault, Law and Power: A Reassessment." *Journal of Law and Society* 23(4):596–614.

—2006b. "The Law-Morality Relation Revisited: A Challenge to Established Traditions by the Australian Sceptical Approach." *Griffith Law Review* 15(1):27–48.

—2007. "Expanding the Classical in Classical Sociology." *Journal of Classical Sociology* 7(3): 243–65.

—2008a. "The Social Must Be Limited: Some Problems with Foucault's Approach to Modern Positive Power." *Journal of Sociology* 44(1):29–44.

—2008b. "Protecting Law from Morality's Stalking Horse: The "Socio" in Socio-Legal Studies." *Law, Text, Culture* 12:104–27.

—2008c. "Are Our Social Sciences as Relevant to Government as They Might Be?" *Australian Universities Review* 50(2):25–32.

Wickham, G. and Freemantle, H. 2008. "Some Additional Knowledge Conditions for Sociology." *Current Sociology* 56(6):925–42.

Winnicott, D. W. 1971. *Playing and Reality.* London: Routledge.

Yeatman, A. 2001. "Who is the Subject of Human Rights?" In *Citizenship and Cultural Policy*, eds. D. Meredyth and J. Minson. London, Thousand Oaks and New Delhi: Sage, 104–20.

—2007. "The Subject of Citizenship." *Citizenship Studies* 11(1):105–16.

—2008a. "The Subject of Citizenship." In *Citizenship between Past and Future*, eds. E. Isin, P. Nyers and B. Turner. London and New York: Routledge.

Yeatman, A., Dowsett, G., Fine, M. and Gursansky, D. 2008b. *Individualization and the Delivery of Welfare Services.* New York: Palgrave.

Young, I. M. 1997. "Asymmetrical Reciprocity: On Moral Respect, Wonder, and Enlarged Thought." *Constellations* 3(3):340–63.

Zachariah, B. 2005. *Developing India: An Intellectual and Social History, c. 1930–1950.* Delhi: Oxford University Press.

—2009. *Playing the Nation Game.* Delhi: Yoda.

Žižek, S. 2001. *Did Somebody Say Totalitarianism? Five Interventions in the Misuse of a Notion.* London: Verso.

—2006. "C'est mon choix . . . to burn cars." *The Liberal* 4:20–5.

Zwaan, T. 2001. *Civilisering en decivilisering, nationalisme en vervolging.* Amsterdam: Boom.

—2003. "On Civilizing and Decivilizing Processes: A Theoretical Discussion." In *Norbert Elias Vol. 4*, eds. E. Dunning and S. Mennell London: Sage, 167–75.

Index